ROUTLEDGE LIBRARY EDITIONS:
INTERNATIONAL TRADE POLICY

Volume 1

AMERICAN BUSINESS AND FOREIGN POLICY

AMERICAN BUSINESS AND FOREIGN POLICY

Cases in Coffee and Cocoa Trade Regulation 1961–1974

JOSEPH SHORT

Routledge
Taylor & Francis Group
LONDON AND NEW YORK

First published in 1987 by Garland Publishing, Inc.

This edition first published in 2018
by Routledge
2 Park Square, Milton Park, Abingdon, Oxon OX14 4RN

and by Routledge
711 Third Avenue, New York, NY 10017

Routledge is an imprint of the Taylor & Francis Group, an informa business

British Library Cataloguing in Publication Data
A catalogue record for this book is available from the British Library

ISBN: 978-1-138-06323-5 (Set)
ISBN: 978-1-315-14339-2 (Set) (ebk)
ISBN: 978-1-138-30060-6 (Volume 1) (hbk)
ISBN: 978-0-203-73329-5 (Volume 1) (ebk)

Publisher's Note
The publisher has gone to great lengths to ensure the quality of this reprint but points out that some imperfections in the original copies may be apparent.

Disclaimer
The publisher has made every effort to trace copyright holders and would welcome correspondence from those they have been unable to trace.

FOREIGN ECONOMIC POLICY OF THE UNITED STATES

American Business and Foreign Policy:

Cases in Coffee and Cocoa Trade Regulation

1961–1974

JOSEPH SHORT

GARLAND PUBLISHING, INC.
NEW YORK & LONDON • 1987

For a complete list of the titles in this series, see the final pages of this volume.

Library of Congress Cataloging-in-Publication Data

Short, Joseph N.
American business and foreign policy.

(Foreign economic policy of the United States)
Originally presented as the author's thesis (Ph.D.--Columbia University, 1974).
Bibliography: p.
1. Coffee trade--United States. 2. Cocoa trade--United States. 3. Coffee trade--Developing countires. 4. Cocoa trade--Developing countries. 5. Foreign trade regulation--United States. 6. Business and politics--United States. I. Title. II. Series.
HD9199.U48S46 1987 302'.41373'0973 87-23792
ISBN 0-8240-8093-9

All volumes in this series are printed on acid-free, 250-year-life paper.

Printed in the United States of America

TABLE OF CONTENTS

(Table of Contents - continued)

ACKNOWLEDGEMENTS

My research has depended heavily upon a generous sharing of time and thought by nearly 100 individuals in business, government, international organizations and universities.

Several individuals have gone much beyond the call of duty to encourage and facilitate this research; and for an empirical study of contemporary business-government relationships, their help has been literally indispensable. As a group, coffee and cocoa businessmen were more responsive to my inquiries than my most optimistic expectations had led me to think they would be. I am especially indebted to the following businessmen: Alwyn N. Fischel, A.C. Israel and Co.; Julian Hemphill, Hershey Food Corporation; John F. McKiernan, former President of the National Coffee Association; George Robbins, formerly of General Foods Corporation; Johann J. Scheu and James Buckley, Nestle (US); and Michael Riess, Metal Traders, Inc.

My access to government officials was extraordinarily comprehensive, including the opportunity to interview all four of the Deputy Assistant Secretaries of State who dealt with the coffee and cocoa issues during the period under study. Among the most accommodating present and former officials of the State Department were: W. Michael Blumenthal; Julius Katz; Henry Brodie; Thomas Mann; Paul Callanan; Edward Fried; Jerome Jacobson; and Richard Scissors. Harold Lamarr, a staff member of the House Committee on Ways and Means, provided valuable insights into Congressional handling of the Coffee Agreement.

Among international civil servants five individuals were particularly helpful: Raul Prebisch, former Secretary-General of UNCTAD; Joao Oliveira

Santos, former Secretary-General of the International Coffee Organization; Nicolas Rivero, Organization of American States; Perce Judd, UNCTAD; and Shamsher Singh, IBRD.

Arnold Mayer, a Washington representative for the Amalgamated Meat-cutters and Butcher Workmen (AFL-CIO), provided an insider's view of union and Congressional involvement with the soluble coffee dispute.

I am especially grateful to my dissertation advisers at Columbia University, among whom have been Professors Robert Cox, Annette Baker Fox, W. Howard Wriggins, and in the early stages, Wayne Wilcox. Neither they nor my many informants, of course, bear any final responsibility for the facts or analysis herein. Professor Leland Goodrich and the late Professor Philip Mosely were my closest academic mentors in earlier years.

My wife, Marilyn, provided constant encouragement and deserves much credit for the completion of this study.

INTRODUCTION

Since World War II Less Developed Countries (LDCs) have waged an active campaign for the global regulation of trade in primary products through "international commodity agreements." Such agreements have the primary purpose of regulating prices in international markets.[1] Heavily dependent upon exports of primary products for foreign exchange earnings, for government revenues, and generally for economic development, the LDCs wish to protect their commodity exports from the frequent ravages of fluctuating or depressed commodity prices. Ideally they hope to regulate the markets for their commodities to achieve higher prices.

---

[1]Such agreements are otherwise known as "commodity stabilization agreements," commodity control agreements," or simply as "commodity agreements." "International commodity agreement" may, and does in other contexts, denote a wide range of agreements that do not seek to influence commodity price behavior, e.g., conservation agreements, or agreements governing the provision of strategic commodities. The latter types of agreement are not encompassed by this study. For a recent survey and analysis of post-WW II agreements see U.N., Conference on Trade and Development, Commodity Problems and Policies: Effectiveness of Commodity Agreements, Report by the Secretary-General of UNCTAD, TD/129, February 16, 1972. Commodity agreements are not a new subject on the international agenda. For an early study see Joseph S. Davis, International Commodity Agreements: Hope, Illusion or Menace? (New York: The Committee on International Economic Policy, 1947.) A historical survey of past agreements is found in Leon Baranyai and J. C. Mills, International Commodity Agreements (Mexico: Centro de Estudios Monetarios Latinoamericanos, 1963). A stimulating interpretation of the evolution of "commodity control" is found in J. W. F. Rowe, Primary Commodities in International Trade (Cambridge: at the University Press, 1965). A survey of major contemporary issues in international commodity agreement policy appears in "Arrangements for Trade in Primary Products," in Harry G. Johnson, Economic Policies Toward Less Developed Countries (New York: Frederick A. Praeger, 1967), 136-162. For an interpretation of the impact of LDC demands on current approaches to the issue of commodity agreements see Alton Law, "International Commodity Agreements: Policies and Problems," Journal of Economic Issues, IV (September, 1970), 87-102.

The very limited progress towards commodity agreements during the 1960's was for LDCs one of the biggest disappointment of a "Decade for Disappointment." Agreements for only five commodities—wheat, sugar, coffee, tin and olive oil—were operative during the decade. Only the tin and coffee agreements, and secondarily the sugar agreement, were of any substantial consequence for LDCs. And repeated international negotiations for agreements covering additional commodities, notably cocoa, were unsuccessful.

LDC proponents of commodity agreements realize that there is a myriad of obstacles to agreements, not the least of which are conflicting interests among LDC producers themselves. But they frequently fault the industrial, commodity-consuming countries, particularly the United States, for the slow progress towards agreements. They tend to see consumer governments as lacking sufficient "political will" to support such aid and trade measures to assist the LDCs.[2] LDCs tend also to believe that much of consumer government resistance to agreements is traceable to the adverse influence of commodity trading and processing firms. Business firms and associations in the consuming countries, in this view, exercise substantial, if not controlling influence on consumer government policies towards commodity agreements.

Even some American observers are certain that "U.S. business" is chiefly responsible for blocking "effective commodity agreement programs [that] would have a far-reaching impact on the distribution of the world's income and living standards."[3]

---

[2] United Nations, Conference of Trade and Development, The Significance of the Second Session of the United Nations Conference on Trade and Development, Report by the Secretary-General of UNCTAD, TD/96/Rev. 1, 1968, 1.

[3] Gabriel Kolko, The Roots of American Foreign Policy (Boston: Beacon Press, 1969), 66. Kolko depicts the United States as an opponent of commodity agreements, seeing this role as a reflection of "America's practice of maximizing its wealth by buying as cheaply as possible while it dumps agricultural goods on the world market and restricts imports damaging to its own producers." Ibid.

Research Purposes. Analyses that conclude that American business has an "important," "decisive," or "controlling" role in deciding U.S. policy towards LDC demands for commodity agreements have prompted this study. As is so often the case with claims about business influence on foreign policy making, these analyses, whatever their merits may be, provide very scant evidence to substantiate their points of view.[4] As with all foreign and public policy, there is regarding the issue of U.S. commodity agreement policy, a great need for "carefully formulated case studies of the roles of businessmen in politics."[5]

This study attempts to respond to this need through a comparative treatment of three cases. It is primarily concerned with how U.S. business firms and associations have behaved, and with what general effects, in relation to U.S. government responses to LDC demands for commodity agreements for coffee and cocoa. The inclusion of a third case, pertaining to U.S. policy and imports of Brazilian soluble (instant) coffee, enables a broader view of business participation in policy-making.

The minimal purpose of this study is to describe major aspects of the relationships between business and foreign policy-making for the coffee and cocoa cases. One would suppose that "business" would be involved somehow in policy-making for commercial issues. But very little has been written about this involvement. Precisely which firms and associations, which only for convenience sake are lumped together as "business," are concerned with the issues? What positions do they take, for what stated or unstated reasons? To which

---

[4]For an example, see Gabriel Kolko's treatment of the subject of commodity agreements in Ibid.

[5]Robert A. Dahl, "Business and Politics: A Critical Appraisal of Political Science," American Political Science Review, LIII (March, 1959), 28.

points in the governmental policy-making process do they seek and gain access? What resources and techniques do they employ to influence policy? What overall relationships exist between business leaders and policy-makers?

The second and more elusive purpose is to illuminate some of the effects of business relationships to policy-making. It was assumed at the outset that business "influence" would have to be analyzed at a fairly high level of abstraction. It would probably not be possible to isolate business influence, if it existed at all, in relation to the plethora of decisions that would constitute U.S. "policy" or "policies" in respect to the Coffee Agreement, the cocoa negotiations, or the soluble coffee dispute.

The best alternative seemed to be an attempt to assess the general impact of business participation in policy-making, that is, to assess whether, to what extent, and how business reinforced, modified, or thwarted otherwise existing orientations in the policy-making system towards the issues. This approach required analysis of the role of certain businesses in policy-making in the context of a wider analysis of sets of factors that might explain policies for the three issues.

The Cases Compared. To explore claims that the United States policies towards commodity agreements have been strongly influenced by the preference of business interest groups, a comparative study of U.S. policies and interest group activity for numerous existing and proposed commodity agreements would be desirable. This research, however, has focused more modestly on two of the most recent commodity agreement cases, and on a related case concerning trade in processed coffee.

The first case for comparative analysis concerns American business relationships to U.S. policy-making in the development of the International Coffee Agreement of 1962. It focuses upon the period of policy-making between

U.S. entry into the Coffee Study Group (1958), which developed the basic drafts for what became the Coffee Agreement, and Congress's provision of enforcement authorization for full U.S. participation in the International Coffee Organization (1965).

The International Coffee Agreement (hereafter "Coffee Agreement" or "ICA") is the first and only comprehensive commodity stabilization agreement, regulating trade in a primary commodity produced almost exclusively in the LDCs, in which the United States has ever participated fully.[6]

The negotiation of this Agreement inspired hope among LDCs that agreements for other commodities could now be achieved with United States support. Raul Presbisch has written that the coffee success "aroused expectations that a similar outcome might be reached for cocoa."[7] Critics of the Coffee Agreement, on the other hand, were fearful that U.S. support of it, perceived as a marked departure from a previous stance of skepticism or outright opposition towards agreements, might presage the development of an extensive system of such agreements.[8] Yet other observers have seen the Coffee Agreement, as Senator Edward Kennedy stated as recently as 1970, as offering "substantial promise of being a model for a host of other commodity agreements between producing and consuming nations."[9]

---

[6] The United States has never joined the International Tin Agreement. It has signed only a few of the several Sugar Agreements since 1933, and has participated only minimally in those. It has been a mainstay of the several Wheat Agreements, but these have aided Developed Countries primarily, not LDCs. It has not signed the International Cocoa Agreement of 1972.

[7] U.N. Conference on Trade and Development, Towards a New Trade Policy for Development, Report by the Secretary-General, 1964, 56.

[8] The Cambridge economist, J. W. F. Rowe has been particularly outspoken against agreements like the ICA. Rowe, op. cit., Chapter 15. For an extensive critique of UNCTAD-type thinking about commodity agreements, see Law, op. cit.

[9] U.S., Congress, Senate, 91st Cong., 2d sess., Congressional Record, December 31, 1970, 21667.

The Coffee Agreement, negotiated in 1962 and renegotiated in 1968, embraced most of the coffee producing and consuming countries in the world (ultimately over sixty countries).[10] The precise objectives of the ICA were constantly at issue, and subject to continuing negotiations within the "International Coffee Organization," established by the Agreement.

The ICA established an "export control" regime to halt coffee price declines resulting from a massive surplus that developed in the late fifties. It assigned coffee export quotas to member producing countries and provided a system for altering quotas within and between years. Producing countries pledged themselves to abide by assigned quotas and consuming countries committed themselves to help enforce the quotas by import regulation. The International Coffee Organization regulated the flow of coffee supplies onto the world market in order to mitigate price fluctuations and to maintain coffee price movements within ranges, which were acceptable to members.

International regulation, such as occurred under the aegis of the International Coffee Agreement, was "political" in the sense that valued things were distributed through the play of power and influence. Most obviously as governments negotiated national and world coffee quotas, not to mention the Agreement itself, they affected the incomes of individuals, business firms and nations. The "politics" of the Coffee Agreement, therefore, encompassed a spectrum of political activity, ranging from the efforts of private business firms to influence government policies to the international politicking of producing countries, individually and collectively, for higher national quotas.

---

[10] Significantly the regulatory regime was discontinued under the third Coffee Agreement (1973).

But economic values were not the only values at stake in the politics of coffee. It has been held by many, for example, that the United States was first and foremost concerned with political or foreign policy values in taking the decision to support the Coffee Agreement. In this view, U.S. decisions to join the Agreement and then to pursue certain policies in the ICO, were primarily attributable to its desire to bolster LDC governments against radical or Communist influence, or otherwise to secure "friends" among the LDCs.

The second case-study concerns relationships between American business firms and associations and policy-making in the negotiations for an *international cocoa agreement* since 1956.

The cocoa negotiations, spanning over fifteen years, must count as a minor epic in diplomatic history. The problems of international trade in cocoa, ironically, were first placed on the international agenda, not by LDCs, but by two consuming countries, Belgium and Switzerland. At the turn into the sixties, however, the quest for regulation of the cocoa market was already evolving as an LDC priority. By this time, several cocoa-producing countries in Africa had joined the major producer, Ghana, as independent states. All of these countries, and others from Latin America and Asia, immediately began to lobby in international organizations for economic assistance, including aid to commodity trade.

Cocoa price fluctuations, not to mention the periods of depressed prices that develop periodically, are especially troublesome and harmful for LDC producers like Ghana that rely heavily upon cocoa exports for economic development, if not economic solvency. Such countries have been in the vanguard of efforts to secure regulation of the market.

From its inception in 1964 the United Nations Conference on Trade and Development (UNCTAD) made the achievement of a cocoa agreement one of its highest priorities. It promoted three world negotiating conferences, either in New York or Geneva, after the FAO-initiated conference of 1963 failed. While the 1966 and 1967 U.N. conferences did not produce an agreement, the conference in September of 1972 did issue in an agreement supported by a substantial majority of major and lesser producer and consumer coventries. The United States has refused to sign the Agreement.

The various draft cocoa agreements have provided for regulation of cocoa supplies on the market through a variety of control mechanisms (export or sales quotas and/or a buffer stock). The Cocoa Agreement of 1972 features export control and buffer stock mechanisms to maintain price levels within a negotiated price range.

If coffee is the "success" case, in the eyes of those who seek commodity agreements, cocoa, at least until recently, has been the "failure." The achievement of the Coffee Agreement, and the failures of the cocoa negotiations—in roughly the same time period and under similar, though presumably not the same conditions—invite comparative study to determine what factors explain the contrasting outcomes.

A central concern of this study is why the United States took a strong leadership role for the Coffee Agreement, but has taken no commensurate role for cocoa. The U.S., some have contended, is either indifferent or opposed to the very idea of a cocoa agreement. To what extent might the contrasting U.S. approaches to coffee and cocoa, if indeed they exist, be attributed to the roles and stances of the American coffee and cocoa industries respectively?

The third case in this comparative study concerns the relationships between American business firms and associations and policy-making in what will be called the "soluble coffee dispute"—a dispute between the United States and Brazil that very nearly scuttled the renegotiation of the Coffee Agreement in 1967-1968.

It will not be evident, at first, how such a dispute, regarding trade in a processed product, could be grouped for comparative purposes with the two commodity agreement cases already mentioned. This can be justified by the central research interest in business and U.S. policy-making, and by the fact that trade in processed products (e.g., soluble or instant coffee) has become an important issue in the negotiations for both coffee and cocoa agreements.

Also consideration of the solubles dispute affords the side benefit of conjoining two issues that are of supreme concern to the LDCs—the regulation of trade in primary products, and the securing of access to major consumer markets for processed and semi-processed products.[11]

The soluble coffee dispute between the United States and Brazil spanned the period between 1966 and 1972. It centered upon Brazil's attempts to export relatively "low cost" soluble coffee to the lucrative market in the United States. For various reasons, disputed by the two countries, these attempts were immediately successful. Brazilian exporters established a substantial toe-hold in the market within one year, and so it seemed, could move on to a really commanding market position in a very short time.

This research has been primarily concerned with how American business responded to Brazilian efforts to break into the U.S. market, and particularly with the allegations that the coffee industry had a central role in arousing U.S. government opposition to Brazilian imports.

Issues and Questions. Each of the cases under comparison surely posed a variety of issues for policy-makers. This study focuses on the nature

---

[11] The International Coffee Agreement has the primary purpose of regulating trade in "green" coffee, i.e., the beans that are subsequently "processed" into ground roast or soluble coffees. The Agreement however, also contains provisions governing processed coffee.

and consequences of American business behavior with respect to selected issues in those cases, stated as follows:

- Whether or not, and on what terms, the United States should support (or even initiate) an international price stabilization agreement for coffee, 1958-1965.
- Whether or not, to what extent, and how the United States should counter Brazil's alleged "subsidization" of its soluble coffee exports to the U.S., 1966-1972. This issue became linked with whether or not the United States should support the renewal of the International Coffee Agreement in 1968.
- Whether or not, and on what terms, the United States should support (or even initiate) an international price stabilization agreement for cocoa, 1956-1973.

Which business firms and associations were concerned with these issues? At what points in the policy-making process did they seek to convey their policy preferences? By what techniques? And last, and most elusive of the questions to be considered, with what general consequences?

Policy Relevance of this Research. The study of business and U.S. commodity agreement policy relates to three policy questions of practical interest. First, if the United States is in a position to make or break commodity agreements, as it seems to be for a large number of commodities, it is a matter of great importance whether, and to what extent, certain businesses are in a position to influence the directions of American policy. Assuming such business enterprises have an influential role, in what directions do they or will they influence policy? There have been numerous studies of the economic and technical preconditions of commodity agreements, and a few of their diplomatic and international political preconditions.[12] This study takes a less familiar perspective

[12] For economic preconditions see John A. Pincus, "Commodity Agreements: Bonanza or Illusion," Columbia Journal of World Business, II (January, 1967), 41-50. For a combination of economic and diplomatic analysis see Jerome Jacobson, "Difficulties in Framing Effective Commodity Agreements," International Development Review, X (June, 1968), 10-15. For international political

that is needed and that is complementary to the other studies. It explores one aspect of the politics of foreign policy-making in the United States, a country whose participation is often deemed crucial for the successful operation of consumer-producer agreements. More studies of the domestic actors and processes through which different exporting and importing countries formulated commodity agreement policy are needed in order to fully understand the international politics of commodity agreements.

The study of business and commodity agreement policy also highlights a potential duality in policy-making for trade issues. Foreign trade policy can be informed by largely political, or what are normally termed "foreign policy" purposes (for example, bolstering LDCs against Communist influence), by self-interested commercial or economic purposes (under this heading can be grouped "national" purposes such as a favorable balance of payments or "sub-national" purposes such as protection of particular businesses or unions), or by some combination of the three purposes.

The cases of coffee and cocoa illustrate this duality and how often conflicting conceptions of the ends and means of foreign policy are reconciled in the play of politics in the policy-making system. Similarly they illustrate how "trade issues can link the smallest business to the largest questions of foreign policy."[13]

---

analysis see Bart S. Fisher, The International Coffee Agreement: A Study in Coffee Diplomacy, Special Studies in International Economics and Development (New York: Praeger Publishers, Inc., 1972); or Stephen D. Krasner, "The Politics of Primary Commodities: A Study of Coffee, 1900-1970" (Unpublished Ph.D. dissertation, Harvard University, 1972). For a participant-observer analysis of U.S. perspectives on commodity agreements see U.S., Department of State, Commodity Agreements: A Partial Answer to the Trade Problems of Developing Countries, by Henry Brodie, Commercial Policy Series Pubn. No. 200 (Washington, D.C.; GPO, 1965).

[13]Raymond A. Bauer, Ethiel de Sola Pool, and Louis A. Dexter, American Business and Public Policy: The Politics of Foreign Trade (New York: Atherton, 1963), 1.

Finally, this study should illuminate certain problems and prospects for international regulation, when such regulation impinges not only upon the material and principled concerns of nations, but also upon those of individuals and groups within nations. The international regulation of trade in coffee, or in cocoa, can affect the fortunes of individuals, trading firms, large processing corporations, political parties, bureaucracies, governments and states. The "free market," of course, also affects the fortunes of men and nations; but the "regulated market" involves governments, and sometimes private individuals and groups, more directly and deliberately in the allocation of values at stake in the market. Commodity earnings are at stake, but so potentially are other values such as survival of a particular government in a producing country, or the continuation of the "old way of doing business" in a consuming country.

Whether or not international regulation will be instituted in the first place, what the nature of such regulation will be, and how an actual regulatory regime will function are issues that will be decided, to a great extent, "politically," that is, in the play of power and influence, among and within states. Different trade regimes will invariably affect various "interests" differentially; hence, the continual political struggle to determine which regime shall prevail.

Numerous studies have shown how certain businesses have taken a lively interest in domestic regulatory activity, even to the point of controlling regulatory bodies that are supposed to regulate them. It would be surprising not to find a business similarly interested in international regulation that might affect it. But how does it try to advance its own conceptions of what the nature, form and effect of regulation should be? And with what effects?

Chapter I provides a modest introduction to the economics of coffee and cocoa trade, both for general background and to prepare the reader for the subsequent case-studies. Chapter II identifies the primary business and governmental actors in these cases. Identifying these at the outset should help set the comparative framework in which the individual case-studies are undertaken. Chapters III, V, and VI undertake in-depth analysis of the Coffee Agreement, soluble coffee and cocoa cases respectively. Chapter IV considers the triangle of relations among business, the State Department and Congress in the development of policy for the Coffee Agreement, and secondarily for the other two issues. In all these chapters the central purpose is to describe and assess the role of certain businesses in U.S. policy-making for commodity agreements.

CHAPTER I

The Economics of Coffee and Cocoa Trade

Commodity trade specialists and economists typically emphasize characteristics of commodity trade systems in discussing the pros and cons of particular commodity agreements. Political analysts should be concerned with how such characteristics determine the participants and processes, and influence the outcomes of U.S. policy-making for the commodities in question.

Patterns of international trade in coffee and cocoa, first, help decide which actors— both proximate policy-makers and interest group actors— will be involved in national policy-making for the two products. For example, because primary coffee and cocoa are largely produced in the LDCs, and consumed in industrial countries like the United States, there is a different configuration of policy-maker and interest group participation in policy-making for these products than obtains, for instance, in the case of sugar, which is produced both in the LDCs and in great quantities within the United States and Europe. For foreign-produced coffee and cocoa the U.S. State Department has played a more prominent role in policy-making than the Department of Agriculture. The roles are reversed in sugar. Similarly, in the case of sugar, Congress, where domestic primary producers seek representation, figures more centrally in sugar politics than the politics of the largely foreign-produced commodities.

No primary coffee or cocoa producers, except the few producers of Hawaii (Kona), are present in the United States to form interest groups that make demands upon policy. Again the contrast to sugar is obvious.

Patterns of international trade in both products, however, do suggest that commercial and processing firms in the industrial countries would be alert to the implications for them of international regulation. American firms and their associations, in fact, have asserted themselves in policy-making for coffee and cocoa, notwithstanding the dubious argument of one observer that "Since coffee is not grown in the United States, the roasters [coffee processors] are not organized in the same sense as sugar-beet or independent oil companies." [14] It does not follow that because there is an absence of primary production in the U.S. that roasters are not organized. American coffee roasters, in fact, are highly organized, and in their own way, have matched the sugar and oil producers in effective lobbying of the government.

Patterns of production and trade in soluble coffee, precipitating the U.S. - Brazilian dispute, are more directly comparable to those in sugar than primary coffee itself. Of central importance to policy analysis is the fact that domestic producers of soluble coffee compete with foreign producers and with other domestic groups that would stand to gain by soluble coffee imports.

Secondly, trade systems may also predispose the actors in policy-making to favor or to oppose commodity agreements, or other trade policies. Policy-makers and interest group leaders form their conceptions of what is desirable and feasible national policy, partly on the basis of perceptions of trade systems. Their conceptions of what is desirable or feasible, by economic or technical standards, are obviously guided by such perceptions. But so, to some extent, are their notions about foreign policy purposes and about what is politically feasible in policy development.

---

[14] John P. Powelson, Latin America: Today's Economic and Social Revolution, (New York: McGraw-Hill, 1964), 161.

The purpose of this chapter is to identify some major attributes of the coffee and cocoa trade systems that help explain why the United States took a leadership role for the Coffee Agreement (1962), and by contrast, why it has assumed a more detached and circumspect posture in the negotiations for a cocoa agreement. Correspondingly, it considers how characteristics of the international trade system in soluble coffee, as linked to the regulated green coffee trade system, helped shape U.S. policies in the U.S.-Brazilian dispute over trade in this processed product.

Coffee and Cocoa Trade Systems

Coffee is a tropical tree product that is not generally suitable for production in the continental United States, though it is the raw material for a vast and diversified trading and processing industry. Coffee processing is a relatively simple and straightforward operation, in which by comparison with cocoa, the stages of processing, and the final products are not highly differentiated.

Imported coffee beans ("green coffee") are either processed into ground-roast, or into one or another type of soluble coffee ("instant coffee").

Two basic types of green coffee are produced by the LDCs: arabica and robusta. Arabica is produced in milder LDC climates, mostly in Latin America, but also in some parts of Africa such as Kenya, Burundi, and Tanzania. American coffee drinkers have been conditioned to prefer arabica tastes during many years of coffee trading with Latin America. Since the 1950's, however, they unknowingly have been purchasing increasing amounts of robusta-type coffee that U.S. manufacturers, for cost-saving purposes, have been buying from Africa and blending into their roast coffees, and especially into their soluble coffees. Increased U.S. demand for robustas have encouraged expansion of

African production, and thereby African competition with Latin America for limited world markets.

Robusta coffee thrives in the warn amd moist tropical climates of Africa, such as in Uganda, Ivory Coast, Malagasy Republic and Portuguese Angola. Europeans have been conditioned to prefer robusta tastes through years of coffee importation from their respective coffee-producing colonies. Until recent years, robustas were generally lower priced than arabicas. Changing patterns of supply and demand, and the operations of the International Coffee Organization, however, have tended to eliminate the price differences.

American are less likely to be aware of the full range of uses for the tropical tree product, cocoa, although chocolate candy bars and "hot cocoa" are about as "American" as coffee and apple pie. Cocoa beans ("nibs") are removed from an outer pod and constitute a distinct primary product when they enter international trade. Two distinct and valuable intermediate, processed products are derived from cocoa beans: cocoa butter (55% of usable bean content); and a non-fat product that is the base for cocoa powder (45%). These intermediate products are used to manufacture chocolate and cocoa powder respectively.

Cocoa powder is used for familiar beverages and for flavoring products such as baked goods and ice cream. Cocoa butter is a major ingredient in chocolate, and chocolate a major ingredient in confections. Cocoa butter is also used in pharmaceuticals and cosmetics. Cocoa-processing firms normally produce both powder and chocolate, in order to get the highest yields from their beans. Cocoa beans, butter, powder base, powder, and chocolate are all traded internationally.

There are two basic types of cocoa beans: "flavor" (also called "fine") and "ordinary." Flavor cocoa of Latin America constitutes only about 10% of all cocoa processed and is blended with the more common "ordinary" cocoa of Africa.

Generally speaking, and, unlike coffee, cocoa can be treated as an "homogeneous" primary product.

When American policy-makers are called upon to adopt policies concerning international trade in certain primary or processed products, it is likely that their responses will depend, at least partly, upon how they perceive the country-compositions and "structures" (patterns and shares of import and export) of the relevant trade systems. They, of course, are bound to be particularly concerned with the position of the United States in the given trade system for which policy is being developed.

How many countries are in a trade system, which countries in which geographical regions, and what their relative shares of exports or imports are, are likely to be variables affecting U.S. policies concerning particular commodity agreements.

Coffee Trade System. U.S. initiative for the Coffee Agreement (1962) was undoubtedly spurred by considerations that coffee was preeminently a Latin American product; that many LDCs throughout the world would benefit from the Agreement; that Brazil, Colombia and strategically located Central American producing countries would benefit; that Brazil as the major producer would be able and willing to effectively lead the producers in a regulatory system; and that it would be practicable to secure the participation of other major importers, as well as the vast majority of traders of coffee.

Latin America has dominated global coffee production and export for many years, although to a steadily diminishing degree. In the sixties alone it accounted for 60-75 percent of all global exports annually.[15] At the time the ICA was negotiated (1962) the six main world coffee exporters, in descending

---

15 Pan American Coffee Bureau, Annual Coffee Statistics, 1969, No. 33 (New York: PACB, 1970), 40.

order of importance were: Brazil, Colombia, Mexico, El Salvador, Portuguese Angola and Guatemala. Brazil and Colombia alone accounted for approximately 50 percent of world exports, and the Central American countries for another 15 percent.

Africa's challenge to Latin America in the world export market was reflected at the 1962 Coffee Conference in the debates over export quota allocation; but it was of more decisive importance in shaping the evolution of the Agreement over the next decade, and in bringing the collapse of the regulatory regime in 1973. Nevertheless, as will be shown in subsequent chapters, policy-makers and interest group leaders were particularly impressed in 1962 with the fact that Latin American producers would be prime beneficiaries of the ICA.

They were also impressed that a very large number of LDCs on three continents were heavily dependent upon foreign exchange earnings from coffee, that these countries were in dire straits over the state of the coffee market, and therefore, that assistance to the coffee market would have very extensive economic and political impact. Coffee during the sixties, was the second most valuable primary export of the LDCs— about $2 billion of trade annually— and from the standpoint of the numbers of countries trading the product, the most important primary export. Thirty-six LDCs eventually received quota allocations under the ICA of 1962. In that year fifteen different countries in Africa and Latin America depended upon coffee for 20 percent or more of their export earnings, and five countries for over 50 percent of their earnings.[16]

---

[16] For a table of coffee export earnings for the major coffee exporters presented to the Senate Foreign Relations Committee, see U.S., Congress, Senate, Committee on Foreign Relations, International Coffee Agreement, 1962 Hearing, March 12, 1963, 88th Cong., 1st sess., 1963, 70. The five countries most dependent upon coffee earnings were Colombia (71% of total export earnings); Guatemala (60%); El Salvador (59%); Ethiopia (51%) and Brazil (51%).

The large number of coffee producers probably favored support of the Coffee Agreement in another way. One view is that the greater the concentration of production and consumption in a commodity trade system, other things being equal, the greater its susceptibility to a regulation by commodity agreement.[17] This hypothesis is based on the assumption that it is easier to reconcile the interests of the few than of the many. The notion seems plausible, and may be generally valid. This research, however, suggests an important qualification to this proposition. Consuming countries, especially under the vigilant prodding of business interest groups, may be anxious about being "locked into" a commodity arrangement under conditions where production and export are concentrated in a few countries.[18] They may fear that a few producers are more likely to be able to concert action in a commodity organization, and thereby enhance their joint bargaining position in relation to the consuming countries. American coffee firms felt reassured in supporting the Coffee Agreement by the fact that there were many producers whose interests were sufficiently diverse to brake tendencies for the producers to act together as an invariably monolithic bargaining agent.

Brazil's sustained leadership in world coffee exports, though on average diminishing during the decades of the sixties, had some vital implications for the development of U.S. initiative for the ICA. Brazil's share of the world coffee

---

[17] An early UNCTAD study contended that concentration in the cocoa market was favorable to the negotiation of the cocoa agreement. U.N., Trade and Development Board, The International Organization of Commodity Trade: Case Study in Cocoa, TD/B/AC.2/3, January 3, 1966, 4.

[18] The most influential single cocoa businessman in the U.S. during the sixties has acknowledged that the American industry has been exceedingly reluctant to encourage collaboration among the few producers by supporting a cocoa agreement. Interview, Julian Hemphill, February 10, 1972.

market in 1962 (35%) was only half of what it had been in 1909 (69%), but it was still the undisputed, leading exporter.[19] Brazil's position in the export market helped convince U.S. policy-makers that a Coffee Agreement was both desirable and feasible.

First, American policy-makers recognized that the major producer of coffee in the world stood to lose a great deal from the collapse of the world market which many authorities believed imminent in 1962. Fifty-one percent of Brazilian export earnings in 1962 came from its coffee trade. For other reasons, as well, the Brazilian economy was quite shaky at the time. If the economic and political future of Latin America was of critical concern to the United States, the future of Brazil, the largest and potentially most prosperous of Latin countries was of particular concern.

Secondly, the policy-makers recognized that Brazil was both able and willing to organize and lead the producers. For this and other reasons a coffee agreement would be "workable." Brazil had had nearly sixty years of experience in governmental regulation of coffee marketing. Even before World War I she had attempted unilateral control of national exports in order to "support" world prices. Between the Wars and after World War II, Brazil played the central role in organizing producing countries internationally to counter adversely fluctuating and declining prices.

It has been posited that the chances for an international commodity Agreement are greatest when the market to be regulated is dominated by a single, major exporter and a single, major importer, both of which are willing and able to support a particular agreement. This condition obtained in the case of the Coffee

---

[19] The closest competitor was Colombia with 14 percent of word exports.

Agreement. Not only was Brazil the major exporter of coffee in 1962, it also held the greatest proportion of world surplus stocks in storage. Brazil's willingness, and importantly, its capacity to hold these stocks off the market were critical to the establishment and functioning of the coffee organization. Indeed the very existence of the gigantic Brazilian stocks was reassuring to American businessmen and policy-makers who otherwise would have thought the agreement was too "risky" or simply "unnecessary." Brazil's willingness to "support" the market throughout the sixties, even at the expense of a steady erosion of its market share, was similarly crucial to the operation of the Agreement.

The obvious corollary to the hypothesis above is that as shares of exports become more evenly spread among all exporters, i.e., as the dominant exporter's position diminishes, it is likely that an existing commidity agreement will become more unstable. If no single country is both willing and able to be the linchpin of export control, control will then depend upon the vicissitudes of multinational cooperation and coordination. The demise of the regulatory aspects of the Coffee Agreement in 1973 may be attributed partly to Brazil's declining capacity and will to support the coffee market unilaterally.

Through the Coffee Agreement American policy-makers could also seek to help several other strategically important and coffee-dependent Latin countries. Columbia, dependent upon coffee for 71 percent of its total export earnings, and several Central American producers, were favored beneficiaries of this policy.

Finally the distribution and pattern of coffee imports in the coffee trade system were, other things being equal, conducive to U.S. initiative for a Coffee Agreement. In 1959 the United States and several countries in Europe took 92 percent of all world coffee imports, and their joint share continued at about this level throughout the sixties (1969 - 89%).[20] Imports into both the U.S. and Europe

[20] PACB, <u>op. cit.</u> 45.

increased during the decade, but Europe's increased at a markedly higher rate. Between 1959 and 1969 the U.S. share of imports dropped gradually from 55.5% to 38%, as the European share rose from 37% to 51%.[21]

In 1962, U.S. policy-makers found European importing countries generally responsive to the idea of a coffee agreement. As the U.S. wished to assist certain Latin coffee countries, so European countries like France wished to assist former or present colonies in Africa from which they were continuing to import coffee. The Europeans and Africans, however, were reluctant about freezing current shares of the export market by an export control agreement. The positive response from Europe, due to the seriousness of market conditions, convinced American policy-makers that the essential number of leading importers and exporters could be attracted to a well conceived coffee agreement.

Cocoa Trade System. The cocoa trade system presents some interesting comparisons and contrasts to the coffee system that help explain U.S. reserve towards proposals for a coca agreement between 1956 and 1973.

First, the cocoa trade system has been more concentrated than the coffee system, both with respect to the number of producers and to the market shares held by these relatively fewer producers. During the sixties just over ten countries accounted for all production and export, in contrast to over 40 producing countries engaged in coffee trade. Consumption was concentrated in the United States, the single most important consuming country, and in Europe, to an extent comparable to the coffee trade. At the time of the first U.N. Cocoa Conference (1963) the U.S. was taking about 27 percent of world imports.[22]

---

[21] *Ibid.*

[22] Gill and Duffus, Ltd., *Cocoa Report* (London: Gill and Duffus, September, 1965), 23.

Western Europe was the leading regional importer, taking just over 50% of all global imports. Germany (13% of world imports), the Netherlands (10%) and the United Kingdom (9.7%) were the leading European importers in 1963, followed by France and Switzerland respectively.

Similarly in 1963 only five countries—Ghana, Nigeria, Brazil, Ivory Coast, and Cameroon—accounted for fully 80 percent of the world's exports.[23] By the end of the decade there was a mild trend towards greater diffusion of production centers, and towards more even distribution among the production leaders, but concentration remained a signally important feature of the trade system.

Concentration, it was indicated earlier, may be conducive to the negotiation of commodity agreements. In the cocoa case, however, the concentration on the producer side has added to American business skepticism of the desirability of a cocoa agreement. The cocoa industry fears that an agreement would aid and abet producer collusion, which would be all the easier because of the few producers in the market.

Second, the cocoa trade system has been dominated on the producer side by African countries, to a degree roughly proportionate to Latin dominance in the coffee market. Throughout the sixties four African countries accounted for approximately 70 percent of annual world cocoa exports. The Latin American countries contributed in the range of 25 percent of world exports annually. Other things being equal, this study suggests, the United States is less likely to favor a commodity agreement that primarily benefits Africa than one that aids Latin America. The United States will be all the more disposed to an agreement that aids primarily Latin America, but also Africa, for example, the Coffee Agreement.

---

[23] Ibid., 6-9.

Third, although Ghana's position in the cocoa trade system appears to have been comparable to that of Brazil in coffee—it has been the premier cocoa producer and exporter for many years—it has not been able to actually exercise the consistent and authoritative leadership among and for producers that Brazil has exhibited in coffee. Certainly Ghana's prominence as a cocoa exporter has not impressed American policy-makers to the degree that Brazil's coffee did.

Several factors have hampered Ghana's ability to play a strong leadership role for an agreement, even when it has been predisposed to have one. In the sixties Ghana exported between 27-35 percent of the world's cocoa annually, a percentage share roughly equivalent to Brazil's share of the coffee market. And yet Ghana's leverage on the market and its role in the cocoa negotiations have been less telling than Brazil's was in coffee.

One important reason for this seems to have been Ghana's relatively greater economic dependence on cocoa income, as compared to Brazil's substantial, but more limited dependence on coffee. The magnitude of this dependence has made it extremely difficult for the Ghanian government to manipulate exports in ways most conducive to "ideal" relations with consuming countries, with or without a cocoa agreement. Also the years of cocoa negotiations have coincided almost exactly with the period in which Ghana has emerged from colonial status (1957) to tackle independently a host of problems in modernization and foreign relations. High national hopes for economic development, partly induced by ambitious governments, and increased government spending, have not made the task of regulating the cocoa industry any easier.

During the Nkrumah years (1957-1966), senior Ghanaian officials were preoccupied with "high" national and international politics, and prone to delegate responsibilities for cocoa diplomacy to junior officials. Since Nkrumah, the country's precarious economic situation and unstable and heavily burdened political system have not been conducive to firm Ghanaian leadership in the international politics of cocoa, although as the conclusion of the 1972 Cocoa Agreement attests, this point should not be overdrawn. Throughout the short period of independence Ghana has also had the onerous task of developing indigenous technical and administrative capacities for cocoa trade and diplomacy, capacities that Brazil has been able to develop, to an impressive degree, over many decades of experience with coffee trade regulation.

Situational factors have also inhibited Ghana's role as a leader for a cocoa agreement. For one thing Ghana has not been able to build up an effective capacity to store surplus cocoa or to store cocoa that is purposely being withheld to support prices.[24] Brazil has had the diplomatic leverage attendant to having massive stores of coffee. At the signing of the ICA (1962) Brazil, and secondarily Columbia, held in storage most of the world's surplus coffee. With these stores she could reassure the consuming countries that a coffee agreement would not result in a short-run shortage of coffee, and at the same time, impress them with her capacity to participate effectively in an export control agreement.

At another level Brazil could use her stored surpluses to pressure other producers into accepting an agreement providing for export quotas, with the implicit or explicit threat that she would otherwise be prepared to release her surpluses onto the market.

---

[24] Cocoa beans are prone to spoil during storage in tropical climates, unless stored in special and very expensive facilities. Nkrumah built a vast complex of storage silos for this purpose, but due to improper design, these have proven virtually useless. Producers can store their product in rented facilities in the consuming countries, but this practice, in addition to the frequent necessity of securing bank loans in industrial countries, lays them open to pressures to sell when they might otherwise prefer to stay out of the market.

At still another level, the producer's capacity to store a product gives it leverage in commodity bargaining with consumers. In the case of cocoa, business firms in the consuming countries often seem to delight in the fact that producers have not been able to concert their efforts in withholding cocoa from the market. The general lack of suitable storage facilities in Ghana and the other producing countries continues to be a major obstacle to these efforts, although divergent economic interests undoubtedly explain the better part of producer disunity.

Ghana's leadership for a cocoa agreement has sometimes not been strong enough (and market conditions not conducive) to overcome the ambivalence of other producers towards commodity agreement proposals. In the early and mid-sixties several African producers, notably Nigeria, Ivory Coast and Cameroon, were attempting to expand cocoa production and export. At the end of the decade Brazil was investing substantial sums in improving its cocoa plantations, and Columbia was contemplating cocoa production for the first time, ironically to "diversify" out of coffee.

So-called "new producers" such as these tend to balk at commodity agreements that freeze shares of the market. Unless there are really compelling reasons for supporting an agreement, such as a long period of large surpluses and seriously depressed prices, as in coffee, the new producers are likely to be unenthusiastic about or quietly opposed to an agreement that restricts production and export expansion.

In conclusion, it has been posited that the composition and structure of the cocoa trade system have not been as conducive to U.S. support of a cocoa agreement, as were the same factors for the Coffee Agreement.

<u>Soluble Coffee Trade System</u>. What have been the salient characteristics of the soluble coffee trade system that are relevant to the analysis of U.S.

policy-making in the American-Brazilian dispute? The international trade system in soluble coffee is relatively new, and by comparison with the green coffee system, quite limited in composition. Secondly, the primary focus of this research must be on the biliteral trade relationships between the United States and Brazil, and only secondarily on the more encompassing global system. Thirdly, it is necessary to understand the linkage between the green coffee system, as regulated by the International Coffee Agreement, and the soluble coffee system, which was central to the development of the dispute, and to the evolution of American policy.

Soluble coffee was not commercialized, to any great extent, until after WWII, first, in Europe, and subsequently, in the United States. While green coffee has moved in international trade for decades, most soluble coffee continues to be processed by companies in industrial countries <u>for local consumption</u>. Where multinational companies have established factories in the LDCs the local market is still the primary target.

The world's instant coffee producing industry has been and remains highly concentrated. The picture is not too different today than it was in 1961 when approximately 75 percent of the world's instant coffee was both manufactured and consumed in the United States. That there has been little international trading of soluble coffee can be illustrated by examining the soluble exports and imports of the United States as the major producer and consumer.

In 1965 the U.S. exported only 12,112 pounds of soluble coffee, from a total production of 184,805 pounds. Canada was the U.S.'s best customer that year, and remains so. In 1969 the U.S. exported only 8,147 pounds out of a total of 171,542 pounds produced.[25]

---

[25] General Foods, of course, has been active in soluble production <u>within</u> other developed countries, e.g., in Canada, Europe and Japan.

Imports of soluble into the United States rose between 1965 and 1969, due to Brazil's entry into the market. But imports as percentages of "available supply for consumption" remained relatively modest. In 1965 imports accounted for less than two percent of available U.S. supply, in 1969 for about 19 percent. The sharp rise in the relative proportion of imports to total supply, mostly from Brazil, is what caused alarm among the domestic producers.[26]

The coffee and cocoa cases conform very much to the typical pattern, lamented by the LDCs, in which developed countries are preeminent in the processing of primary products that are produced in the LDCs. The soluble coffee case concerns the efforts of Brazil to challenge this pattern by processing its own coffee and exporting into the developed American market, in competition with domestic producers.

In the late fifties a number of Central American countries and Brazil began to set their sights on exporting soluble coffee to the United States. El Salvador and Mexico took the initiative, but faltered and withdrew when pressured by the U.S. National Coffee Association to remove tax and other incentives they were giving to their exporters.[27]

Not until the early sixties did Brazil take the decision to expand soluble coffee procution and to enter the U.S. market. From 1965 to 1967 Brazil's share of the total U.S. Market jumped from a mere one percent to 13 percent, setting the scene for the U.S.-Brazilian dispute.

---

[26] Data for U.S. exports and imports of soluble coffee extrapolated from Table 32, as found in Pan-American Coffee Bureau, op. cit., 57.

[27] American soluble coffee experts believe that a foreign producer of soluble coffee cannot compete effectively, if at all, in the U.S. market unless he is "subsidized." Interview, Edward Aborn, October 4, 1971. This is one reason why U.S. coffee companies have shown no great interest in investing in soluble plants in the LDCs where local markets are less promising.

Brazil's advance into the U.S. market was propelled by government policies that enabled Brazilian exporters to enter a substantially lower cost instant coffee in the competition for the lucrative U.S. market. At Brazilian initiative the instant was marketed through American companies that packed the product under their own label. Some of the latter companies, as was intended, then developed material interest in the continuation of Brazilian imports.

How were the green coffee and soluble coffee trade systems linked in the solubles dispute? A large segment of the American coffee industry, and eventually the U.S. government itself, held that Brazil was exploiting the Coffee Agreement to subsidize its exports of soluble. A contributor to the IBRD Coffee Papers subsequently described Brazilian solubles policy as a case of "reverse protection."[28]

The basis for the American complaint was that Brazil was taxing its exports of green coffee, but not its exports of soluble coffee. American solubles producers were placed at a competitive disadvantage, both because they had to buy the taxed Brazilian beans for their raw material, while Brazilian producers were exempt from export taxes and otherwise permitted the use of good quality, low cost beans, and because they were restricted in using non-Brazilian sources of beans by the country quota arrangements of the Coffee Agreement. American critics claimed that Brazil's scheme would not work, if it were not for the exports quota of the ICA; otherwise American producers would be able to secure unlimited amounts of low-cost beans from non-Brazilian sources, and thus be able to neutralize Brazil's "discriminatory" export policies.

---

[28] Baranson, "The Soluble Coffee Dispute and the Case of Reverse Protection," in International Bank for Reconstruction and Development, "The Coffee Problem: Essays and Official Papers, Vol. II of The Coffee Papers: An Inquiry into the Economics of Commodity Markets, CSSS-7, edited by Dragoslav Avramovic for the International Bank for Reconstruction and Development (3 vols.; Washington, D.C.: IBRD, 1969).

Paradoxically, commodity agreements for primary products sought by the LDCs may tend to discourage LDC processing and exporting of the product under regulation. At the 1967 U.N. Cocoa Conference the Netherlands and the United States, two major cocoa processing countries, sought provisions in the agreement proposal under discussion that would inhibit LDC measures to promote the production and export of processed products. Certainly the U.S.-Brazilian dispute over soluble coffee suggests the unlikelihood that industrial countries will allow the LDCs to use commodity agreements as facilitating devices for subsidization of exports of processed products from the same primary products regulated by such agreements.

The complex interplay of primary product and processed product trade systems may also divide the ranks of the LDCs. In the soluble coffee case the African coffee producers, who had not yet gotten into the export of processed coffee, were undoubtedly threatened by Brazil's surge into the American soluble coffee market, even though they carefully avoided identification with the American diplomatic campaign against Brazilians. The Africans had expanded their robusta markets in the United States, primarily due to increased demands from the soluble coffee manufacturers such as Maxwell House.

At the same time, Brazil made little secret of the fact that its venture into the U.S. soluble market was, to some extent, an attempt to compensate for shares of the U.S. green coffee market that had been lost to the African producers in previous years.[29]

---

[29] Stavisky & Associates, Inc., "U.S. Switches Tactics in Battle to Ban Brazil's Instant Coffee," Press Release issued for Brazilian Soluble Coffee Industry, December 29, 1967.

This interface between the green coffee and soluble coffee trade systems, it will be shown, put the U.S. policy-making system in a double-bind. In retrospect, it does not seem that political circumstances would have permitted both preservation of the Coffee Agreement and the fullest possible accommodation of Brazil's desire to become a major exporter of soluble coffee in the United States.

Market Organization: The Role of the Futures Markets

Several features of the organization of the markets for coffee and cocoa, respectively, have undoubtedly influenced American policy-makers and interest group leaders, as they have contemplated the desirability and feasibility of coffee or cocoa agreements. It is probably of special significance for policy-making, however, that the American futures market in coffee was at its nadir at the time the Coffee Agreement was negotiated, while the cocoa futures market has continued to flourish throughout the years of the cocoa negotiations. While the key coffee firms felt they had no stake in how an agreement might affect a moribund commodity exchange, the American cocoa industry remains anxious that a cocoa agreement would undermine the futures market that is central to their present and preferred way of doing business.

Futures markets for coffee developed in New York, and secondarily in Le Havre. More recently a futures market for African coffees has developed in London. Cocoa markets developed in London, Paris, New York and Amsterdam. Importantly the New York coffee futures market, under the aegis of the New York Sugar and Coffee Exchange, was generally dormant during the sixties, only showing some signs of revival during the early seventies. The New York Cocoa Exchange has been thriving.

"Organized futures markets developed," Professor Rowe has said, "primarily in order to facilitate the price-making activities of merchant speculators."[30] But once they were established, he notes, another set of transactions was made possible.[31] Traders of actual commodities found that they could buy and sell futures to insure themselves against falling prices while they were holding physical stocks of a commodity. "Hedging," as this practice came to be known, is theoretically useful to the several parties involved in trading and processing commodities. Notably in the case of cocoa, American businesses of all types, even the large processing corporations, use the Cocoa Exchange for hedging purposes.[32]

One major reason for vociferous trader opposition to an international commodity agreement for cocoa is their fear that an agreement would, by constricting price movements ("stabilization"), discourage speculators from entering the market. While they themselves do not speculate much, they recognize the importance of the speculators for keeping the market alive with enough transactions to facilitate their own vital hedging operations. Traders make their profits through the hedging medium, by making small percentages on many coordinated transactions in both actuals and futures markets. Generally they make their profits through wise use of hedging procedures, as the market moves either upwards or downwards. Traders of actual commodities are not concerned so much with the direction of price movements, so long as prices are fluctuating sufficiently to keep the futures market lively and their hedging medium in a healthy condition.

---

[30] Rowe, Primary Commodities in International Trade, 49.

[31] Ibid., 50.

[32] See Henry B. Arthur's recent and superb account of how particular American firms use cocoa futures as a management tool. This account deals with the complex variety of hedges and their several uses, as well as other management uses of futures. Henry B. Arthur, Commodity Futures as a Business Management Tool, Division of Research, Harvard Graduate School of Business Administration (Boston: Harvard University, 1971), 261-289.

Other cocoa using firms have also been skeptical of agreements that might hamper the operation of the futures markets. Some manufacturers themselves use the futures market for a variety of management purposes. They are also aware of the significance of the market to the trader class whose services they continue to value, if for only self-interested reasons.

Certain cocoa users and traders have liked to leave the impression that a commodity agreement would inevitably snuff out the cocoa futures market. In fact, while this is certainly a very real possibility, developments would depend very much upon the nature of the commodity agreement. The more ambitious the purposes of the agreement in respect to price "stabilization," e.g., as in seeking to confine price movements in the market to a very narrow range, the more threatening an agreement would surely be to a futures markets.

But traders and other supporters of present futures marketing arrangements for cocoa are surely on shakier ground in contending, as many have done, that the demise or dormancy of the coffee futures market in the United States, evident from the early sixties, may be attributed exclusively to the operations of the Coffee Agreement. Opponents of a cocoa agreement like to use this argument because it is superficially plausible; but at bottom, it is a partly misleading argument.

In fact, the coffee futures trading on the N. Y. Sugar and Coffee Exchange was in evident decline as early as the late fifties, before the signing of the Coffee Agreement. By 1963 there was only negligible trading in the market. The ICA may well have diminished an otherwise faltering futures market in the United States. If this is so, it is interesting to consider why it did not also "close" the coffee futures market in London. That market has continued to trade futures actively, mostly in African robusta coffees.

The decline of the New York market in futures was due, in the first instance, to Brazil's trade policy innovations of the late fifties. Saddled with a tremendous surplus in storage, and faced with declining and depressed prices, Brazil instituted a policy of guaranteed export prices. American traders, for instance, that bought Brazil at one price were guaranteed reimbursement in kind (coffee) for the differential between that price and what the going price at the time the traders could sell to customers in the United States. Brazil was obviously attempting to assure a higher volume of exports, to partly offset the impact of lower prices then prevailing. Guarantees to reimburse in kind enabled it to draw on a wasting asset, its huge stores of the product.

Firms receiving the guaranteed prices now did not need the future market as a medium for hedging, and reduced their transactions on the Exchange accordingly. This had considerable impact since Brazil's "contract" was the primary contract being traded in New York.[33]

Another reason for the demise of the coffee futures market would seem to have been the increasing inclination of manufacturers like General Foods to buy their coffee beans directly from producers or at least, their disinclination to use the futures market for either speculative hedging, or other management purposes. Since General Foods, in particular, was such a substantial force in the market, its lack of support for a futures market—such as Hershey, Nestle and interestingly GF itself have given to the cocoa futures market—was bound to be felt in the market.

---

[33] J.M. Clark, Vice-President of Anderson, Clayton & Co., and former president of the NCA and the New York Sugar and Coffee Exchange respectively, believes Brazil's guaranteed prices and the stabilizing effects of the Coffee Agreement best explain the demise of the coffee futures market in New York. Interview, September 28, 1971.

While the International Coffee Agreement may have further dampened the New York coffee futures market by discouraging prospective speculators from playing the game, the previous points suggest that it was more a contributing factor than the decisive factor in the decline of the market.

In summary, it is probable that the nature of market organization in coffee and cocoa respectively has substantially affected the evolution of U.S. policies for the two products. The positions and roles of the futures markets for the two commodities have been of particular importance. At the time the ICA was negotiated the New York coffee futures market was already on the decline. Brazil's selling policies and General Foods' lack of interest in using the market for its own business operations meant that the ICA could hardly have been perceived as the primary and most immediate threat to the existence of the market, much less the only threat. Although certain parties were giving lip service to the importance of a futures market, there were none with substantial political influence that sought to spare the market the further blow of a price stabilizing commodity agreement.

General Foods and other large processing corporations simply had no compelling business reasons for wishing to prop up the futures market, not to mention the fact that they had positive reasons for supporting the development of the ICA. The traders, on the other hand, stoically accepted the demise of the futures market, and to some extent, contributed to this development by participating in Brazil's system of guaranteed export prices.

The cocoa case presents a marked contrast to that of coffee. The existence of an active cocoa futures market in the United States, supported by the processors and traders alike, has been a central reality with which American policy-makers and cocoa negotiators have had to come to terms. Cocoa processors and traders have generally seen the very idea of a commodity agreement as antithetical to the present organization of the market which they have preferred. All types of cocoa business firms, it has been said, use the market in the management of their own operations. The processors, for their part, have wanted to keep some traders in the field, and have recognized the value, indeed the necessity of the market for the traders. Nevertheless, the processors could adjust to the loss of the market more easily than the traders; and for this reason, the latter are constantly alert to and anxious over the possibility that Hershey, Nestle and General Foods might one day accede to a regulated market system that could spell the doom of the cocoa futures market.

Market Conditions: The Central Problem of Prices

What market conditions have helped shape the prospects for international commodity agreements in coffee and cocoa, and particularly for U.S. support of such agreements? Commodity trade specialists tend to emphasize how such conditions affect actor perceptions of the desirability and feasibility of certain agreements. "I just never thought a cocoa agreement was needed, as I did the Coffee Agreement," a U.S. State Department commodity trade specialist has remarked, indicating that he thought variable market conditions for coffee and cocoa respectively were the most immediate reasons for U.S. support of the Coffee Agreement, and coolness towards the cocoa negotiations.[34]

Keeping in mind that different actors may reach quite different policy conclusions concerning market conditions, even though they perceive those conditions alike, it is still important to try to isolate any "objective" differences in market conditions that may explain variable policy responses. This study focuses

---

[34] Interview, Paul Callanan, January 26, 1972. Callanan was the State Department's cocoa trade specialist between the late fifties and 1968.

upon possible connections between market conditions and U.S. policy responses; nevertheless, it would seem obvious that market conditions affect the dynamics of international negotiations for agreements, as well as national perspectives on agreements.[35]

"All, or nearly all, primary commodities are alike in one important respect," states the Cambridge commodity specialist, J. W. F. Fowe. "In the absence of any successful organised control scheme, their market prices fluctuate very widely, not only in the short term of a few weeks or months, or say within one year, but also in the longer term of several years."[36]

For the average LDC that depends heavily upon export earnings from one or a few such primary commodities price fluctuation, in and of itself, can pose serious economic difficulties. In an age of economic planning for development a major problem is that the best laid plans can be undercut when the prices of a major export product take an unexpected or unpredictable turn for the worse.

Still it is not so much price fluctuations per se that excite interest in commodity agreements. Rather it is the level of prices— "adverse" in the perspective of either producers or consumers— that has done so. Price fluctuations are troublesome to the economic planners; but the real concern is with price swings for the worse, or with sustained periods of extremely high prices (consumers are concerned) or extremely low prices (producers and sometimes consumers are concerned).

---

[35] There seems to be a direct correlation between periods of low commodity prices and producer-country enthusiasm for such agreements. Consuming countries are more likely to show interest in agreements in periods of high or rising commodity prices, or possibly, as this study indicates, in periods of exceedingly depressed prices. Fluctuating prices, therefore, tend to destabilize bargaining situations both among and between producers and consumers respectively.

[36] Rowe, op. cit. 66.

While both the coffee and cocoa markets have historically exhibited patterns of market price fluctuation in short and longer periods of time, the comparative purposes of this inquiry require closer examination of market conditions for the two products in the period since the late fifties.

Coffee. Chart I shows the pattern of price movements in the spot market for coffee over the period in which the International Coffee Agreement was negotiated and implemented. High demand for coffee after WWII and relative coffee shortages sent the prices soaring to the high of 1954. High prices called forth expanded production on a massive scale and resulted in an extended period of "oversupply" and "low" prices, the full ravages of which were probably contained by the Coffee Agreement.

The major cause of price fluctuations in the coffee market over the long-run, according to a recent IBRD study, has been the "coffee cycle." [37] Coffee cycles, the IBRD report holds, "have been engendered partly by the fundamental technological characteristics of the industry and partly by a special constellation of demand and supply price elasticities." [38] Coffee is a tree crop and as such has a long period of gestation, in which the first yields come 3-5 years after planting, and full bearing up to 2-5 years later. This means that production can adjust only slowly to changing price conditions.

---

[37] International Bank for Reconstruction and Development, The Coffee Problem Revisited," Vol. I. of The Coffee Papers, op. cit., 14-17. "The outstanding feature of the coffee industry in the last seventy years," the authors conclude, "has been a sequence of long price and production cycles lasting about 20-25 years each." Ibid., 15.

[38] Ibid., 15.

CHART I

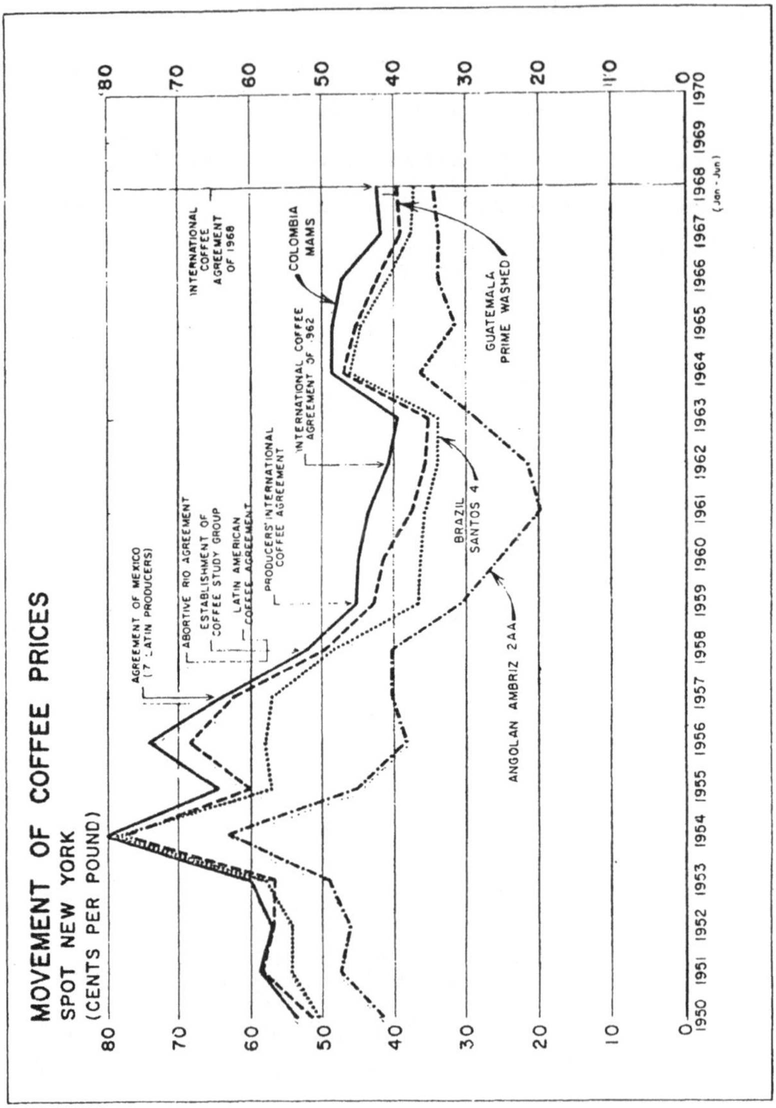

SOURCE: (R) IBRD 3966

The primary effect of high or low prices for coffee is altered rates of investment in production, the consequences of which are only slowly registered. High prices, especially over long periods, elicit greater investment in coffee production (land, plantings, buildings, infrastructure). In the aforementioned "cycle," the onrush of new production from the new trees coming to maturity puts pressures on prices and has historically ushered in a period of oversupply and low prices. The low prices, to complete the circle, discourage investment, bring the gradual onset of shortages, and then another period of high prices.

This coffee cycle is reflected in the 25 years following World War II. As the European market was reopened after the War, and transportation restored globally, release of pent-up demand for coffee sent the prices soaring to the highs of the early fifties. These high prices not only affected demand adversely, but they called forth a new phase of investment in the developing countries, growing supply and then "oversupply" in the late fifties. The latter conditions, of course, prompted the negotiation of the International Coffee Agreement. Unless the Coffee Agreement has some yet unforeseen moderating effect upon the investment behavior of the producers, it may be supposed, as the IBRD Coffee Papers do, that a fifth coffee cycle in this century is now unfolding, with a price "upswing phase emerging on the horizon." [39]

One factor in the first post-WWII coffee cycle is of particular note in this study. This is that the response of "new producer" to the high prices of the early fifties added to the tendency to increased investment in production among the already established producers. Several African countries (or more properly their colonial metropoles), eager for development revenue, were among the countries which sought to capitalize on what appeared to be a promising market for coffee.

---

[39] Ibid.

The net effect of a multitude of different investment decisions in numerous LDCs, neither coordinated through diplomacy nor regulated by an international agency, was a great outpouring of investment, and then inevitably, oversupply and low prices. If one producing country is prone to "over-react" to high or low prices in the coffee market, as Brazil was when it was the unchallenged source of most of the world's coffee, it is all the more likely that many producers, acting independently without production guidelines, much less production quotas, are likely to do so.

Decentralized decision-making in world coffee production exacerbates long-term price fluctuations that may be disadvantageous to both producers and consumers. Awareness of this has given impetus to the efforts to establish a regulatory system, facilitating, at least, some coordination of national export and production policies. Narrowing price fluctuations, for example, by setting floor prices or price ranges for international support, may help to even out the irregular patterns of investment that, to a great extent, account for variable production over the long-run, and hence, fluctuating prices.

The "coffee cycle" explains the long-term fluctuations of coffee prices; but it is useful to understand one important and common reason for short-term fluctuations of coffee and cocoa prices: annual supply variability due to natural disasters (frost, disease, drought) or political upheaval. These short-term fluctuations have sometimes been more troublesome for commodity agreement policy development than the longer-term fluctuations. Because there is a low price elasticity of demand for green coffee and for cocoa, over a relatively wide range of the demand curve, variations in supply at any one time, can have a marked effect upon prices. In the case of cocoa, speculative success on the futures market is largely a matter of anticipating supply availabilities.

What specific conditions in the coffee market seem to have been conducive to U.S. support of the Coffee Agreement? Such conditions were mediated through the perceptions (and values) of proximate policy-makers and interest group leaders whose support of an Agreement would be required.

First, in the period when the United States actively participated in negotiations over the problems of coffee (1958-1962), coffee prices were in a state of serious and steady decline. Between 1954, a year by most standards of exorbitantly high prices, and 1962, Colombia MAM's and Brazilian Santos 4 dropped in price, at least, by half (from approximately 80 cents per pound to 40 cents or less). For the last half of the decade prices of all types of coffee were in steady decline at varying rates. The generally accepted prognosis was that in the absence of international action, including consumer governments, prices would drop even lower. Most authoritative observers agreed on the possibility or likelihood of a "collapse of the market."[40] There were differences over what the United States should do about the situation, but little dissent from the view that the market was in a serious state of dislocation.

Second, and obviously contributing to the declining price, was a severe oversupply of coffee in relation to current and anticipated demand. The market now reaped the whirlwind of several previous years of expanded planting throughout the world. From the mid-fifties exportable production began to exceed actual exports in most years, except in those years when a natural disaster affected major production areas. By the coffee year 1958-59, total world coffee <u>stocks</u>, most of which were being held by Brazil, <u>equalled</u> total exports. Over the next

---

[40] This was the view of General Foods' Director of Green Coffee Operations, George Robbins. Interview, February 25, 1971; and of Sam Israel, the chief trader for the New Orleans firm of Leon Israel & Sons, Inc. Interview, October 21, 1971.

six years the cumulative world surplus of unexported coffee, climbed to 80 million bags (Kg. 1965). Since actual coffee exports in this period ranged between 40 and 53 million bags annually, it can be seen that stocks by themselves had become large enough to satisfy one to two years of global coffee requirements.[41]

There was no mistaking that the structure of the coffee market (supply and demand relationship) was in a state of serious dislocation. The problem, the OAS Special Commission on Coffee had forecast as early as 1955, was no temporary imbalance of supply and demand. An enormous surplus was a tangible reality by 1960.[42]

Low and declining coffee prices, and enormous stocks overhanging the market, and little prospect of a short-run change on these conditions, were key economic factors contributing to the American decision to support the Coffee Agreement.

It is possible to suggest some of the decisive ways in which these conditions registered upon the U.S. policy-making system. First, the international coffee market was in a state of crisis. Observers commonly observed that coffee prices were moving to "disastrously" low levels. And scores of producing countries would be affected adversely.

Crisis, it has often been observed, is a galvanizing force in both diplomacy and national policy development. Crisis in the coffee market favored diplomatic concessions in the coffee negotiations that countries might otherwise have been

---

[41] Data on stocks extrapolated from IBRD Chart 3967, "World Supply and Demand for Coffee," reprinted as Chart 2, in International Bank for Reconstruction and Development, International Coffee Agreement, 1968: Background and Analysis, Report EC-165 Prepared by Shamsher Singh (Washington, D.C.: IBRD, August, 1968).

[42] The OAS Special Commission forecast in 1955 that a large oversupply of coffee was imminent. Organization of American States, "The Coffee Economy and the Future" (Washington, D.C.: OAS, 1955) as cited in Ibid., 2.

unprepared to make, had the future of the market either been more hopeful or more uncertain. A crisis of depressed and declining prices encouraged producers to make concessions. The conditions were serious enough that the "new producers"—those that might stand to lose by an agreement that could freeze shares of the market—were sufficiently impressed with the gravity of the price situation to temporarily forego export expansion in favor of bolstering market prices.

A crisis of depressed and declining prices might seem an economic boon for consuming countries, even when there are obvious "political" reasons for their being concerned about them. But the consuming countries are also aware, especially in the case of coffee where there have been distinct historical cycles of ups and downs for many years, that a period of very low prices will usually be followed by disinvestment in coffee production, supply shortage, and then resulting high prices. The vivid memories of the high coffee prices of 1954—American consumers paid well over $1.00 per pound of regular coffee in that year—have caused American policy-makers to view periods of very low prices in the perspective of their longer run consequences.

Certainly the large roasting corporations and the large trading firms have been atune to the fact that they have self-interested, economic reasons for desiring that excessively low prices not develop in the market. In this connection, General Foods is known to have wished, by supporting the Coffee Agreement, to head off a collapse of the market and the longer-term consequences of coffee shortage.[43]

General Foods turns over a tremendous volume of coffee, making its profit on a "cents added" (to the cost of green coffee) basis. Excessively high green

---

[43] Interview, George Robbins, February 25, 1971.

coffee prices, such as may result in the long-run from severely depressed prices, can price coffee out of the consumer market. U.S. coffee demand was permanently diminished by the high prices of 1954. While there is a low price elasticity of demand for coffee in the U.S., extreme prices can and do shift the level of demand. Also during the sixties coffee was hard pressed in the consumer market by other beverages, notably soft drinks and tea. A General Foods has to consider the possibility that any increase of demand for coffee during extreme low-price periods may be offset, or more than offset, by a price swing in the opposite direction. This is one of several reasons why GF strongly favored the Coffee Agreement.

Generally speaking, crisis in the coffee market was conducive to the Coffee Agreement. It tended to convince crucial governments, and within the U.S., key policy-makers and interest group leaders, of the desirability of government action. At another level it created an atmosphere in which American policy-makers could conclude that a Coffee Agreement was "feasible" both in terms of negotiability and operability, and in terms of securing sufficient political support in the Executive and in Congress for American participation.

Within the general crisis of the market another condition probably was conducive to an agreement: the large coffee surplus itself. Not only were prices relatively low and trending downwards, but the enormous stocks overhanging the market and the current pace of production, not to mention the apparent incapacity of the producers to develop by themselves an effective export control system, convinced most participants and observers that there was unlikely to be any marked reversal of price trends in the foreseeable future. There was no feeling that the market would "bounce back" shortly, as until recently, manufacturers and traders thought the cocoa market would invariably do, after a short period of depressed prices.

Huge coffee surpluses and the scale of current production underlined the need for governmental measures to regulate the flow of coffee supplies into the market. They also reassured the consumers that market conditions basically militated against the "misuse" of a commodity agreement as an unabashedly price-raising instrument. The consumers, so the unexpressed reasoning went, had a generally superior bargaining position. So long as coffee surpluses existed, the producers would need an agreement more than the consumers. Implicit in this situation was the possibility that the consumers could easily withdraw, if not satisfied with the operations of an agreement.

The great coffee surplus during 1958-1965, militated against wide swings in price. The price rise in 1963 was temporary and due to weather damage to the Brazilian main crop. Were it not for the existing stocks, it is probable that the price rise would have been steeper, and more lasting. The coffee surplus indirectly helped to stabilize the conditions for negotiating the Coffee Agreement by, in effect, freezing the national economic and commercial interests long enough to facilitate compromise.

The point is made clearer by a comparison with cocoa. In the absence of protracted surpluses of cocoa, year after year, cocoa prices have moved up and down, each time on the up-side tending to upset a fragile consensus of support for a cocoa agreement. A commodity surplus, by nature, is a factor conducing to lower prices in a market. Its effects, of course, may be mitigated by sales or export control schemes.

The great coffee surplus and attendant low prices, also favored diplomatic consensus for an agreement, by compelling the producers to subordinate their conflicting interests over market shares to their common interests in better prices. It also heightened the consumers' awareness of their economic and political interests in supporting an agreement. The existence of the large surplus, at the same time, encouraged the consumers to believe that they prospectively had a favorable bargaining position in any organization of the market, or at least, that the surplus protected against "any significant rise in coffee prices in the foreseeable future," irrespective of an agreement.[44]

Cocoa. Chart II shows spot price movements for cocoa over the period in which four major U.N. negotiation conferences for a cocoa agreement have been held. It will be noted that three of the four conferences (1963, 1966, 1972) followed closely upon periods of declining cocoa prices, or one might say in the perspective of the producing countries, periods of relatively "low prices." The 1967 Conference, as a follow-up of the conference of the previous year, occurred, by contrast, at a time when a new phase of price increases was in the making. Rising prices upset the producer consensus for an agreement that had developed during the previous two years.

The timing of the cocoa negotiations would seem to suggest that commodity agreement negotiations will normally come about, if at all, in a period of "low" or "declining" prices. This is a time when producers are most likely to feel strong pressures for an agreement, and take collaborative initiatives accordingly. Consumers are most disposed to commodity agreements, if at all, as a means of preventing shortages of a commodity, and attendant high prices, or for political reasons; so they may be amenable to negotiations in periods of low price, and for other economic, as well as political reasons, be responsive to producer appeals for commodity agreement talks.

---

[44]This assertion was made by Secretary of State, Dean Rusk, in a letter to President John F. Kennedy, October 2, 1962, as found in U.S. Congress, Senate, Committee on Foreign Relations, International Coffee Agreement, 1962, 3-6.

CHART II

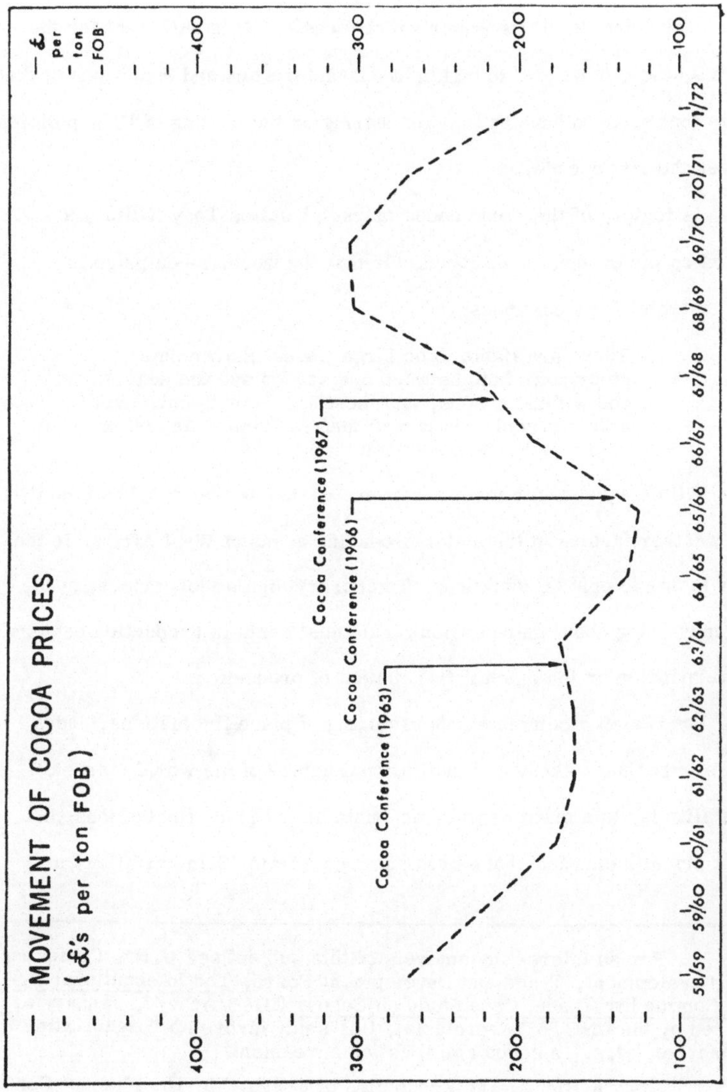

SOURCE: Derived from Chart in Sir Eric Tansley, "Is a Cocoa Scheme Necessary," Unpublished Paper, 1972.

The subject of cocoa price-determination and fluctuations is extremely complex, at least, in all its important nuances.[45] It is sufficient for the purpose of this study, however, to highlight characteristics and conditions of the cocoa market that seem to have had major bearing on the making of U.S. policies for cocoa over the last decade.

"A feature of the world cocoa market," states Tony Killick, a British expert on the economics of cocoa, "is that the world cocoa price is chronically unstable." He continues:

> There are liable to be large [price] movements up or down both between one season and the next and within seasons, and these movements have over a long period been larger than for almost any other major primary export commodity.[46]

Killick agrees with most observers in finding that supply variability, often due to weather factors in the major producing areas of West Africa, is the single major factor in price fluctuations. Temporary high or low prices, at the same time, may bring about more serious maladjustments in production centers, such as overexpansion or too much retrenchment of production.

But "to get a complete understanding of price fluctuations," adds Killick, "it is important to know the institutional nature of the world market."[47] Supply variability is, to a great degree, accountable for price fluctuations, but why is it that price fluctuations have been so much greater than variations in

---

[45] For an interesting analysis of this subject see U.N., Conference on Trade and Development, Trade and Development Board, The International Organization of Commodity Trade: Case Study on Cocoa, TD/B/AC 2/3, January 3, 1966. Produced by the UNCTAD secretariat, this study favors an "organization of the cocoa market," i.e., a cocoa stabilization agreement.

[46] Tony Killick, "The Economics of Cocoa," in The Study of Contemporary Ghana, Vol. I: The Economy of Ghana, ed. by Walter Birmingham, [illegible] N. Omaboe (London: George Allen & Unwin, Ltd. 1966), 379

production levels? The primary reason, in Killick's view, is that expectations of productive levels more than actual production, are most important in influencing short-run price changes.

A very high percentage of cocoa dealings are in "forward transactions" through the cocoa exchanges, sometimes up to twelve months in advance. Participants in the exchanges, including speculators, engage in a constant process of educated "guessing" about what equilibrium prices for cocoa will be sometime in the future. The tendency has been for forecasts of supply to consistently "differ from the eventual result," and in consequence, "to exaggerate the extent of actual change of supply, whether the change was an increase or decrease.[48] This has tended, of course, to result in exaggerated swings in market prices.

Another factor in the cocoa market also contributes to exaggerated short-run swings of price, and points up another peculiar difficulty of "organizing" the cocoa market. Unlike coffee which moves directly into consumption after only a relatively small amount of processing, cocoa beans undergo a great amount of processing and differentiation, and are transformed into a variety of retail products, some of which are only partly derived from cocoa (even the chocolate candy bar contains a variety of non-cocoa ingredients). This and other factors typically contribute to a lag between the adjustment of final demand for cocoa-derived products and the constantly changing prices of cocoa beans. Frequently, this lag amplifies swings in short-run bean prices. For example, bean prices may be rising, as a result of an anticipated shortfall in the West African cocoa crop; simultaneously demand for cocoa by chocolate manufacturers may be increasing as a delayed response to a fall in cocoa prices six to twelve months earlier. The effect, of course, is an increase in the price rise. The process works in a similar manner in the opposite direction.

Ibid.,, 380.

In the search for contrasting market conditions between coffee and cocoa, respectively, that may help explain U.S. support of the Coffee Agreement, but its reserve about a cocoa agreement, some very considerable contrasts spring to attention. Basically, these suggest that at no time during the long period of negotiations for a cocoa agreement has the cocoa market been so severely dislocated as the coffee market was during the years in which the Coffee Agreement was negotiated and implemented.

Certainly there have been wild swings in cocoa prices, and periods of extremely high or low prices. These indeed have given impetus to the cocoa agreement negotiations. But as in coffee during the late fifties and early sixties, there has so far developed no severe and sustained imbalance of supply and demand. Periods of cocoa shortage or oversupply, in relation to current demand, have tended to be relatively short-lived. And most importantly no period of oversupply has been so serious as that which surrounded the negotiation of the Coffee Agreement.

Cocoa surpluses have tended to be much smaller and, by no means, "chronic." Throughout the sixties the cumulative surplus of cocoa never so much as constituted even 40% of world cocoa requirements for any one year.[49] Proponents of the free market, such as Sir Eric Tansley, have not hesitated to argue that:

> the free market in cocoa has been an efficient means of bringing supply and demand into balance: it has avoided the development of chronic surplus conditions or the wasteful build-up of excessive unwanted stocks.

---

[49] The largest cumulative surplus during the sixties was registered in 1964-65: 485,000 tons against actual consumption in that year of 1,321,000 tons. Chart entitled "World Cocoa Production and Consumption," Sir Eric Tansley, "Is a Cocoa Scheme Necessary," Unpublished paper, London, 1972.

Opponents of a cocoa agreement have argued that the absence of chronic cocoa surpluses is one of the distinguishing characteristics of the cocoa market which sets it off from the case of coffee in the late fifties.

Cocoa surpluses or shortages over the last decade have either been mild, or if extreme, short-lived. The two periods of extreme prices— the price collapse in 1965 and the excessively high prices of 1969— were as much as anything due to extreme supply changes as a result of weather conditions. According to Tansley, the "exceptional crop" of 1964/65, "probably a weather freak," came unfortuitously at the end of a period of "substantial expansion in production." Production levels fell sharply in 1968-69, by contrast, due to adverse weather conditions in West Africa.[50]

In the absence of a sustained glut of market, such as existed in the case of coffee, there has so far developed no strong and sustained sense of urgency, among both producers and consumers, for formulating a cocoa agreement. Ironically, frequent alternating shortages and surpluses, and attendant price swings, have tended to create unstable conditions for negotiating an agreement. Periods of high prices have not been propitious for agreement negotiations— consumers have been generally unenthusiastic about a cocoa agreement and have usually been in a position to "ride out" these periods; producers lose enthusiasm for arguments when the market is strong— and periods of low prices have either not been severe enough or long enough to propel agreement.

In summary, the "objective" economic conditions of the cocoa market, during the period of this survey, have been less conducive, than those of the coffee market were, to either global diplomatic consensus for an agreement, or particularly U.S. support thereof. This is not to say either that these conditions

---

50 Tansley, op. cit., 1-2.

have altogether precluded an agreement—there is, at least, the Cocoa Agreement of 1972—or that they have been, by themselves, decisive either way.

In the broader view, characteristics of the coffee trade system were more favorable to U.S. support of a Coffee Agreement in 1962 than have been those of the cocoa system to similar U.S. support of a cocoa agreement. Likewise the development of U.S. policy in soluble coffee dispute was shaped, to a great extent, by the inter-connection between the green coffee and soluble coffe trade systems.

CHAPTER II

Primary Actors: Business and the State Department

Which have been the key business firms and associations that have had substantial stake in regulation of the coffee and cocoa trade systems? What characteristics of the American coffee and cocoa industries help explain patterns of relationships between business and policy-making for the issues under study?[51]

This study confirms that the largest processing corporations are preeminent in the national economy and politics of coffee and cocoa. Since World War II there has been a pronounced trend in the coffee and cocoa industries towards integration and concentration.

Small trading firms have tended to give way to the large, multi-product trading firms, and both these types of firms have had to contend, to varying degrees, with direct dealings between the large processing corporations and selling agents of the LDC producers. Small processing corporations, though still relatively numerous in coffee, have tended to give way to the middle-sized or giant processing corporations. In a related trend, small and large processing corporations, in increasing numbers, have been absorbed in the country's largest, multi-product industries. Similarly, certain coffee and cocoa processing industries have integrated vertically, thereby eliminating numerous autonomous firms.

---

[51] The perspective of this research, comparing business-government relationships in three cases, excluded an in-depth analysis of the sources of business behavior. For an interesting article that employs theories of the "behavior of the firm" to explain corporate policies towards the Coffee Agreement, see Stephen D. Krasner, "Business Government Relations: The Case of the International Coffee Agreement," Unpublished Paper, Center for International Affairs, Harvard University, Spring, 1973.

Several trading and processing firms are actors in two, or in all three cases under study. Many trading firms, e.g., A.C. Israel and Co., have traditionally dealt in a range of primary products, or even raw materials; and some large processing corporations such as General Foods and Nestle produce a diverse line of food, beverage and other products, and use both coffee and cocoa as primary products. This presents the possibility of comparative analysis of the behavior of particular firms in different cases of proposed international regulation, involving different products that they trade or process.[52] What factors, for example, explain General Foods and J. Aron support for a Coffee Agreement, but their opposition to a cocoa agreement?[53]

The Coffee and Cocoa Industries

Coffee Industry. The coffee industry of the United States is a multi-million dollar industry, widely dispersed throughout the United States. In 1967, 267 different coffee roasting establishments, employing 16,100 employees, produced and shipped roasted coffee valued at $1,802,400,000.[54] The roasting industry meanwhile was linked to a wider "economy of coffee," including allied industries of grocery marketing, shipping and banking.

---

[52]For an introduction to some of the questions involved when a diversified, multi-product company confronts a general foreign policy issue— "free trade"— see the pioneering study, Bauer, et al. American Business and Public Policy, 1963.

[53] J. Aron & Co. of New York City is one of the largest American traders of coffee and cocoa.

[54] U.S., Department of Commerce, 1967 Census of Manufacturers Preliminary Report, (Washington, D.C.; Bureau of the Census), November, 1969, as reproduced in Tables R-5-1 and R-5-2, in Pan-American Coffee Bureau, Annual Coffee Statistics, 1969, No. 33 (New York: PACB, 1970), A-76 and A-77.

There are two main types of business firms in the coffee "industry," which for convenience, can be called "roasters" and "traders."

Roasting firms roast, grind and blend coffee beans into the "regular" coffee familiar to Americans. A few of the larger firms are also engaged in the capital intensive production of soluble coffee ("instant coffee"). Many more roasting firms package and market soluble coffee supplied by soluble producing firms.

The roaster category of business includes a wide variety of types and sizes of business, ranging from the giant General Foods Corporation, which produces over 300 grocery items and 30 different brand-name food products, including several different brand-name coffees, to the middle-sized roaster such as Hills Bros. of San Francisco that has coffee as its major product, to the relatively small and parochial roaster that markets in a very limited geographic area.

General Foods, as Table I indicates, has held in the range of 30 percent of the total U.S. market for regular coffee. According to another estimate, GF brands accounted for 34 percent of all regular coffee sales in 1965.[55] Coffee sales (including instant) constituted just over one-third of total GF sales of packaged food and beverage procuts in 1965, or for approximately $500 million in sales. These sales provided about half of GF's profits for that year.[56]

General Foods is likely to be a force to reckon with in the political economy of coffee, both because of its large share in the coffee market and

---

[55] Harvard Business School, General Foods Corporation, Case No. ICH 10G104 / Am-P/ 188R2, 1964, 4.

[56] Extrapolated from figures provided in Ibid., 1-4. Krasner estimates that 28% of GF sales by value in 1970 were in coffee. Krasner, op. cit., Table 4.

TABLE I

Regular Coffee: Market Shares in the U.S. by Company, 1968-1970

Company/Brand	1968(%)	1969(%)	1970(Est)
General Foods	29.0	29.4	29.4
Maxwell House	24.0	24.0	24.0
Sanka	3.0	3.2	3.2
Yuban	2.0	2.2	2.2
Proctor & Gamble			
Folger	18.0	19.5	19.8
Hills Bros.			
Hills Bros.	12.5	11.5	10.3
Standard Brands			
Chase & Sanborn	5.5	5.5	5.5
Coca-Cola	5.5	5.0	4.0
Maryland Club	2.5	2.0	1.7
Butternut	3.0	3.0	2.7
S.A. Schonbrunn & Co.			
Savarin	1.5	1.0	0.8
All Others	28.0	28.1	29.8
	100.0	100.0	100.0

Source: Table, as found in John C. Maxwell, "Overview: Market Share Trends, World Coffee and Tea: Guide to Coffee/USA (August, 1971), 40.

because coffee is the company's single most important product. Beyond this General Foods is among America's fifty largest corporations, and the resources of the larger company can be brought to bear upon issues concerning the coffee sector of the company only.[57]

The Folger Coffee Co. has ranked second to GF in overall coffee sales throughout the period under study. It illustrates one of several significant trends in the structural development of the American coffee market which probably has substantial implications for governmental policy-making regarding coffee trade. In the mid-sixties Folger Co. was purchased by Proctor and Gamble, becoming one of several divisions of that giant corporation.

There have been several other instances of large corporations "diversifying" into coffee processing, either as a marked departure from old lines of business (P & G) or as a more ostensibly logical extension of current activity. Instances of the latter include Coca-Cola's new ventures into regular <u>and</u> instant coffee production, and Nestle's purchase of Cain's Coffee, once an independent coffee manufacturer in the southwest. Even the leading chocolate manufacturer, Hershey Food Corporation, has now acquired a coffee plant. Mergers such as these and the expansion of large, previously non-coffee corporations into the coffee field, are undoubtedly, reflective of the pervasive trend to consolidation throughout the American economy. It would seem, at the same time, that the entry of more large corporations into coffee processing could bear upon the politics of policy-making for coffee.

Hills Bros. of San Francisco has been a third major manufacturer of regular coffee. Unlike General Foods or Folger, Hills Bros. so far has remained a "closely-held" company. Until recently, it did not press for a national market and concentrated its marketing on the west coast. Now it has joined the

---

[57] The Chief executives of General Foods normally rise through the Maxwell House Division of the Company.

great media battle of the early seventies for a major share of the national market. Coffee is the main product of the firm.

The fourth major producer of ground roast coffee, Standard Brands, is also a major U.S. corporation; but it has remained aloof from the politics of the Coffee Agreement. According to one observer, the company has never even had a representative on the Foreign Affairs Committee of the National Coffee Association, the influential group that has advised the State Department from the inception of negotiations for an Agreement.[58]

A & P's prominence in the national coffee market grew over the sixties and represents another significant factor in the American coffee market, the participation of the mammoth grocery chains in coffee processing itself. A&P, Kroger and other such chains have previously packaged and put their brand names on regular and instant coffees provided by special suppliers; but some of the larger companies, like A & P, are now finding it more economic to engage in actual production.

While a few large corporations account for the lion share of national coffee sales, a number of small, regional manufacturers, though considerably fewer than several years ago, together hold a substantial share (1969 - 19 percent) of the market. These corporations still depend heavily upon traders for securing supplies of appropriate types of coffee beans when they are needed.

The other major type of business firm in the American coffee industry has been the trading firm. Trading firms also vary considerably in nature and functions, although generally it has been their role to secure coffee beans, and to arrange for their transportation and delivery to various roasters in the United States. Most of these firms are based in one of the four major coffee import centers (New York, New Orleans, Houston or San Francisco), but may also

---

[58] Krasner, op. cit., 21.

operate in foreign exports centers, and certainly in the inland United States where they find customers.

The most important distinction among the trading firms is surely size. The very small firms that once flourished in such locations as "Front Street" in Wall Street have been dying out rapidly over the last 20 years. The increasingly substantial capital requirements of conducting trading operations, the promise of greater investment returns in other pursuits, and certain developments in the international trade of coffee, for example, increased producer government involvement in the trade once conducted by private merchants, have all militated against the small trader.

The most viable trading firms in the coffee industry, not surprisingly, have been large firms which more often than not trade in numerous primary products besides coffee. Over the last decade the trading firm of J. Aron & Co., Inc. has been the foremost importer of green coffee into the United States. A. C. Israel Coffee Co. of New York and Leon Israel & Bros., Inc. of New Orleans, have been leading importers for many years. The new A. C. & Leon Israel Coffee Co. (ACLI) resulting from the merger of the two aforementioned companies, has catapulted to the top echelon of the list of importers. In 1972 the new company was second in amount of imports.[59] ACLI International which embraces this coffee combination is also a major trader in many other products, including cocoa, sugar and rubber.

Still there are numerous relatively small trading firms in the field, as well as larger trading firms that "dabble" in coffee. While J. Aron and ACLI <u>each</u> imported over 2 million bags of green coffee in 1972, several old family

---

59 For a list of the top 50 importers of coffee for the coffee year, 1972, see the table prepared by George Gordon Paton & Co., as reproduced in <u>World Coffee and tea: Guide to Coffee/USA, IV</u> (August, 1972), 26.

firms accounted for considerably smaller, but substantial shares of imports: Scholtz & Co. ranked ninth in imports with 647,000 bags; S. F. Pellas Co. was 24th with 207,000 bags; and A. L. Ransohoff Co., Inc. was 39th with 92,000 bags. The large and diversified British trading firm of Gill & Duffus, with a branch office office in New York City, meanwhile ranked 17th in U.S. imports with 312,000 bags.[60]

In the import rankings for 1972 only four firms imported more than one million bags. Two of the firms in this category, in addition to J. Aron and ACLI, were the major coffee roasters, General Foods (1.2 million bags) and Folger (1.9 million bags). Their participation in direct importing underlines the fact that trader activity has been constricted by direct corporate buying operations. But the raw materials needs of the large corporate processors are still not fully met by direct purchases or "special deals." Indeed, according to Frederick Otterbein, Vice-President of General Foods for green coffee operations, most of his company's green coffee purchases in the late sixties and early seventies were still made through trading firms. All of its Latin coffees were secured through trader channels, and <u>half</u> of its African coffees.[61]

A high percentage of imports through trading firms must ultimately be consumed by the leading roasters. It is obvious that the larger roasters must, therefore, have a great deal of leverage upon the many traders, large and small, that seek business with them. This, it may be supposed, is a major reason why large roaster support and leadership in behalf of the Coffee Agreement was so crucial to developing business consensus for the Agreement.

---

[60] Ibid.

[61] Interview, Frederick Otterbein, September 22, 1971.

For several decades the peak trade association of the coffee industry has been the National Coffee Association (NCA) headquartered in New York City. Virtually all roasters and trading firms in the United States, and numerous "allied" firms in banking and shipping, are members of the NCA. The Association, which maintains a representative Board, numerous joint Committees, and a small professional staff, is generally authoritative in representing industry views in word and action. Historically, the Association has had a central role in representing industry views to government, regarding a variety of issues, including armed services coffee supplies, health and packaging regulation and domestic or international market regulation.

The NCA is the authoritative voice of the whole industry, but to the chagrin of the numerous trader members, a relatively few giant processing corporations, led by General Foods, actually dominate Association policy-making. These corporations bear a relatively larger share of NCA costs, have the financial and personnel resources to seize leadership, and in the end, the crucial buying power to require trader support for positions they desire.

There are three major regional associations of traders: the Green Coffee Association, the Pacific Coast Coffee Association and the Green Coffee Association of New Orleans. The roasters maintain memberships in these associations, but generally accept that they will represent a trader point of view in most instances. These associations supported the first Coffee Agreement, although more hesitantly than the roasters, and opposed the second.

Soluble Coffee Industry. Processing of soluble coffee is a sub-industry of the larger coffee industry. The global rise of instant coffee production is mostly a post-WWII phenomenon, initiated first in Europe by the Swiss Nestle Co., and spread rapidly to the United States, especially in the 1950's. From the beginning the industry was capital-intensive and pervaded by keen technological competition among a few companies. Competition has been marked by successive developments of different types of instant coffee: spray-dried ("powdered"), freeze-dried and more recently, agglomerated. Each of these types has had the potential of markedly changing, if not "revolutionizing" the quest for sales. Instant coffee sales in the United States rose rapidly in the 1950's, levelled off in the early 1960's, and were given a boost again in the late 1960's by freeze-dry innovations. Instant coffee sales have come to account for nearly 30 percent (by value) of all coffee sales in the United States, but coffee experts do not expect this percentage to rise above 40 percent, at least, in the foreseeable future.[62]

Production in the U.S. instant coffee sub-industry is highly concentrated, but there has been intense competition among industry leaders such as General Foods and Nestle (US). Table II indicates the high degree of concentration in the industry, partly obscured by the fact that General Foods and Nestle, between them, sell seven different "brands" of instant coffee.

General Foods has a more commanding position in the production and marketing of soluble coffee in the United States than it does in regular coffee. Among other things, this may be attributed to the tremendous capital resources at the disposal of the company leadership which the latter has chosen to commit heavily to technological innovation in soluble production. In the sixties GF invested millions in the development of freeze-dried instant coffee, which coincidentally, was just being put on the market when the major challenge of lower cost Brazilian imports (powder) presented itself.

---

[62] Interview, George Robbins, August 11, 1971.

TABLE II

Instant Coffee: Market Shares in the U.S. by Company, 1968-1970

Company/Brand	1968(%)	1969(%)	1970(Est)
General Foods	53.0	51.8	51.5
Maxwell House	27.5	23.5	24.8
Maxim	10.0	13.0	10.5
Sanka	11.5	8.8	9.0
Yuban	4.0	4.0	2.7
Freeze-dried Sanka	-	2.5	4.5
Proctor & Gamble			
Folger	7.5	7.4	7.7
Hills Bros.			
Hills Bros.	2.5	1.8	1.5
Nestle	14.0	16.5	23.0
Nescafe	11.5	11.0	11.0
Taster's Choice	1.0	4.0	10.5
Decaf	1.5	1.5	1.5
Standard Brands			
Chase & Sanborn	4.0	3.2	3.2
Borden			
Kava	1.0	1.5	1.3
All Others	8.0	17.8	11.8
	100.0	100.0	100.0

Source: Table, as found in John C. Maxwell, "Overview: Market Share Trends, World Coffee and Tea: Guide to Coffee/USA (August, 1971), 40.

GF's closest competitor in the U.S. instant coffee market has been Nestle (US), with headquarters in White Plains, New York. Nestle (US) is a semi-autonomous "national" company within the "multinational" Nestle Alimentana S.A., which is incorporated in Switzerland and headquartered in Vevey. Nestle (US) has a high degree of autnonomy in relation to the parent holding company in Vevey. For example, it is largely responsible for its own profit picture. But it is also subject to directives from the multinational's headquarters. Nestle Alimentana is the parent holding company among three holding companies that together comprise "Nestle." It manages national companies (partly through the other two holding companies) in over thirty different countries, which together operate 208 factories. Subsidiaries and allied companies of Nestle market a vast variety of food and drink products, but the specialties of the larger company have always been beverage and cocoa products.[63]

Nestle pioneered instant coffee sales in Europe and today is still first in that market. It has shown a stronger inclination than General Foods to establish subsidiary companies in the LDCs, and importantly for this study, has maintained instant coffee (Nescafe) operations in Brazil since 1948, as well as in the Ivory Coast and Central America.

In the United States Nestle (US) has recently presented a sharp challenge to General Foods, especially in the freeze-dried market. Nestle's Taster's Choice (freeze-dried) is waging a fierce market battle with GF's freeze-dried entry, Maxim. Both companies have undertaken major television campaigns for their products, both to bolster the flagging consumer preference for coffee and to promote their own brand names.

---

[63] Information on Nestle extrapolated from Standard and Poor's, Corporation Records, Oct.-Nov., 1971, 2104-5.

The GF-Nestle (US) competition is, undoubtedly, important to the analysis of business behavior in the U. S.-Brazilian dispute over solubles. In the early stages the two companies worked together through the National Coffee Association to press the U. S. government for countermeasures against Brazilian policy. In 1970, however, Nestle adopted a more conciliatory attitude towards Brazilian imports and led a coup within the NCA Board of Directors to gain acceptance for its views.

Due to the large capital requirements of soluble coffee production only fourteen U. S. companies have entered the field. These operate 20 highly automated factories throughout the country. The "brand-name roasters"— GF, Nestle, Hills Bros., and Standard Brands— account for most of this production.[64] While all of these companies seem to have imported the controversial Brazilian soluble, at some time or another, Hills Bros. was unique among the large roasters (before 1971) in relying wholly upon the Brazilian product, rather than on its own production.

Until the mid-sixties Hills Bros. had engaged in soluble production on a modest basis, and in the early seventies returned to it. With the introduction of the low cost Brazilian soluble, however, it closed its own processing operations and began to package and sell the Brazilian product as its own. By 1971, anticipating restrictions on the Brazilian imports it had returned to soluble production itself. In the meantime, Hills Bros. had been one of the most vocal advocates of Brazilian imports. From the perspective of business competition, it would seem that Hills Bros., as a medium-sized roaster and modest soluble producer, was attempting to enhance its competitive terms in relation to the giant coffee producers like General Foods.

---

[64] For a listing of companies and factory locations see the Table, USA's Instant Coffee Plants," in World Coffee & Tea: Guide to Coffee/USA (August, 1971), 36.

A substantial threat to the brand-name roasters' ascendancy in instant coffee sales has arisen from a second category of participants in the soluble coffee trade, the "private label" companies. Many small roasters and food chains have lacked either the means or the inclination to make large investments in soluble production, which run 10 to 20 times greater in capital requirements than a comparable regular coffee plant. Nevertheless, these companies have wished to sell their "own" coffees; and many, in fact, have bought and sold the product of the "private label suppliers."

It has been the "private label" sales of the large food chains such as A&P that have caused the most anxiety and consternation among the large brand-name producers. The latter have chafed over the fact that the private label firms have benefitted from, but not helped finance the expensive media campaigns to promote soluble sales. They have also been watchful of any competitive advantage these firms might gain from new factors in the marketing equation. Naturally they were anxious about the possibility that the private label firms would capitalize heavily upon the low cost Brazilian imports; and private label behavior was not reassuring in this regard.

The private label firms used to depend heavily upon the "private label suppliers." During the instant coffee boom of the fifties four private label suppliers provided virtually all of the instant coffee packaged by the private label companies. At that time they accounted for as much as 20 per cent of the total instant coffee production in the United States. Tenco, purchased by the Coca-Cola Company in 1960, at one time accounted for 85% of the private label business.[65] The other three private processors were Sol Cafe Manufacturing Corporation and Coffee Instants, Inc., both of which have since been bought out by Chock Full O'Nuts, and United Instant Coffee Corporation. In the sixties other

[65] The President of Tenco, from the late fifties to the present, Edward Aborn, was the first chairman of the National Coffee Association's Soluble Coffee Committee.

private label suppliers entered the field. Nestle (US) itself became the second or third most important supplier, as a side-line to its brand-name business.

It can be inferred that the availability of low cost Brazilian soluble would present real difficulties for private label suppliers with substantial investment in domestic productive capacity. The central problem for them has been the loss of customers who turn to importing the lower cost supplies. Another new trend, food chain investment in production facilities (e.g., the Kroger Co. and Safeway Stores, Inc.) has also weakened the position of the private label suppliers. The Brazilian imports have also affected the positions of the suppliers relative to each other, favoring those with less capital investment in plant productive capacity.

Have coffee traders been concerned with the soluble coffee dispute, as they have been with the establishment and operation of the Coffee Agreement? Generally speaking, green coffee traders have resisted what they perceive to be "subsidized" exports of soluble coffee to the United States. As early as 1956-1957 west coast traders were calling for action against imports of soluble from Mexico and Central America. Their concern was that imports of soluble coffee would displace a corresponding volume of green coffee trade feeding domestic soluble production.

The traders were doubly alarmed over the Brazilian imports, due to their sheer volume. In time, however, the unity of opposition to Brazilian imports began to deteriorate, if only partially. At the end of the sixties a number of traders were developing a new trade in soluble coffee.[66] The vast majority of traders, nevertheless, remained adamantly opposed to Brazilian imports.

---

[66] In 1971 at least eight New York City traders were importing soluble coffee: Imperial Commodities Corporation, Standard Importing Co., R.F. Downing, Liberty Import Co., Richter Bros., Jaret Imports, Escriptoric Supplicy, and S.F. Pellas. International Trade Center, UNCTAD and GATT, The Market of Soluble Coffee in Canada and Japan (Geneva, 1971).

Some have suspected that the political behavior of certain U.S. participants in soluble coffee production and trade during the U.S.-Brazilian dispute may have been influenced by the nature of their foreign investments.[67] Patterns of international investment do seem to have had some important implications for U.S. policy-making in the solubles dispute.

There has been only modest U.S. corporate investment in soluble production in Brazil. Although both Tenco (before its acquisition by Coca-Cola in 1960) and Standard Brands contemplated establishing soluble plants in Brazil in the late fifties, neither carried through at that time.[68] Not until 1968 or 1969, when Coca-Cola Tenco acquired the Fruzol plant in Brazil did an American company make a major commitment to soluble production there.[69]

General Foods' pattern of domestic and international investments presented it with a different set of calculations in the face of low cost Brazilian imports. Importantly GF has had no investments in soluble coffee production in Brazil. It controls Industrial Alimenticias Gerais, S.A., and its partner in this combination since 1957, Kibon, S.A. Gerais is prominent in ice cream, cereal, chewing gum and Kool-Aid sales.

---

[67] During the Senate Foreign Relations Committee Hearings on the International Coffee Agreement, 1968, on June 8, 1968, Senator Albert Gore questioned State Department witnesses concerning whether "American financial interests own the processing plants in Brazil." The witnesses, Anthony Solomon, the Assistant Secretary of State for Economic Affairs and Acting Deputy Assistant, George Jacobs, seemed somewhat unsure of their answer, but concluded: "...the Brazilian-processed coffee producers are Brazilian owned, to our knowledge." From a statement by George Jacobs, Acting Deputy Assistant Secretary of State for Economic Affairs, as found in U.S., Congress, Senate, Committee on Foreign Relations, International Coffee Agreement, 1968, Hearings on Executive D, 90th Cong.; 2d sess., June 4 and 12, 1968, 19.

[68] Interview, Edward Aborn, October 4, 1971.

[69] Tenco's rival, United Instant Coffee Corp., seems to have had half-ownership of Fruzol immediately before Tenco took over, but this has not been authoritatively confirmed.

Around 1968 the Brazilians labored to get GF to buy into a soluble plant in their country; but then, as before, GF displayed its general reluctance to invest in LDCs and a specific disinclination to invest in that industry in Brazil. There were many reasons for the GF response to Brazil. One of these was that GF had already made substantial investments in domestic soluble coffee plant expansion; another was that GF had never been eager to subject itself to the economic and political vicissitudes of doing business in the LDCs, especially in the absence of a very promising market for the product in question.[70]

GF prefers to establish its foreign operations in the industrial countries, e.g., in Canada, Europe or Japan. There is, however, as the Gerais investment attests, no absolute prohibition within the Company against investments in the LDCs, especially in the more advanced of these countries. In this connection, during the solubles dispute the Brazilians complained that General Foods and other American firms had invested in Mexican and Central American soluble coffee plants and that this explained why there was no hue and cry about imports of soluble from those countries, as there was about imports from Brazil.

It has proven impossible to gain a comprehensive picture of investments in Central American and Mexican soluble plants. But it seems probable that the very small volume of U.S. imports from that area is a better explanation for the absence of American industry opposition than factors of ownership. Before 1966, when the surge of Brazilian imports began, annual soluble imports never accounted for more than 3.2 percent (1959) of annual national sales in the U.S.

By the late sixties Brazil was accounting for over 60 percent of soluble imports into the United States while El Salvador, its nearest Latin competitor was contributing only about 5 percent, and Mexico a negligible 1.3 percent.[71]

---

[70] Interview, George Robbins, August 14, 1971.

[71] See Table, "Soluble Coffee Imports," in World Coffee and Tea: Guide to Coffee/USA (August 1972), 26.

It is true that GF and other American firms have invested in soluble production in Mexico and Central America, but solid information about the companies and individuals that have invested is difficult to secure. In 1962 Americans held part ownership (20-50 percent of capital shares) in each of the four soluble plants then in existence in Mexico, Guatemala, Salvador and Nicaragua respectively.[72]

Tenco, IBEC (Rockefeller enterprises), MJB of San Francisco and General Foods have at various times had soluble coffee investments in one or more of the four countries. In 1963 General Foods acquired an 85 percent share in Cafes de Mexico, S.A., a company founded in 1957 by an association of coffee growers. Cafes and two other companies comprised General Foods de Mexico. By 1965 Cafes de Mexico, which briefly supplied soluble powder to the parent company in the U.S. for mixing in its own solubles, was closed down.[73]

The role of Nestle (US) in industry and official policy-making in the solubles dispute may well have been shaped as much by the perspectives and directives of the parent company, Nestle Alimentana, S.A. as by the autonomous decisions of its executives in White Plains. At least, it would seem that Nestle's "multinational" composition, including soluble coffee operations in <u>both</u> the United States and Brazil, must have had some bearing upon the U.S. company's behavior in the solubles dispute.

According to a Nestle source, Nestle (Brazil) which began producing Nescafe for the local market in the late forties, was not authorized by the Brazilian government to export this product until the mid-sixties. This authorization

---

[72] A.S. Rupley (Executive Vice President of W.R. Grace & Co.), "Soluble Coffee," Unpublished Memorandum, 1962, 6, attached to Memorandum of transmittal from Louis Harris and Associates, Inc., to Ralph Dungan, Special Assistant to the President, White House, July 12, 1962. John F. Kennedy Library, Waltham, Mass. Files (Tariffs) TA 1654, Box 1959.

[73] Harvard Business School, General Foods Corporation, Case No. ICH/10G104/AM-P/188R2, 1964, 20.

came in conjunction with the Brazilian decision to increase its export earnings through solubles exports.[74] From 1965 or 1966 Nestle (US) began to import Nescafe from its counterpart in Brazil which at the time began to receive all of the inducements for export (tax and raw material) that were being given the new Brazilian solubles companies.[75]

Significantly Nestle (US) lobbied strenuously with the State Department for U.S. counter-measures against Brazilian solubles export policy until 1970, that is, for some four or five years after it had begun to import its own Nescafe from Brazil. In 1970, for reasons not altogether clear, the company reversed its position and lobbied successfully for NCA acceptance of the Brazilian concession to American pressures, an export tax of 13 cents per pound on its solubles. In neither phase did Nestle (US) give any indication of being "neutral" about the solubles issue, as one company official has insisted it was.[76]

Cocoa Industry. The cocoa industry in the United States consists generally of three classes of firms: bean dealers or traders, chocolate manufacturers and confectioners.[77] This classification is used within the industry,

---

[74] Interview, Johann Scheu, September 24, 1971

[75] The Nestle (US) Vice President for Purchasing has explained that Nescafe (US) had a production "undercapacity" for the American market that could now be offset by an "overcapacity" in Nescafe (Brazil). Interview, James Buckley, September 30, 1971.

[76] According to James Buckley, Nestle Vice President, "Our position on Brazilian solubles was 'neutral' in that we could benefit, either way the resolution of the issue went. We were importing less Brazilian soluble than General Foods, so we could not be particularly hurt by the restriction of the imports; or vice versa." Ibid.

[77] Since the confectioners, e.g. M & M/Mars, Peter Paul, and Russell Stover, have tended to remain aloof from the politics of cocoa agreements, this study has focused upon the activities of the trading and manufacturing segments of the industry. It should be kept in mind, nevertheless, that the confectioners, and their National Confectioners' Association, would probably oppose

but is partly misleading. The major chocolate manufacturers—Hershey Food Corporation, Nestle (US) and General Foods Corporation—are both "processors" of their own "proprietary" or "franchise" products (i.e., they process their own chocolate confections) and to greater or lesser degree, "converters," firms that grind cocoa beans into "bulk" products that are sold to confectioners, cosmetic and pharmaceutical firms, and other users of cocoa products.

The "confectioners" have in recent years integrated vertically in the opposite direction. M & M/Mars used to buy its chocolate from Hershey, but now has its own chocolate manufacturing operation, formerly Klein Chocolate Company, Inc. Wards and NABISCO have also secured their own chocolate manufacturing plants.

The leading chocolate manufacturer and producer of cocoa products in the United States for many years has been the Hershey Food Corporation.[78] Hershey, which since the mid-sixties has undertaken to diversify into the manufacture and sale of pasta products, baked goods, coffee brewing equipment,

---

any international commodity agreement. According to one spokesman for the traders and manufacturers who has himself lobbied against an agreement, the confectioners are ardently resistant to government "interference" with free market mechanisms. They are so "conservative," he asserts, that "they have opposed everything from social security forward. They even think Barry Goldwater is a revisionist." Interview, Thomas D. Finney, January 27, 1972. Individual confectioners are members of the New York Cocoa Exchange, but except for the period around the first UN Cocoa Conference, 1963, they have not joined the traders and manufacturers in their collaborative lobbying of the bureaucracies and Congress. Interview, Julian Hemphill, February 8, 1972. State Department officials, according to Paul Callanan, nevertheless have a high regard for the confectioners' capabilities to stir up Congressional opposition to any agreement that might be negotiated. The confectioners, he says, would be able to mobilize the confection wholesalers and retailers widely dispersed throughout the country. To offset this opposition, he believes that "substantial" business support from other quarters would be essential to secure Congressional support of a commodity agreement for cocoa. Interview, Paul Callanan, January 26, 1972.

[78] Before 1968 the Hershey Chocolate Corporation.

small household electrical appliances and other products, is still best known for milk chocolate, chocolate almond bars, and breakfast cocoa. Hershey is not the giant in the manufacture of chocolate and other cocoa products that General Foods is in coffee, but it is the single most important company in the American economics and politics of cocoa.

Hershey, according to its Director of Purchasing, grinds about 35-45 percent of all beans ground in the United States each year. It buys about 80 per-cent of its bean supplies through cocoa dealers, the remainder directly from the producers. Ninety per cent of Hershey's chocolate production goes to its own proprietary (or "franchise") products such as "Hershey bars." For the remaining 10 percent of its production Hershey functions as a converter.

Hershey uses approximately 100,000 tons of cocoa annually, accounting in 1971-72 for approximately one-fourteenth of the world's consumption of the product. Hershey's buying policies have a substantial impact upon the behavior of the market and upon the fortunes of producing countries and American cocoa traders alike.

Julian Hemphill, Hershey's Director of Purchasing and the foremost cocoa businessman in the United States over the last decade, has recalled an occasion that well illustrates the importance of the company in the cocoa market. In 1964-65, when manufacturers and traders alike were becoming anxious about the then drastic decline in the price of cocoa beans, Hershey entered the market to buy large amounts of the commodity, hopefully to stop the decline at 15 cents per pound. "In a very real sense," Hemphill says, "Hershey acted as a buffer stock agent." In the event, "Nkrumah decided to put Ghana's next year's crop on the market immediately, thus undermining our efforts to stop the decline."[79]

---

[79] Data provided by Julian Hemphill, Interview, February 8, 1972.

In 1961 under similar circumstances, Hershey assumed the similar role of attempting, by large purchases to support the market. What is especially significant for this analysis is that Hershey has the buying power to substantially affect the movement of prices at any one time, except under conditions of extreme surplus or shortage.

Hershey has storage capacity for a two-year supply of cocoa beans, and likes to maintain a large inventory to keep supplies flowing dependably and smoothly into its manufacturing facilities. Storage capacity and use of the cocoa futures market enable it to select the more propitious times for entering the market to buy beans. In this connection, Hershey normally does not use the futures market to hedge its inventories, as the standard text may suggest it would; rather according to a recent study of Hershey management policies, it primarily "looks upon the futures market as an aid in carrying out the simply stated objective of purchasing its bean requirements at the lowest possible prices."[80] Substantial storage capacity gives it more time and leeway to capitalize on favorable price movements.

Until the mid-sixties the Hershey management was generally satisfied that company interests were best served by an unregulated market. Before the early sixties, when management changes occurred, the company was adamently laissez faire in disposition.[81] Market conditions in the second half of the decade, however, culminating in a serious decline of company profits in 1968-1969 (from $19,898,149 in 1968 to $12,041,411 in 1969) prompted, among other things, a reassessment of the company's long-time opposition to the idea of a commodity agreement. Until that time the company had always been able to ride out periods of cocoa shortage and high prices. After prices dipped to a post-World War II low in 1965, nevertheless, there followed four years of cocoa

---

[80] Arthur, op. cit., 286-287.

[81] Interview, Julian Hemphill, February 8, 1972.

shortage and sharply rising prices to the record peak of 1969. Despite Hershey's large storage capacity, Hemphill recalls, it was not able to stay out of the market for so long a period as four years. Finally the Company was forced to buy in a very high-priced market.

The high cost of cocoa beans around 1969 spelled the end of the "five-cent chocolate bar" and the beginning of a somewhat more accommodating Hershey attitude towards the commodity agreement negotiations. Reasoning that periods of extreme low prices (1964-65) are likely to be followed by shortages and high prices (1969), "We came to accept," states Julian Hemphill, "the idea of simple agreement to cut off the bottom of price movements."[82] In fact, Hershey has remained skeptical of the types of agreements that LDCs propose.

Though Hershey does not normally use the futures market to hedge its inventories, it knows that the dealers from which it buys 80 percent of its supplies depend upon it heavily. The Director of Purchasing, during the period under study, asserts that Hershey has preferred to use the services of the dealers rather than to absorb their functions into the company proper.[83]

The other two major chocolate manufacturers in the United States are General Foods and Nestle (US), the two corporations that are also prominent either in the production of both regular coffee and instant coffee (GF), or instant coffee alone (Nestle). Together GF and Nestle grind 35-45 percent of the cocoa beans ground in the U.S. annually, or about as much as Hershey grinds by itself. Together the three companies may account for as much as 80 percent of the national grindings in any one year. The Blommer Chocolate Co. of Chicago

---

[82] Ibid.

[83] Ibid. Hemphill states that Hershey would require, at least, 30 new employees to perform the tasks being done by the traders. He cites the convenience factor for using the traders and the advantage of not having "to deal with the corrupt practices of the exporters."

ranks a distant fourth in grindings, and a few other companies follow in the rankings. Chocolate manufacturing is a highly concentrated industry with the big-three companies predominating.

General Foods' involvement in cocoa product manufacture, as well as the other two products under study, presents possibilities for interesting comparisons of corporate behavior. General Foods, in fact, entered the chocolate business before its expansion into coffee. As the Postum Co., Inc., it purchased Walter Baker & Co., Ltd. (Baker's chocolate and cocoa) in 1927.

Cocoa purchasing and manufacturing operations are today lodged in GF's Jell-O Division. The company takes about 40,000 tons of cocoa per year, some 85 percent of which is used in converting operations. By contrast with both Hershey and Nestle, most of GF's business consists of converting beans to bulk products for secondary users.[84] The smaller proportion of its production (15 percent) goes to its own franchise products such as home-cooking products, syrups and chocolate chips.

It has been suggested that GF's specialization in bulk products places a premium upon its effective use of the cocoa futures market for hedging purposes. According to Professor Henry B. Arthur:

> Thin gross margins usually prevail in the industrial market and this imposes pressures on General Foods to be efficient in its conversion operations, to keep capacity fully scheduled, to give service and timely delivery, and to buy beans with high yield and quality characteristics. With these considerations, a firm cannot afford to have a transaction wrecked by price swings.[85]

One might suppose that these pressures would just as well conduce to GF support for a price-stabilizing commodity agreement; in fact, they have not. GF

---

[84] Arthur, op. cit., 280-281.

[85] Ibid., 281.

has developed a complicated and sophisticated system of planning production and cocoa purchasing, a system that Arthur believes depends very heavily upon the skill of its cocoa traders and their facility in hedging cocoa transactions in the futures market.

GF's contrasting stands on the Coffee Agreement and cocoa agreement negotiations respectively—strongly favoring one and opposing the other—pose an interesting, if not surprising, contradiction. They obviously suggest that GF, as a company, has no strong ideological preference, either for or against commodity agreements. It can only be assumed that there are contrasting variables in the two instances that explain the Company's contrasting stands. Despite considerable effort, however, it has proven impossible to develop a completely satisfactory explanation for the contrasting stands. Variable market conditions in coffee and cocoa respectively, variable factors in coffee and chocolate manufacture and sales, variable company leadership and preferences in different sectors of the firm, and other factors, may help account for the differences.

Certainly General Foods is aware of the contradiction of favoring a coffee agreement and opposing a cocoa agreement, and self-conscious about it.

The Company has also been extremely sensitive to its position in a highly concentrated industry, and the possibility of anti-trust actions against it and the other two major manufacturers. According to several informants, GF has tried to maintain a "low profile" in the industry, especially with regard to associational action in relation to government policies. During the early and mid-sixties, for example, GF withdrew from the Chocolate Manufacturers Association, out of fear of being vulnerable to anti-trust action.

Nestle (US) is the third major chocolate manufacturer in the U.S., as well as General Foods' main competitor in the instant coffee market. It uses about 50,000 tons of cocoa annually, while the larger multinational corporation uses fully one-half the world's supply of cocoa. From 50-70 percent of Nestle (US) production is for its own proprietary products such as chocolate bars and cocoa powder, the remainder for bulk sales to other companies. By contrast with General Foods which buys 35-45 percent of its supplies directly from producers like Ivory Coast on a firm-price basis, Nestle buys virtually all of its supplies from cocoa dealers.

Nestle (US) has always been an enthusiastic supporter of free market mechanisms for trade and especially of the futures market. In fact, the company uses the cocoa exchange primarily to hedge its transactions connected with converting operations, that is, for about 30-50 percent of its production. Price risks for the proprietary products are not handled by hedging, rather by varying profit margins, by altering the processing mix, or by both methods.[86] Nestle also uses the futures market as a procurement tool, that is, as a means of securing the most favorably priced supplies.

Nestle (US) has generally opposed the very idea of cocoa agreement. Nevertheless, it has had to be responsive to the directives of Vevey. This, at least, has meant that it has assumed a "statesman-like" posture towards the cocoa negotiations, that is, an outward appearance of cooperativeness concerning the negotiations. It has also meant that the American cocoa firms always harbor some doubts about the "national" or "political" loyalties of the U.S.-based firm.[87]

---

[86] Arthur, op. cit., 285.

[87] Julian Hemphill, who has been the primary American industry spokesman in international negotiations for several years, says he would like to "step down" from leadership. The problem, he says, is that the best qualified successors, for example, the Director of Purchasing for Nestle (J. J. Scheu), are discounted because of their association with "foreign" firms. Interview, Julian Hemphill, February 9, 1972.

Cocoa dealers, clustered around the New York Cocoa Exchange in the Wall Street area, constitute a second class of firms of interest in this study. Three firms stand out among these, accounting for over 60 percent of all beans traded through middlemen: A.C. Israel, Gill & Duffus, and J. Aron.[88] General Cocoa, Holco Trading Co. Inc., Lonray, Inc. and Truebner & Co. are companies of the second rank, each handling 5-19 percent of all cocoa traded by dealers annually. General Cocoa has been the most prominent of these firms with a market share of about 10 percent. A third rank of firms includes those that account for a very modest percentage of the cocoa traded, for example, Produce Unitrade and Curacao Trading Co., Inc.[89]

The small dealer, it can be supposed from these rankings, is an endangered species. The old family firms are steadily passing off the scene and leaving the field to the large multi-product traders. A.C. Israel cocoa operations are now conducted within A.C. and Leon Israel (ACLI). Gill and Duffus (US) is an affiliate of the large British firm, one of whose directors is Sir Eric Tansley, former head ("Czar") of the Ghana Cocoa Marketing Board. J. Aron, of course, is a giant trading firm in several products.

Cocoa trading is concentrated among a few trading firms based in New York City. While the chocolate manufacturers could conceivably get along without them, by direct purchases from the producers, Hershey and other companies

---

88 J. Aron, the leading coffee trader, purchased the family cocoa trading firm of Rayner & Stonington, Inc., in 1968. In April, 1971, J. Aron became the "agent" for the sale of all Ghana coffees in the United States, removing itself from the market as a "dealer." The relationship with Ghana has since ended, leaving J. Aron an uncertain future as a dealer in cocoa.

89 Rankings, except for J. Aron, provided by Julian Hemphill. Interview, February 8, 1972.

try to spread their business among several trading firms, to keep alive a flexible trading network. Hershey has pursued a deliberate policy of trying to strengthen trading firms still in the field, and there is some evidence that it has given financial assistance to firms attempting to enter the competition.

The dealers may be few, but they have been ardent and politically effective opponents of a cocoa agreement. The cocoa dealers thrive on price fluctuations and are heavily reliant upon the Cocoa Exchange for hedging purposes. They see their function as being to service buyers and sellers, and their profits as coming from skilled merchandising and use of the Exchange. Some of the larger firms, for example, A. C. Israel, may speculate to a modest degree.

The dealers, united in the belief that an international cocoa agreement would pose a threat to the Cocoa Exchange, have acted to bolster the manufacturers already existing skepticism of the proposals for an agreement. Dealers are highly susceptible to manufacturer leadership on this issue, because a few manufacturers buy most of their cocoa; but they have played a relatively autonomous role in opposition to an agreement.

The U.S. cocoa industry, in contrast to the coffee industry, has never had a national association that authoritatively represents all its segments. Instead there are associations that represent the three major functional groupings within it: the Chocolate Manufacturers Association of the United States of America; the Cocoa Merchants Association of America; and the National Confectioners Association of the United States.

Industry needs for consultation and collaboration, across functional groupings, are partly satisfied through the representative bodies of the New York Cocoa Exchange, Inc., to which firms of all types belong. The National Confectioners Association tends to remain aloof from the Manufacturers and Merchants associations; but the latter are normally in close contact with one another through regular and informal contact among their respective leaders in the Wall Street area where the Cocoa Exchange is located. The prospect of international regulation of cocoa trade prompted the cocoa associations, especially the Manufacturers and the Merchants, to make joint representations to the government, and even to share the costs of a Washington lobbyist.

The State Department

The State Department has been the primary bureaucratic actor in policymaking for the coffee and cocoa issues. Certain subdivisions of the Department have had primary responsibilities for policy development for all three issues. And contrary to the findings of a recent study, these have had to be concerned with the views of business firms and associations that have assiduously lobbied them on these issues.[90]

In the "new diplomacy" the State Department increasingly uses economic and other instruments of foreign policy—commodity agreements, as the specific case in point—that elicit concern on the part of domestic interest groups that feel that they may be materially affected in the process. If interest groups gravitate to points in the policy-making process where critical decisions affecting them are made, there is no reason to assume that in the cases under study they would necessarily consider the State Department off limits to their lobbying efforts. The State Department, in fact, has been the primary target of business

---

[90] In a recent study Harmon Zeigler has reaffirmed the earlier observation by E. Pendleton Herrington that the "position of the State Department renders it immune to the influence of...pressure groups, and its contacts with these...are of little significance in the administration of the department's work." E. Pendleton Herrington, Public Administration and the Public Interest (New York: McGraw-Hill Book Company, Inc., 1936), 77, as quoted in Harmon Zeigler, Interest Groups in American Society (Englewood Cliffs, New Jersey: Prentice Hall, 1964).

efforts to influence coffee and cocoa policies, although other bureaucracies and certainly Congress have been approached as well.[91]

Commodity specialists were first brought into the State Department to staff U.S. participation in the Combined Food Board during World War II. By the sixties these specialists and foreign service officers on temporary assignment to commodity affairs were genuinely integrated into the State Department establishment. Primary responsibilities for coffee and cocoa negotiations, and for administration of U.S. participation in the International Coffee Organization, came to be lodged in the Department's Bureau of Economic Affairs.

By 1962, when the ICA was negotiated, one of the several Deputy Assistant Secretaries of State in that Bureau, had been assigned primary responsibility for overseeing State Department action on commodities, ranging from petroleum to tropical products like coffee and cocoa. In 1968, the "Deputy Assistant Secretary of State for International Resources and Food Policy," as this officer came to be called, had an expansively defined field of action. According to an unclassified internal State Department Memorandum, this officer

> Develops policy recommendations and administers approved policies and programs relating to international problems of production and trade in primary products ...

---

[91] Theoretically, the "bureaucratic politics" model would be useful for analyzing U.S. policy-making for the coffee and cocoa issues. Besides Congress, the White House, and the Departments of Agriculture, Commerce and Treasury have been important actors in policy-making. Also various divisions of the State Department have at times contended with one another to influence policy outcomes; for example, U.S. policies in the soluble coffee dispute were partly determined by the inter-play between certain "desks" for economic and Brazilian affairs respectively. Although this model has not been explicitly adopted, due to lack of appropriate data, and a primary research emphasis on interest group relationships, it is implicit in the analysis of relations among business, the State Department and Congress.

> Supervises and, in important matters, personally handles the U.S. Government participation in multilateral and bilateral negotiations on commodity trade problems, and also the presentation to Congress of international agreements requiring Congressional approval (e.g., the International Coffee Agreement.)[92]

The Deputy Assistant Secretary is also charged to supervise and coordinate the work of three subdivisions of his office: the Office of Fuels and Energy (FSE); the Office of Food Policy and Programs; and the Office of International Commodities (ICD).

One of the three divisions within ICD, the Tropical Products Division (TRP), has been intensely and continuously involved with the coffee and cocoa negotiations. It is worthwhile to quote at length from the State Department's own statement of the responsibilities of this division. It then will be easier to understand why it, along with the Office of the Deputy Assistant Secretary, has been a primary point of contact in the State Department for businesses seeking to influence coffee and cocoa policies.

The Tropical Products Division (TRP), according to this Department Memorandum:

> 1. Develops and applies policies with respect to international production, consumption and trade in tropical products (including sugar and excluding rubber and timber) which present special problems in our foreign relations; coordinates the Department's activities in this field and on a global basis; advises on the inter-relationship of international and domestic developments; and guides U.S. participation in international activities relating to these products, including the development, negotiation, and administration of international commodity agreements.
>
> 2. Represents the U.S. or backstops the U.S. representative in international organizations concerned with the problems of production and trade in tropical products,

---

[92] U.S. Department of State, Bureau of Economic Affairs, "Office of the Deputy Assistant Secretary for International Resources and Food Policy (ORF)," Unpublished internal memorandum, 1968, 1.

including the International Coffee and Sugar Councils, and the Cocoa, Tea, and Banana Study Groups. In particular, coordinates all U.S. positions relating to the U.S. membership in the most active, functioning commodity council, the International Coffee Council.

3. Backstops the Department's representative or represents the Department in interagency committees concerned with problems in the Division's field of competence.

4. Coordinates and develops U.S. policy to eliminate preferences affecting trade in tropical agricultural products and to substitute other arrangements which will give countries now enjoying preference equivalent advantages but will avoid discrimination against trade of non-preference suppliers.

5. Maintains liaison with private industry groups concerned with international implications of trade in tropical products.

Importantly, TRP is charged to "maintain liaison" with private industry groups, but not with any of a number of other groups that might have a continuing interest in commodity trade, for example, foreign affairs, consumer or union groups. The explicit mandate concerning industry groups, at very least, reflects the fact that business groups have insisted on the right of consultation which other groups have usually not done—the Amalgamated Meatcutters in the soluble coffee dispute being an exception—and furthermore, that business views and expertise are valued and respected in a special way.

Although the Deputy Assistant Secretary for International Resources and Food Policy has often been identified as the "chief policy-maker" for the coffee and cocoa issues, and this characterization is basically valid, authority in decision-making obviously cannot be so easily pinpointed. Decisions to press for the Coffee Agreement were taken in the higher reaches of the State Department in consultation with other interested Departments, and ultimately by President Kennedy himself. Assistant Secretaries of State for Economic Affairs, though they have delegated considerable responsibilities to their Deputies in coffee and cocoa matters, have not infrequently engaged directly in coffee and cocoa decision-making or diplomacy themselves. For example, Thomas Mann, as Assistant Secretary for Economic Affairs in the late fifties, is credited with a considerable personal role in laying the groundwork for U.S. participation in the Coffee Study Group. In the mid-sixties Assistant Secretary Anthony Solomon was involved personally in negotiations to facilitate a cocoa agreement.[93] Policy initiatives and implementation have been routinely "cleared" through higher ranks of the Department, and at times senior officers have participated substantively in policy-making, and certainly as advocates of the Coffee Agreement, before Congress.

Primary responsibilities for coffee and cocoa policy-making have been assigned to the "functional" Bureau of Economics; but since policies for these issues impinge upon the concerns of the "area" Bureaus of Inter-American and African Affairs respectively, the latter have attempted, to varying degree, to secure solid footing in the policy-making process.

The Bureau of Inter-American Affairs collaborated closely with the Bureau of Economic Affairs in the negotiations for a Coffee Agreement. A systematic study of bureaucratic policies in the State Department, on the other hand, would probably conclude that the Bureau of African Affairs has either not been strongly committed to the idea of a cocoa agreement or that it has not been effective in advocating the idea before otherwise reluctant policy-makers.

The only pronounced inter-bureau contention over the issues studied developed in the soluble coffee dispute. In this case, the Brazil country desk in the Department contended strongly for a policy on Brazilian soluble imports that would minimize adverse effects on U.S.-Brazilian relations. It conceded that the fragile American consensus favoring the Coffee Agreement was being jeopardized

---

93 Interview, Raul Prebisch, April 20, 1971.

by Brazilian soluble coffee policy, but pressed the Bureau of Economic Affairs not to adopt an excessively narrow definition of what "solution" would be acceptable to American business critics of Brazilian policy. Although the precise effect of this advocacy cannot be ascertained, at least one prominent Brazilian coffee expert and diplomat, Ambassador George Maciel, believes that it substantially moderated U.S. policy towards Brazilian soluble policy.[94]

During the 1960's the Department of State clearly prevailed over other interested Executive departments in the initiation and development of policies regulating coffee and cocoa trade. One reason for this, Thomas Mann has observed, is that the "demand for such regulation came primarily from outside the country."[95] Because little coffee and no cocoa are produced in the United States, the Department of Agriculture has neither desired nor sought the important role it has traditionally played in wheat and sugar trade regulation.

The Departments of Agriculture and Commerce have played distinctly subsidiary roles in policy-making. Agriculture has provided commodity trade statistics for national decision-making, and also for international negotiations. Both Agriculture and Commerce have provided technical expertise in the development of the coffee control system and for assessing various cocoa agreement proposals. A former State Department officer recalls that in the early years of international cocoa negotiations the American cocoa industry "advised" the U.S. government through formal meetings at the Bureau of International Commerce of the Department of Commerce. The State Department, however, succeeded, by informal initiatives in transferring those meetings with the business advisers to Foggy Bottom. In so doing it wrested control of the advisory relationship with

---

[94] Interview, George Maciel, July 16, 1971.

[95] Interview, Thomas Mann, August 20, 1971.

business from Commerce.[96] If the State Department had proven unreceptive to business views, it is probable that Commerce would have sought a more prominent role in policy-making in their behalf.

The Treasury Department has not had a highly visible role in cocoa and coffee policy-making, although its Customs division has administered import regulation under the Coffee Agreement. Nevertheless, it is widely known that during periods of the Eisenhower administration, the Treasury Department, notably under Secretary George Humphrey, had and used a strong position in discouraging any accommodation to Latin appeals for commodity agreements.

In the next chapters analysis focuses upon the interactions of business and governmental actors, especially upon the triangle of relations among businesses and their associations, the State Department and Congress.

---

[96] Interview, Paul Callanan, January 26, 1972

CHAPTER III

American Business and the International Coffee Agreement

Between 1958 and 1962 the United States government moved from a stance of general skepticism towards international commodity agreements to initiatives for the International Coffee Agreement. What factors help explain this ostensible change of posture? What business firms and associations promoted or opposed the change? How, and with what consequences? And what conditions favored or thwarted a role for business in policy-making?

To describe the relationships of business firms and associations to the policy-making process for the Coffee Agreement, and specifically to assess their impact, it is necessary to sketch out the major events and issues in the evolution of U.S. coffee policy in this period, and to understand what policy orientations developed among officials, irrespective of business preferences and pressures.[97]

This research has to take account of two prevailing modes of dealing with the role of business in the formulation of American policy in the establishment of the Coffee Agreement. One mode has been to ignore the question altogether. American leadership for the Coffee Agreement contradicts either the

---

[97] The practical limits of this enterprise are acknowledged. The ideal, however, as Prof. Wootton has suggested, is to conceive research so that interest group influence is assessed in terms of what the "Target's" orientation is, independent of interest group influence. For example, "To what extent did the particular Target have to change ground under the interest-group's impulsion?" or "What did the change [of ground] cost the Target in terms of normative commitment?" Graham Wootten, Interest Groups, Foundation of Modern Political Science Series (Englewood Cliffs, N.J.: Prentice-Hall, 1970), 79.

assumption that business "controls" American policy for commodity agreements, or the assumption that it invariably will oppose LDC appeals for agreements for their primary exports, or possibly both. Those who cherish both assumptions prefer to ignore the Coffee Agreement case altogether.

The other approach reaches the more plausible conclusion that the U.S. government was so intent on achieving the Coffee Agreement that business had to "go along to get along."

This research supports a third perspective, that depicts business's role as being somewhere between "controlling" policy and "going along" under duress. An accurate account of the relationship between business and government in the development of policy for the ICA probably has to depict a more subtle process of mutual accommodation, rather than a "slam-bang" type influence moving in either direction.

Research indicates also that there were, at least, two major phases in the development of U.S. support for the Coffee Agreement, in each of which business-government relationships were somewhat different than in the other. In the first phase the Eisenhower administration moved from strong ideological opposition to commodity agreements for LDC products to a cautious participation in the discussion of coffee "problems" in the Coffee Study Group. The Kennedy Administration, in the second phase, took initiatives for a Coffee Agreement as part of the Alliance for Progress. Between the two phases, there was both continuity and change in the official American approach to LDC appeals for a coffee agreement. The making of American policy in the establishment of the Coffee Agreement spanned a period from 1957 to 1962, or if Congress is viewed as a participant in policy-making, to 1965.[98]

The first section of this chapter describes the major events and issues in the evolution of U.S. support for the first Coffee Agreement. The next section attempts to identify the major, "non-business" factors that explain U.S. policy for coffee. And this is followed by analysis of the nature and consequences of the business relationship to policy-making in the bureaucratic and diplomatic stages.

The next chapter considers the crucial triangle of relations among business, bureaucracy and Congress. A lengthy account of Congress's reception of the Coffee Agreement is justified for what it indicates about the development of policy for the ICA itself, but also for what it indicates about how Congressional participation in policy-making increases the opportunities for business to influence bureaucrats and diplomats in the development of agreements, or as a last resort, to "veto" agreements that have been negotiated.

The Evolution of U.S. Coffee Agreement Policy. The United States government has never been enthusiastic about international commodity agreements whose antecedents can be traced to the period around World War I.[99] Nevertheless, as early as the 1930's it entered agreements for two commodities.

In 1933 the U.S. government broke a tradition of abstention from international commodity agreements by taking the country into the International Wheat

---

[98] This study deals only with business and policy-making during the years in which U.S. support for the first Coffee Agreement (1962) evolved, 1957-1965. For a general introduction to the international politics of the Coffee Agreements see Fisher, op. cit. He discusses briefly the role of American business in the founding and operation of the International Coffee Organization (ICO) at different points.

[99] For an excellent history of the development of commodity control schemes see Rowe, op. cit., 77-183.

Agreement, a short-lived but precedent-setting export control agreement among nine exporting and importing countries. In 1939 the U.S. initiated an international cotton congress, which but for the outbreak of World War II, would probably have resulted in an agreement such as for wheat, including U.S. participation.

Meanwhile in May of 1931 producer associations of Cuba, Java (Netherlands) and Europe had agreed to the first International Sugar Agreement, providing for export quotas, production limits equal to export quotas, and the planned reduction of existing stocks. This first Sugar Agreement, as all subsequent agreements, did not encompass the U.S. and British sugar "empires," only the residual "free market." "By 1937," according to a U.S. government economist, "the United States and Great Britain had stabilized their programs for their domestic sugar industries sufficiently to be willing to take more active roles in developing solutions for international sugar problems."[100] In May the U.S. adhered to the second Sugar Agreement, committing itself to manage its own sugar program in a manner supportive of international regulation. The U.S. did not commit itself to take imports from exporting members of the Agreement; rather it agreed that it would not reduce imports from countries then paying the full-duty tariff rate in its market, "and that countries subject to its full-duty rate would be assigned any deficit in U.S. imports of sugar from the Philippines Independence Act."[101]

Since World War II the United States has been a mainstay in seven consecutive International Wheat Agreements. It has been a member of two of three

---

[100] U.S. Department of Agriculture, Economic Research Service, A History of Sugar Marketing, Agricultural Report No. 197 by Roy A. Ballinger (Washington, D.C.: GPO, 1971.), 46. The International Sugar Act should not be confused with the U.S. Sugar Act (Jones-Costigan Act, 1934 and subsequent amendments) which allocates the U.S. sugar market among domestic and foreign producers.

[101] Ibid., 47.

Sugar Agreements negotiated since 1953. The United States participated in negotiations for the 1968 Sugar Agreement, but did not sign the resulting pact because it felt that Cuba was treated too generously.

At the end of World War II "economic expansion" and "free trade" were among the dominant credos of American and European statesmen and politicians planning a new world economic order. American policy-makers desired a "self-regulating and stable world economy that would give scope to American enterprise and that would require a minimum of institutional control."[102] In the words of one such policy-maker at the time, the central thrust of U.S. policy was towards "expansion of world trade, the attainment of high levels of employment and income, and the maintenance of economic stability."[103]

If "expansion" and "free trade" were to be the themes of post-War economic planning, would commodity control agreements have any role? In view of all the rhetoric about trade liberalization, it seems somewhat surprising that the idea of commodity control agreements was not rejected out of hand. At the very least, the notion of agreements conjured up images of trade restriction; at worst, they evoked repugnance for cartel-fasion exploitation of consumers. Most of the pre-WWII commodity control schemes were producer agreements, and Americans tended to class them with the infamous, industrial "cartels."

Policy-makers proved reluctant to reject the cumulative experience of commodity trade regulation, even if that had been a controversial experience.

---

[102] Ernst B. Haas, Tangle of Hopes: American Commitments and World Order (Englewood Cliffs, N.J.: Prentice Hall, Inc., 1969), 120.

[103] Bernard F. Haley, "United States Policy Regarding Commodity Agreements," Proceedings of the Academy of Political Science, XXI, 3 (May, 1945), 429. See also Bernard F. Haley, "Relations between Cartel Policy and Commodity Agreements," American Economic Review, XXXVI (May, 1946), 717-734. This is an analysis of the commodity agreement segment of "Proposals for Consideration by an International Conference on Trade and Employment" (1945), the U.S. proposals for the Havana Conference.

Reflecting a turn of mind that would be prevalent among coffee policy-makers in the early sixties, they believed that less than perfect tools might have to be used to deal with concrete problems in the international economy. Two widely held perspectives reinforced this view. First, virtually all observers, whatever their predisposition toward commodity agreements as such, were anxious to avoid the severe instability of prices, especially of commodity prices, that had characterized the inter-war period.[104] American policy-makers were anxious that commodity problems, particularly price instability, should not become serious sources of economic maladjustment that could "undermine the general program for economic expansion.

Secondly, at the time the post-War economic order was being planned, numerous observers were forecasting a new phase of commodity market dislocation, including surpluses. The State Department's Director of the Office of International Trade believed that there were bound to be commodity surpluses. Whatever the positive benefits of expansion of trade and production, there would be "a residual of individual commodity problems which will have to be dealt with by means of international collaboration, and in some cases, by commodity agreements."[105] In developing a general policy orientation towards commodity agreements, policy-makers could not escape the claims of immediate and concrete policy problems.

While it is probably true, as a prominent commodity trade expert observed in 1947, that the climate of official and unofficial opinion in the U.S. at the end of the War was against the development of an ambitious network of commodity agreements, actual American policy reflected a willingness to countenance the selective use of commodity agreements under certain carefully defined

---

[104] Rowe, op. cit., 155. [105] Ibid., 529.

conditions.[106] In the same spirit in which Lord Keynes and the British had attempted at the Hot Springs Conference on Food and Agriculture (1943) to advance commodity agreement ideas, specifically the idea of a global "buffer stock" system, that would enhance trade expansion rather than restriction, the United States now took the approach of trying to reconcile the use of commodity agreements with its image of the new world economic order.

Chapter six of the draft charter for an International Trade Organization, adopted by the Havana Conference of the United Nations in 1947-48, reflects the general American orientation to commodity agreements at the time. Although ITO never came into being, the principles of its draft charter concerning commodity agreements were incorporated into the General Agreement on Tariffs and Trade (GATT).

The central idea of ITO was trade liberalization. The abuses of inter-War economic nationalism and trade restriction, including those of commodity control schemes, would have to be avoided. A commitment to the efficacy and efficiency of "market forces" meant that commodity agreements would be given a "backseat" or "last resort" position in the new scheme of things.

The ITO designers foresaw only two conditions under which commodity agreements would be allowable: either there would have to be a "burdensome surplus" of a commodity, resulting in serious hardship for producers, of whom a substantial proportion would have to be small producers; or there would have to be widespread unemployment or underemployment in a particular primary industry causing undue hardships to producers. If any member of GATT should

---

[106] For an early critique of commodity agreements and for the view that there was a post-war climate of opposition to commodity control schemes in the United States, see Joseph S. Davis, op. cit. Davis was then Director of the Food Research Institute, Stanford University.

conclude that one of these rather vaguely defined conditions obtained, it could appeal to the United Nations for a "study group" to examine the problems of the primary industry in question. Any such study group would have the prerogative of recommending a U.N.-sponsored, inter-governmental conference to negotiate a commodity agreement.

The ITO designers also enunciated certain principles that should govern the establishment of control schemes: international negotiations for agreements should occur under the aegis of the U.N.; consuming countries should participate and have voting powers equal to those of producers; and vaguely, any agreement should assure "adequate supplies" at "reasonable prices." Numerous other guidelines to action were set down, each conceived to correct or hedge in one or another presumed deficiency of commodity agreements as tools for regulating the international economy. Several of these, including the provision that no agreement or its renewal should exceed five years in duration, manifested the expectation that agreements were to be remedial and temporary, not permanent fixtures on the international scene.

The codification of the latter principle indicated, for the time being at least, that the idea of a comprehensive and permanent system of commodity agreements, for numerous products, had been soundly rejected. At the same time, American policy called for qualification of the free trade thrust in the Havana Charter, to the extent of allowing for commodity agreements in emergency situations.[107]

---

[107] The provisions on commodity agreements, however, were among those that triggered the decisive opposition of Congress to the Havana Charter.

Another diplomatic episode, also precipitated by World War II, reflected American readiness to regulate commodity trade, under exceptional circumstances, despite theoretical reservations about government interventions in the free market. The Inter-American Coffee Agreement (IACA, 1940-49), embraced by the United States and fourteen Latin American countries, allocated the U.S. coffee market among Latin and other producers. While the stated purpose of the IACA was to provide for the "orderly" marketing of Latin coffee in the United States— German occupation of Europe had closed that market to Latin coffee— analysis of the American purposes in that Agreement suggests remarkable parallels between policy-maker perceptions then and subsequently, in the instance of the global Coffee Agreement of 1962.

The late Republican Senator, Arthur Vandenberg, who favored the IACA, spoke as if U.S. support of the Agreement were a concession to Latin America, an "act of grace."[108] Congressional support of that Agreement was neither exclusively nor primarily based upon U.S. altruism towards Latin America, any more than its support of the ICA in the 1960's would be. Senator George provided a glimpse of the self-interested purposes of the U.S. in the IACA, when he pointed out that adversities in the Latin coffee economies could substantially reduce U.S. exports to that region. Moreover, he said, "we are interested also in the maintenance of economic and political stability in the coffee-producing countries."[109] Sen. O'Mahoney was even more explicit: "I assume that the principal purpose of this treaty is to promote Western Hemispheric solidarity."[110]

---

[108] U.S., Congress, Senate, 75th Cong., 2d sess., Congressional Record, February 3, 1941, 475.

[109] Ibid., 475.

[110] Ibid., 479.

It remained for the Stanford University commodity specialist, Vernon Wickizer, to characterize the essentially "political" motivations of the U.S. in the IACA. Writing in 1951, just after the termination of the Agreement, he stated: "From the United States' standpoint any program that increased payments to Latin-American countries to compensate in part for the loss of the normal European outlets [resulting from German occupation] would strengthen their ability to resist Axis pressure, promote the Good Neighbor policy, and render the United States' strategic position secure."[111] The IACA, he concluded, "was inspired, and perhaps made possible by abnormal conditions arising from the war."[112]

The IACA was something of a precedent for the global ICA, although it is not clear to what extent U.S. policy-makers were swayed in any direction by that experience. George Robbins, the General Foods executive who promoted an international coffee agreement during the late fifties and early sixties, recalls that he was greatly impressed by the performance of the Inter-American Coffee Board, and had urged the State Department to seek retention of that administrative structure for consultative purposes when its regulatory functions were suspended in 1949. His advice was stoutly resisted by State Department officials who were then becoming increasingly negative about international commodity trade regulation.[113]

In the early fifties the United States entered the first of the post-war wheat (1953) and sugar (1954) agreements; otherwise a rather rock-ribbed,

---

[111] W. D. Wickizer, Coffee, Tea or Cocoa: An Economic and Political Analysis (Stanford: Stanford University Press, 1951), 94.

[112] Ibid.

[113] Interview, George Robbins, February 25, 1971.

ideological opposition to commodity agreements began to take hold. George M. Humphrey, Eisenhower's first Secretary of the Treasury (1953-57), personified a generally held antipathy for commodity control agreements. In the early sixties Humphrey would be remembered as having abhorred commodity agreements so much that he would not allow that they be discussed in his presence.[114]

At the end of the fifties a special report to the Senate Foreign Relations Committee could still conclude that U.S. policy with regard to LDC appeals for "forthright international action commodity problems" was "negative" and "lacking in initiative."[115] The report declared: "we [United States] discourage discussion of international action [on commodities], we leave the initiative to others, and our approach to a direct attack on commodity problems is essentially negative."[116] Furthermore, it said, "when a commodity crisis is upon us we are apparently willing to endorse direct action. But we seem to resist even the thought of regulation until a crisis, however foreseeable, has actually occurred."[117]

Nor were conditions in several commodity markets, notably the coffee market, propitious for commodity agreements in the ten years immediately following WWII. In 1954, primarily because of weather damage to the Brazilian main crop, coffee prices rose to an historic high. American diplomats and politicians were then more anxious over why American consumers were having

---

[114] Interview, W. Michael Blumenthal, October 17, 1971.

[115] U.S., Congress, Senate, Committee on Foreign Relations, United States-Latin American Relations: Commodity Problems in Latin America, Study prepared at the request of the Subcommittee on American Republics Affairs by International Economic Consultants, Inc., No. 2,86thCong., 1st sess., December 12, 1959.

[116] Ibid., 65-6.

[117] Ibid., 66.

to pay over a dollar per pound for their coffee than with the prospect that high prices were reinforcing an emerging trend to massive overproduction of coffee. Since the late forties old coffee producers and several newcomers, the latter mostly in Africa, had been planting heavily to respond to the heavy post-war demand. The high prices of 1954 momentarily hid a more fundamental trend to oversupply, and probably reinforced a tendency to short-sightedness in the U.S. policy-making system.

During 1954 Latin coffee producers, already detecting a trend to oversupply, prodded the Inter-American Economic and Social Council (IA-ECOSOC) of the Organization of American States (OAS) into sponsoring a study of the coffee situation. The OAS's Special Coffee Committee concluded that oversupply would develop, if as expected, the trends of 1955 continued.[118] In response to this report, in April of 1956, the IA-ECOSOC voted to draft an international coffee agreement, despite the expressed position of the United States that it would neither take the lead in negotiating an international agreement nor join one.[119] According to Thomas C. Mann, a former Assistant Secretary of State for Economic Affairs (1957-1960), this position remained U.S. "policy" toward coffee until January of 1958.[120]

From 1956 prices for arabica-type coffees moved steadily and sharply downwards. Colombia MAMS, for example, dropped from an average price of

---

[118] Report of OAS Special Coffee Committee, 1955, as cited in International Coffee Organization, International Coffee Council, History of Recent International Coffee Agreements: Their Background, Provisions, Operations and Related Developments, 1954-63, ICC-1-1, June 28, 1963, Washington, D.C., 1.

[119] The U.S. position was set out in a letter from Ambassador Harold M. Randall to IA-ECOSOC, April 27, 1956, as cited in Thomas C. Mann, "The Coffee Study Group," Coffee Annual, 1958 (New York: George Gordon Paton, 1959), 73.

[120] Ibid., 73.

70 U.S. cents per pound in 1956 to 40 cents in 1962. Robusta coffee prices held relatively steady from 1955 to 1958, after sharp declines from the exceptional highs of 1954, but plunged downwards after 1958.[121] A crisis in the coffee trade system was sensed by the producers as early as the mid-fifties, but was evident to all after 1958.

During 1955-1957 several Latin producers engaged in "gentlemen's agreements" to support the market prices. In October of 1957 the seven major Latin producers established formal machinery under the Agreement of Mexico, providing for quarterly adjustable export quotas, but no minimum prices. At Rio in January of 1958 fourteen Latin Producers and Portugal (for Angola) agreed to a non-regulatory arrangement for, among other things, the exchange of statistical information on world coffee production and trade.

The large size of the 1957-58 coffee crop, and the growing threat of surpluses over an extended period, propelled even the United States to consider more substantive measures for the ailing coffee market than the producers had initiated in the months before. The ICO historian is correct that there was "increasing concern within government and trade circles in both producing and importing countries" as a result of the steadily declining prices of early 1958.[122]

Significantly, in the United States individual coffee businessmen seem to have prodded the government to reconsider its position on coffee problems before it was otherwise prepared to move. A commodity expert in the State Department remembers that prominent businessmen unsuccessfully attempted

---

[121] See Chart 2, "Price Trends of Principal Types of Coffee, 1946-62," in ICO, History of Recent International Coffee Agreements.

[122] Ibid., 3.

to get State to seriously undertake international negotiations on coffee problems, as early as 1956 or 1957.[123]

In January of 1958 the Board of Directors of the National Coffee Association (NCA), the authoritative association of the American coffee industry, voted "to work with the United States Government and the governments of the producing nations in studying the [coffee] problems and seeking sound solutions."[124]

The policy guidelines set down by the NCA Board of Directors the following May reflect the adaptive, if fundamentally defensive position that the NCA was taking at the time. The NCA Board declared:

> (1) The Association is opposed to the idea of import quotas, as it is opposed to all governmental regulations that are affecting the trade in our industry.
>
> (2) That we advise the State Department that we are anxious to cooperate with them in studying and trying to find a solution to the problems with which the world would be faced if there were a collapse in coffee prices.
>
> (3) If the State Department informs the Committee [Foreign Affairs Committee] that it is convinced that the only solution they have to this problem is the imposition of import quotas, the Committee should advise the State Department that: if we must have import quotas, we request the opportunity to work with the U.S. government in developing a plan governing these quotas, to the end that the plan be the most equitable and to the best advantage of all segments of the industry.[125]

---

[123] Interview, Paul Callanan, July 12, 1971. Callanan remembers George Robbins of General Foods and two coffee traders, Arthur Ransohoff and Fred Silence, coming to State.

[124] Resolution, NCA Board of Directors, January 15, 1958, as printed verbatim in Tea and Coffee Trade Journal, CXVI (June, 1959), 35.

[125] Resolution, NCA Board of Directors, Pebble Beach, California, May 19, 1958 as quoted in Tea and Coffee Trade Journal, CXVI (June, 1959), 35-36.

George Robbins of General Foods, the most influential individual in the councils of the NCA then, seems to have felt that the NCA was not prepared for stronger leadership towards a direct commitment to market regulation. However, by 1958 Robbins was arguing openly, as he did in an article for Tea and Coffee Trade Journal, for international price regulation— setting reasonable floor and ceiling prices for coffee— to avoid risks to U.S. economic health and security.

On a more pragmatic note, Robbins concluded that "Politically... the application of the ceiling/floor system to coffee might be quite an unpopular program, until the worsening of political and economic conditions in Latin America forces the people of the United States to the realization of the imminence and magnitude of the problems of Latin America."[126] Robbins was clearly beyond the mainstream of NCA thinking and inclination in 1958, and clearly prophetic.

The NCA Board decision to consult with governments on current problems coincided with the guest appearance of Assistant Secretary of State for Inter-American Affairs, Roy Rubottom, Jr., at the NCA's annual convention at Boca Raton, Florida. NCA leaders discussed their concerns with Rubottom and formally established a Foreign Affairs Committee (FAC) to carry on national and international consultations.[127]

---

[126] George V. Robbins, "Floor/Ceiling Coffee Prices," Coffee Annual, 1958 (New York: George Gordon Paton, 1959), 82 and passim.

[127] FAC became the most prestigious committee of the NCA and has performed advisory and diplomatic functions for the Association for over 15 years. For a laudatory article on FAC see John F. McKiernan, "The U.S. Coffee Industry's 'Diplomatic Task Force,'" Coffee Annual, 1969. (New York: George Gordon Paton & Co., 1970), 37-39. The circumstances and purposes of FAC's establishment, and its subsequent relationship with the State Department, call to mind Joseph LaPalombara's observation about clientele relationships between groups and governments: "...in order to function well as a clientela, the group involved must be physically close to the locus of administrative decision-making, and will to some extent articulate its organizational structure to facilitate interaction with the bureaucracy...with which the clientela relationship is maintained." Joseph LaPalombara, Interest Groups in Italian Politics, Princeton: Princeton University Press, 1964), 302.

Shortly thereafter (February 25) the Foreign Affairs Committee, through the good offices of Rubottom, met in Washington with the new Assistant Secretary of State for Economic Affairs, Thomas C. Mann. Numerous observers would later consider Mann the single most important official in lobbying for U.S. entry into serious discussions to deal with the problems of international coffee in the late fifties. Mann was "the first well-placed State official to be receptive to American business appeals for serious attention to the problems of the coffee trade."[128] Although no enthusiast for commodity agreements, Mann was impressed by the contention of the FAC delegation that coffee market conditions could not be ignored any longer. As a Latin Americanist he was hardly unfamiliar with the significance of commodity exports, and especially of coffee exports to Latin America. He would come to believe that coffee market conditions warranted an international coffee agreement, as a "crutch" to overcome a temporary crisis.[129] Mann later rejected the idea that the ICA was fundamentally a Cold War artifice; but he did concede that "if you have economic chaos, you may be presented with a difficult problem from the standpoint of national security." Further, he would say of his support for the Coffee Agreement, "I am a great believer in the importance of Latin American to the United States, or generally in the importance of geographic proximity in foreign relations."[130]

After the FAC conversation with Mann in early 1958, a small task force of State Department officers set to work on proposals for dealing with the growing crisis in the coffee market. The important, if seemingly modest recommendation of this group, was that the United States should help organize a coffee

---

[128] Interview, Paul Callanan, July 12, 1971.

[129] Interview, Thomas C. Mann, August 20, 1971.

[130] Ibid.

study group. According to the NCA President at that time, the Association proposed this line of action to the State Department.[131] When Mann and his superior, Under Secretary Douglas Dillon, approved this undertaking, the only remaining obstacle was to secure the approval of the powerful Council on Foreign Economic Policy, an interdepartmental body, chaired by the President's special adviser on foreign economic affairs, Clarence Randall. Randall was an industrialist of strong free trade proclivities, and according to Mann himself, "against commodity agreements in principle."[132]

In a little known instance of private lobbying, General Foods helped assure Council approval of Mann's enterprise. According to George Robbins, then Director of Green Coffee Operations for GF, he personally "introduced Mann to the White House." Robbins' first point of access at the White House was Clarence Francis, a General Foods executive, who then served as a special adviser to Eisenhower, and subsequently, as the Chairman of the Board at General Foods. Francis, anxious about the appearance of a "conflict of interest," in turn, introduced Robbins to another Presidential adviser, Myer Kastenbaum. Robbins met with Kastenbaum several different times, and at this early date convinced him of the need for a coffee agreement, or at least of the merits of

---

[131] "The Editor Interviews: Jack McKiernan," Tea and Coffee Trade Journal, CXXII (January, 1962), 15. In response to this interview a coffee trader complained that the NCA initiative had not been widely publicized within the industry, implying that there would have been considerable opposition. Charles J. Meono, "Who Will Benefit from Agreement?" Tea and Coffee Trade Journal, CXXII (March, 1962), 16. It does appear that NCA initiatives for a U.S.-based coffee study group were undertaken quietly by a small number of prominent coffee businessmen who would engineer industry consensus for the ICA four years later.

[132] Interview, Thomas C. Mann, August 20, 1971. In 1954 Randall had chaired a Commission on Foreign Economic Policy that recommended against U.S. participation in commodity agreements. See U.S., President's Commission on Foreign Economic Policy (Randall Commission), Report to the President and to Congress (Washington, D.C.: GPO, 1954), 35.

entering into serious international discussions of the problems of the coffee market. Kastenbaum, in turn, arranged for meetings between Thomas Mann and Clarence Randall. [133]

Robbins is certain that his personal intervention propelled the State Department into action and secured the Randall Council's blessing for U.S. entry into the Coffee Study Group.[134] Encouragement from the premier coffee businessman in the United States, representing the country's largest coffee processor and food corporation, probably did weigh heavily in the scales for Council approval of a change of U.S. coffee policy; but it cannot be known just how decisive it was. It is more likely that this timely intervention was one of several major factors contributing to the change.

The year 1958 brought the beginning of a series of changes in United States foreign economic policy towards Latin America, spanning the late Eisenhower and early Kennedy administrations, only one of which was the move from unwillingness to engage in serious talks about coffee problems to initiatives for the Coffee Agreement. According to R. Harrison Wagner:

> A series of innovations appeared between 1958 and 1961 in two main stages, each apparently connected with what was interpreted to be a crisis in the relations between the United States and the countries of Latin America. The first major change was associated with the rough treatment given Vice President Nixon during his visits to Peru and to Venezuela in 1958. Shortly thereafter the United States Government agreed to the establishment of an Inter-American development bank and began a series of discussions with the countries of Latin America concerning both international commodity agreements and the broad questions of economic development raised by the Brazilian proposal of an 'Operation Pan America.'

---

133 Sometime around the end of May the Council approved U.S. participation in a coffee study group, though it did not, for the time being, authorize the State Department to work towards a regulatory regime. Interview, George Robbins, February 25, 1971.

134 *Ibid.*

> The second major change began in the summer of 1960, when the full dimensions of the problem presented by the Cuban Revolution became apparent, and continued into the first months of the new Kennedy administration. During this time the United States initiated the discussions that resulted in the Act of Bogota, and then opened a second round of discussions, which in August 1961 produced the Alliance for Progress. About the same time a definite decision was made by the Kennedy administration to sign an international agreement regulating the coffee market.[135]

"The change of policy most directly influenced by the Nixon riots," Wagner adds, "seems to have been that concerning commodity agreements."[136] The U.S. decision to enter the Coffee Study Group was taken about the time of Nixon's South American journey, in May of 1958, and may or may not have been precipitated by the hostile demonstrations he met there. Certainly the latter riveted policy-maker attention on Latin American policy.

According to a staff member on the Senate Foreign Relations Committee at that time, the Nixon riots prompted the FRC's Subcommittee on American Republics Affairs to undertake a full-scale review of Latin American policy.[137] The Subcommittee commissioned two studies of U.S. policy, one of which significantly, dealt with "Commodity Problems in Latin America."[138] He believes that the Committee had a part in persuading the Executive of the merits of considering commodity agreements for Latin America. "Thomas Mann and C. Douglas Dillon [Under Secretary of State for Economic Affairs in 1957-58]," he added,

---

[135] R. Harrison Wagner, _United States Policy Toward Latin America: A Study in Domestic and International Politics_ (Stanford: Stanford University Press, 1970), 134-35.

[136] _Ibid._, 139.

[137] Source withheld.

[138] Committee on Foreign Relations, "Commodity Problems in Latin America," _op. cit._

"were trying to turn us around on Latin American Policy," and in that context were receptive to the idea of exploring commodity measures which before had been rejected out of hand. "The true turning point of policy, affecting the chances for U.S. support of commodity agreements," he concluded, "came in July of 1960 when the concept of aid to 'social development' was accepted in the Act of Bogota."

Again Professor Wagner is correct that the "crisis in the coffee market" was even more important than the Nixon riots in compelling the United States to reconsider its earlier refusal to consider substantive commitments to bolster that market.[139] Increasingly, as C. Douglas Dillon observed, policy-makers were seeing general commodity problems, adverse balance of payments and general economic difficulties in Latin America as "more permanent."[140] In this context, there were strong doubts that the coffee market could recover of its own accord, in any short period of time.

Assistant Secretary of State Roy Rubottom, Jr., described the U.S. decision to enter the Coffee Study Group as "an historic step in our economic policy."[141] Perhaps this seemed no hyperbole to his Colombian audience. To policy-makers such as Thomas Mann at the ground-level, however, U.S. entry into the Coffee Study Group was a modest beginning at exploring what the United States could do to help bolster the coffee market. No authorization to work towards U.S. participation in a Coffee Agreement had been given, and Mann doubts in retrospect, that that could have been secured in that period.[142]

---

139 Wagner, op. cit., 140.

140 U.S., Congress, Senate, Committee on Foreign Relations, American Republics Cooperation Act, Hearings, 86 Cong., 2d sess., 1960, 11, as cited in Ibid., 143.

141 Press Conference, Bogota, Colombia, February 9, 1959, as quoted in National Coffee Association, News Letter, No. 629, February 27, 1959.

142 Interview, Thomas C. Mann, August 20, 1971.

Mann advised Latin American coffee diplomats that they would have to be patient and work deliberately, step-by-step, if they expected to secure United States support for more ambitious efforts to strengthen the coffee market.[143] At least one prominent Latin coffee expert remembers that Mann labored diligently to secure the fullest possible mileage from the restrictive mandate that the Council on Foreign Economic Policy had given the State Department.[144]

In June of 1958 the Coffee Study Group (CSG) was formally inaugurated, with Thomas Mann as chairman. In the CSG the United States, at first, played the unlikely role of promoting producer agreements, providing for either product retention or fixed export quotas. When at the end of the year Latin and African producers (i.e., France and Portugal for their African colonies) failed to resolve their differences over proposals for regulatory measures, the fifteen countries signed a Latin American Coffee Agreement (1958-59), providing for retention of exportable production. The following year France and Portugal, for their African colonies, joined the Latins in the first producer International Coffee Agreement (1959). This Agreement, which did not include consuming countries, was renewed twice and phased into the ICA of 1962. The United Kingdom took its East African colonies into the Agreement in 1960, and several newly independent Francophone countries joined. The producer International Coffee Agreements provided for fixed export quotas, and for administrative and representational arrangements that anticipated the International Coffee Organization of 1962.

Meanwhile officials of producing countries were expressing the view that producer agreements were not the "ideal solution" for dealing with "the

---

[143] Ibid.

[144] Interview, Dr. Joao Oliveira Santos, April 30, 1971. Santos, a Brazilian economist, was the first Secretary-General of the International Coffee Organization (1963-1968).

really big problems of coffee."[145] In December of 1958 Lt. Col. Jose Maria Lemus, President of El Salvador, expressed openly what was on many minds: the necessity for the United States and other consuming countries to cooperate in regulation of the coffee market. Specifically, he proposed that there be established "import quotas in the continental territory of the United States applicable to all coffee-producing countries, similar to those established by the Inter-American Coffee Agreement signed in Washington in 1940, at the beginning of World War II."[146] The following March Lemus pressed this proposal and others on the U.S. government, during an official visit to the United States.[147]

Proposals for coffee import quotas were widespread at this time. The NCA and other associations that opposed import restrictions were becoming anxious about "rumors" that the government was actually contemplating import controls.

In March Weldon H. Emigh, President of the Pacific Coast Coffee Association, queried the State Department about its intentions. Thomas Mann replied that the State had drafted "tentative standby provisions" that could be employed, if it were "deemed necessary" to impose import restrictions. Mann indicated that the moment of necessity had not arrived, but might arise in the event of "chaos and bankruptcy because of collapsing prices."[148]

According to the NCA President, John F. McKiernan, the State Department on April 23 assured the NCA's Foreign Affairs Committee that it did not

---

[145] Remarks of Renato Costa Lima, President, Brazilian Coffee Institute, September 24, 1958, concerning the Latin American Coffee Agreement, as cited in ICO, History of Recent International Coffee Agreements, 7.

[146] Council of the Organization of American States, Special Committee to Study the Formulation of New Measures for Economic Cooperation, CECE-79 (English) Rev. 1, as cited in Ibid., 11.

[147] New York Herald Tribune, March 17, 1959, as cited in Ibid., 12.

[148] Letter from Thomas C. Mann to Weldon H. Emigh (date in March 1959, unspecified) as cited in National Coffee Association, News Letter, No. 640, May 15, 1959.

intend, at that time, to seek legislative authorization for import controls. Furthermore, he indicated, Assistant Secretary of State Mann pledged in writing that the State would "consult in advance with the Foreign Affairs Committee" before taking any such action.[149] Parenthetically, McKiernan felt that the State's formal commitment to consult with the NCA before taking major initiatives regarding the coffee market indicated a "significant accomplishment" for the Association, that it was gaining the authoritative standing with the Department that it desired.

The NCA Foreign Affairs Committee urged that standby regulations only be implemented in "an emergency situation," and stated that the NCA was prepared to discuss in advance the possible basis of these standby regulations. It also declared its opposition "to any import regulations that would limit shipments to specific United States ports, areas, individual importers or other members of the United States Industry based upon prior record of purchases." Finally, it said, "Any import quotas imposed should be on a basis of countries of origin with all members of the U.S. Coffee Industry having free access to coffee made available within the quotas."[150]

After the flurry of excitement and activity over proposed coffee import controls in the first half of 1959, U.S. policy development for coffee problems settled on a plateau for the remainder of the Eisenhower Administration. The producer agreements continued to function, with the tacit encouragement of the U.S., and coffee diplomats and technicians continued to explore the means for

---

[149]John F. McKiernan, "Equal Opportunity for All in the Trade," Tea and Coffee Trade Journal, CXX (May, 1961), 17.

[150]Views of NCA Foreign Affairs Committee, as quoted in Tea and Coffee Trade Journal, CXVI (June, 1959), 36.

more ambitious international regulatory measures. Throughout 1960 an ambitious, multi-volume study, "The World Coffee Problem: Present Status of the Industry and Future Prospects," was in preparation; and the first volumes of that were distributed to members of the CSG in January of 1961, just as producer hopes were rising that the new Kennedy Administration would be more disposed to joining in coffee market regulation.

In its last years, the Eisenhower Administration made incremental adjustments of foreign economic policy toward Latin America that would indirectly contribute to the evolution of U.S. policy toward participation in a Coffee Agreement. During 1960, as numerous studies have indicated, the Administration was becoming increasingly anxious about expanding ties between Castro's Cuba and the U.S.S.R., and about the implications of these for a Latin America mired down in an exceptionally severe phase of economic difficulties. For two or three years there had been a growing concern among key administration officials and advisers that policy innovations to spur Latin "economic growth" were not sufficient in and of themselves, particularly in view of perceived Soviet efforts to exploit popular discontents. Douglas Dillon, who became Under Secretary of State for Economic Affairs in 1957, is frequently credited with effective initiatives to adapt U.S. policies.[151]

Dr. Milton Eisenhower, who visited Mexico and Central America in 1957 and 1958, was one of the first to cautiously articulate the view that the U.S. should directly aid measures that would benefit the Latin majorities who were not otherwise being helped in the new prosperity founded on economic growth.[152]

---

[151] See Arthur M. Schlesinger, Jr., A Thousand Days: John F. Kennedy in the White House (Greenwich, Conn.: Fawcett Publications, 1967), 179-180.

[152] Milton Eisenhower, The Wine is Bitter (Garden City, New York: Doubleday and Company, 1963), 209.

But even as late as 1959, his concrete proposal for aid to public housing was beat down by the Department of Treasury and lending agencies which were opposed to American aid to "social development." [153]

Soviet involvement in worsening U.S.-Cuban relations probably propelled President Eisenhower and the policy-making system into policy adjustments that would have been unthinkable a couple of years earlier.[154] In its last months in office, the Eisenhower administration secured funding authorization from the Congress for aid to social development in Latin America. In September it joined Latin countries in the framing of the Act of Bogota, which called for U.S. assistance to Latin social development, and Latin commitments to social reform. The Act of Bogota, Democrats would later admit reluctantly, set the stage for Kennedy's Alliance for Progress.

The election of John F. Kennedy continued and amplified some of the trends in foreign economic policy toward Latin America that were becoming evident at the end of the Eisenhower Administration. It was particularly significant for the fortunes of coffee market regulation.

The general orientation of the new Administration towards commodity agreements, and particularly the proposals for a consumer-producer coffee agreement, was shaped partially in the period between the election and the inauguration, by the deliberations of the Kennedy Task Forces on "Foreign Economic Policy" and on "Immediate Latin American Problems." [155]

---

[153] Ibid., 222-23. I am indebted to Prof. Wagner for pointing out the Eisenhower advocacy of social development measures. Wagner, op. cit., 145-6.

[154] Wagner, op. cit., 149.

[155] Report to the President-Elect of the Task Force on Foreign Economic Policy, Submitted by George Ball (Chairman), January, 1961, Unpublished Document, John F. Kennedy Library, Waltham, Massachusetts; and Report to the President-Elect of the Task Force on Immediate Latin American Problems, Submitted by Adolph Berle (Chairman), January, 1961, Unpublished Document, John F. Kennedy Library, Waltham, Massachusetts.

The Ball Task Force on Foreign Economic Policy observed that "The intensive drive toward nationalism in the less-developed areas confronts us with a shift in the world balance of power" and that the "urgent task" was to "to direct this drive... into constructive channels."[156] Among other things, the Task Force concretely proposed that the United States be prepared to make unilateral tariff concessions to LDC imports and to develop arrangements to stabilize their export income.[157]

It is useful to quote at length the Task Force's comments and recommendations regarding commodity agreements and arrangements, since these anticipated the tone and substance of actual policies subsequently adopted by Kennedy.

> In the past the United States Government has in principle opposed commodity agreements and arrangements for the stabilization of the export income of single commodity producing countries. It is the view of the Task Force that this principle has been too rigidly applied. The Kennedy Administration should explicitly recognize the desirability of income stabilization and show hospitality to well-conceived proposals to attain that end. Two techniques for income stabilization are available:
> (i) Commodity agreements to stabilize prices.
> (ii) Loans to offset fluctuations in income.
>
> The Task Force emphasizes that commodity agreements are not a panacea and that effective agreements may be possible for only a limited number of widely traded commodities. Certainly, the problem of developing and administering agreements will vary in difficulty, depending upon the commodity in question, e.g., its perishability, storability, the number and nature of producers, the geographic areas of production, etc. As a result the Task Force feels that no categorical statements can be made regarding the general utility of commodity agreement techniques.
>
> Not only are stabilization techniques vital to the economic development of less-developed areas, to which the United States is committed, but we have at least two additional interests in encouraging the employment of such techniques where they can be effective. (i) The United States is either a principal producer or a principal

---

[156] Ball Task Force on Foreign Economic Policy, 3-4.

[157] *Ibid.*, 4 and 35.

> consumer of every product likely to be the subject of commodity agreements, and, hence, our participation in such arrangements is often indispensable to their success; (ii) The United States has a direct interest in the income stability of many raw materials producing areas since those areas in turn provide important markets for American production.
>
> While the United States should be hospitable to proposals for commodity agreements where such agreements are practicable, it should not encourage efforts to employ commodity agreement techniques that support prices at artificially high levels. This would amount merely to ill-designed economic assistance paid for by the consumers of the commodity in question—ill-designed because it would tend to enrich a handful of individual producers without necessarily benefitting the total economies of the producing countries.
>
> In many instances income stabilization might be better achieved by techniques other than commodity agreements. The Task Force feels that much greater consideration should be given to the possibilities of using the resources of the International Monetary Fund for short-term loans to cushion income fluctuations resulting from cyclical variations in production conditions or the terms of trade of raw material producing countries.[158]

The Berle Task Force on Immediate Latin American Problems contended "that the greatest single task of American diplomacy in Latin America is to divorce the inevitable and necessary Latin American social transformation from connection with and prevent its capture by overseas Communist Power politics."[159] The Task Force assumed that "the new Administration will undertake a new approach in dealing with the serious problems that already confront the United States in the Latin American field, and others that may arise."[160]

Among the recommendations for economic and social policy was the advice that in spite of the "slight embarrassment at building on a program initiated by the previous Administration," President Kennedy should warmly support

---

[158]Ibid., 41-43.

[159]Berle Task Force on Immediate Latin American Problems, 2.

[160]Ibid., 3.

the beginnings made in the Act of Bogota. This agreement, the Task Force believed, "contains the essential elements of the kind of program the new Administration should support."[161] "It is also necessary," concluded the Kennedy advisers, "to demonstrate our break with past inadequate programs and dramatize our intention to organize a new 'Alliance for Progress' in the Americas."[162]

The Berle Task Force Report, a frankly political document, contained a substantial section entitled "Commodity Market Stabilization." The Berle group agreed with the Ball Task Force: "It would be most unwise to undertake a blanket endorsement of the market stabilization for all major Latin American exports, but instead indicate our willingness to discuss such arrangements whereever needed."[163]

The Task Force was more explicit about coffee policy. "In the case of coffee," the Report observed, "we are threatened with a catastrophic avalanche [author's emphasis] of production in the 1961-62 crop year." It continued:

> The present rather frail international coffee agreement [producer ICA, 1960] may not be able to withstand this avalanche. In addition to the generally agreed steps of seeking to persuade the Germans and other Europeans to reduce coffee excise taxes, and pressing the European Common market to abandon its discrimination in favor of French African coffee, we should consider emergency strengthening of the international agreement by applying United States (and if possible European) import resrictions to enforce the quotas, provided that effective plans are undertaken to reduce the chronic overproduction. At the same time, we should devote a significant part of the agricultural assistance programs to helping find better long-run uses for the relatively high-cost coffee producing land.[164]

Prof. Lincoln Gordon, a member of the Berle Task Force and draftsman for certain passages of its Report, believes that the Report helped crystallize President Kennedy's thinking on Latin American policy innovations that he

---

[161] Ibid., 24. [162] Ibid., 25. [163] Ibid., 30. [164] Ibid., 30.

had already promised in general terms, during the campaign.[165] Regarding commodity agreements, in particular, a member of the staff for the Senate Foreign Relations Committee recalls that Senator Kennedy of the Committee had taken a lively and positive interest in the report of 1959 on Latin American commodity problems prepared by International Economic Consultants.[166] More pointedly, in a campaign speech in Tampa, Florida, during October of 1960, Senator Kennedy announced his hopes for an Alianza para Progreso, including among new departures in U.S. policy, stabilization of "the prices of the principal export commodities."[167]

In March of 1961 President Kennedy launched his Alliance for Progress in a speech before the Latin American diplomatic corps at the White House. Fifth among ten points in the new program, was the assertion that "the United States is ready to cooperate in serious, case-by-case examinations of commodity market problems." And further, "Frequent violent changes in commodity prices seriously injure the economies of many Latin American nations—draining their resources and stultifying their growth. Together we must find practical methods of bringing an end to this pattern."[168]

Numerous key policy-makers believe that the President's inclusion of the call to action on commodity problems in his Alliance program gave great

---

[165] Oral History Interview, Lincoln Gordon, John F. Kennedy Library, Waltham, Massachusetts, 1964.

[166] Interview, Staff Member, Senate Foreign Relations Committee, July 8, 1971. Name withheld upon request.

[167] Schlesinger, Jr., op. cit., 183-184.

[168] Department of State Bulletin, XLIV (1961), 471 and 473.

impetus to the fortunes of proposals for U.S. participation in a coffee agreement. W. Michael Blumenthal remembers the mutually reinforcing efforts of seeking, at once, coffee market regulation and a more broadly conceived Alliance for Progress. "The Alliance for Progress and the meeting at Punta del Este in August 1961," says Blumenthal, "were indeed factors which caused us to move quickly and more positively [regarding coffee problems]. I was the U.S. Representative on Committee Three, negotiating the Third Chapter of the Alliance. Our positive attitude on commodity problems in that Committee, which I was authorized to evince, was a helpful factor in getting the Alliance going."[169]

A commitment to "examine" specific "commodity market problems," of course, did not immediately commit the U.S. to participate in a coffee agreement, although as the Berle Task Force had indicated, there was hardly a more obvious or more likely candidate than coffee, if the new policy were to mean anything at all.

W. Michael Blumenthal, one of several young Kennedy appointees, and who served as a Deputy Assistant Secretary of State in the Bureau of Economic Affairs, was charged to look at the whole question of commodity agreements anew. "We listed and studied all the possibilities," he recalls, "and then tried coffee for a starter." "Coffee was hot politically," he added, "was technically suitable for control, and a product of great importance to Latin America." "George Ball [Under Secretary of State] and Edwin Martin [Assistant Secretary for Economic Affairs], of course, made it clear that the Administration expected to do more for Latin America."[170]

---

[169] Letter from W. Michael Blumenthal to author, October 20, 1971.

[170] Interview, W. Michael Blumenthal, October 13, 1971. Blumenthal had been Vice-President of Crown Cork Co., and after government service became President of Bendix International.

According to Blumenthal, "The decision to press for an agreement [coffee] was made in the summer of 1961 [probably July, 1961] after about three months of review and discussion within and outside the Government." Within the government, he indicates, "there obviously were differences" over whether the U.S. should join a coffee agreement. He recalls:[171]

> State tended to be the leader and most favorable to an Agreement. AID was in full agreement. We had little trouble from Agriculture since they have no real interest in coffee. The most negative reactions came from Commerce and Treasury. The former, because they tend to be most business oriented; the latter, because implementation of the Agreement involved import quotas administered by Customs. Bringing the rest of Government along was our constant problem.

However, he continued,

> It wasn't too difficult during the period involved since it was known that the White House supported the idea. Incidentally, the Council of Economic Advisors was of good help.[172]

Within the State Department itself, "there were only minor differences of viewpoint between E [Bureau of Economic Affairs] and the geographic areas. The area desks let E take the lead but they were fully in support of what we were doing. The African Desks were not as active as ARA [Bureau of Inter-American Affairs]. They were also a little more nervous about the Coffee Agreement because they worried that we might favor the Milds over the Robustas."

Outside the government, the State Department consulted closely with the NCA's Foreign Affairs Committee, and with individual officers and members of the Association, as it developed its policy for coffee.[173]

In the first part of 1961, the NCA leadership, which had made a special point of visiting most of the Kennedy Administration officials who might conceiv-

---

[171] Letter from W. Michael Blumenthal to author, October 20, 1971.

[172] Ibid. [173] Ibid.

ably influence decisions affecting coffee, was fully aware of the shift in attitude towards commodity agreements and the likelihood that this would affect the coffee negotiations. An increasing number of key businesses indeed were sympathetic to the change, as it might affect coffee, and some like George Robbins of General Foods, actively encouraged the emerging commitment of the U.S. to a coffee agreement.[174]

FAC, of course, had been monitoring developments in the Coffee Study Group negotiations, and had already advised the State Department that it would oppose market regulation that would call for either a coffee buffer stock, such as in the International Tin Agreement, or for import quotas.[175] At the end of May or in early June the NCA received assurances from Deputy Secretary Blumenthal that he would value the advice of the Foreign Affairs Committee concerning the current deliberations in State on coffee policy. On or about June 6, President McKiernan met with Blumenthal at State and with Richard Goodwin, Assistant Special Counsel to the President with responsibilities for Latin American policy. On June 20, eight members of the FAC met with Blumenthal, and at that time were assured by him that the State Department would make no major decisions regarding coffee without prior consultations with the Committee.[176]

---

[174]Robbins had been involved in a substantial amount of transnational diplomacy to promote a coffee agreement. In mid-1960, for example, he joined a group of Latin Americans in visiting France to promote its participation in an agreement. Robbins met high level government and foreign office officials for this purpose. Interview, George Robbins, August 11, 1971.

[175]Report by George Robbins to NCA Board of Directors, (date unspecified), as cited in Speech by John F. McKiernan to Southern Coffee Roasters Association, June 2, 1961, as cited in NCA, News Letter, No. 749, June 5, 1961.

[176]NCA, News Letter, No. 752. June 20, 1961. Members of FAC attending the meeting were George Robbins, chairman; Edward Aborn; Arthur A. Anisansel; Jack R. Durland; Peter Folger; Reuben Hills III; John McKiernan; and Austin A. O'Brien.

By the end of June, John McKiernan reports, the NCA's Board "had become convinced that our Government's participation in a new, long-term, International Coffee Agreement was necessary if the economic and political stability of the coffee producing nations—not only of Latin America but of Africa as well—was to be achieved." At that time it recommended to the State Department in writing "That the United States become a signatory of the International Coffee Agreement [existing producer agreement] or its equivalent under conditions which will insure:[177]

> That the United States has sufficient controlling vote to protect the interests of the United States consumers;
>
> That the United States use every effort to encourage the producing countries to take effective steps to reduce future overproduction and existing coffee surpluses;
>
> That other consuming and producing countries not now parties to the International Coffee Agreement should be encouraged to become signatories to the International Coffee or its equivalent;
>
> That to implement policing of the export quota plan the United States and other consuming countries agree to impose temporary import quotas only on producing countries not signatories to the International Coffee Agreement or its equivalent and also on those countries which violate their export quotas. Any import quota imposed on any country to be removed when that country joints the International Coffee Agreement or corrects its violation of its export quota;
>
> That the United States develop an organized plan to encourage the consuming countries of the world to reduce import and other taxes on coffee as a commodity, the reduction of which would increase consumption and thereby further expand world trade in coffee;

---

[177] Statement by John F. McKiernan, President, NCA, to Senate Foreign Relations Committee, March 12, 1973, as found in U.S., Congress Senate, Committee on Foreign Relations, International Coffee Agreement, 1962.

> That in the event the United States becomes involved in lending financial assistance to any coffee producing country it shall be arranged so as to insure that the U.S. Government will not become the owner or responsible for the disposal of coffee because such action would not contribute to the ultimate solution of the problem.[178]

In July the NCA President conveyed to the State Department a resolution of the Green Coffee Association of New York, expressing the view that a precondition for U.S. entry into a coffee agreement should be a provision indicating that "no producing country be allowed to import coffee into this country by any of its Governmental organizations either official, quasi-official or any other sort of agency that can be so construed.[179] U.S. coffee traders were becoming increasingly exercised by the growing tendency of producing countries to establish selling offices in the U.S. and Europe, in order to deal directly with coffee processors. Fearing that they would gradually be supplanted by these official agencies, they clamored for prohibitions against this practice in any future coffee agreement. The NCA adopted the traders' position on this issue, less because the industry leaders (i.e., major processors) had strong convictions about it than out of a desire to bring the reluctant traders into the industry consensus supporting a coffee agreement.

It is unlikely that the extent of business "influence" in forging the various elements of the U.S. "position" in the Coffee Agreement negotiations can be determined conclusively; nevertheless, it is certain that the NCA advocacy of a provision against producer government selling offices <u>was</u> largely responsible for its inclusion in the U.S. position. Even then the resulting Article 53(2) of the Coffee Agreement (1962) was brief and ambiguous. The Article,

---

[178] NCA recommendations submitted to State Department, June 27, 1961, as quoted in NCA, <u>News Letter</u>, No. 757, July 31, 1961.

[179] Resolution of the Green Coffee Association of New York, July 19, 1961, as quoted in NCA, <u>News Letter</u>, No. 757, July 31, 1961.

calling on members to conduct their business "in a manner consonant with the established channels of trade," could be interpreted to allow trade by government selling offices, which much to the consternation of the American traders, is what happened when in 1964 Uganda became the fourth producing country to open a selling office in New York City.

George Robbins, a member of the FAC advisory group at the U.N. Coffee Conference (1962), remembers that it was "only by the sheer weight of the United States' influence" that any provision on this matter at all was included in the Agreement. "Most of the nations wanted it out completely," he reported to the NCA Board of Directors.[180] Many American traders felt betrayed by the American delegation, and their defeat on this issue contributed to their determination to oppose renewal of the Agreement in 1968.

Deputy Secretary Blumenthal informed the NCA that the State Department intended to officially indicate its willingness to work towards what Secretary of the Treasury Dillon later called a "proper coffee agreement" at the August meeting of the Inter-American Economic and Social Conference at Punta del Este. This occurred, and the Third Committee of the Conference, in which Blumenthal represented the United States, discussed coffee market regulation in general terms, and then referred the matter to the Coffee Study Group.

Among the resolutions passed at the Conference of Punta del Este, Resolution C. 1 expressed the Conference's

> decision to support the meeting of the Coffee Study Group which is to convene in Washington in September, 1961, for the purpose of assuring

---

[180] Extract of a report from George Robbins, Chairman, Foreign Affairs Committee to NCA Board of Directors, New Orleans, October 31, 1962, as found in "NCA Committee Report on UN Coffee Conference," Tea and Coffee Trade Journal, CXXIV (January, 1963), 68. This Report provides an invaluable perspective on American business views and concerns in that conference.

> the preparation, in the shortest possible time, of a long-term World Coffee Agreement.[181]

This and other resolutions also stated a number of principles that should guide the signatories in working towards a long-term coffee agreement.[182]

At the State Department's request, the entire Foreign Affairs Committee met with Blumenthal and his colleagues on September 8 to help plan for U.S. participation in Coffee Study Group negotiations. FAC was convinced that its earlier six-point proposal had been absorbed into State Department views, but reasserted its opposition to U.S. financed or owned buffer stocks, and its desire for adequate protection against producer selling operations in the United States. McKiernan requested, and apparently received approval to attend all future meetings of the Coffee Study Group.[183] Blumenthal would be the chief U.S. delegate in the CSG talks and Paul Callanan, Assistant Chief of the Foodstuffs Division at the State Department, his alternate.

In the September 27th meeting of the GSG's First Committee, Callanan outlined current U.S. thinking on coffee market regulation. A new agreement would be needed, he said, to remedy the two main deficiencies of the existing producer agreement: a membership limited to exporters and an ineffective quota system. He assured African members of the Group that President Kennedy's pledge to seek workable solutions to commodity problems applied to Africa, as well as to Latin America. The United States was ready to join a "workable"

---

[181] OAS, "Alliance for Progress: Official Documents Emanating from the Special Meeting of the Inter-American Economic and Social Council at the Ministerial Level, "ES-RE-Doc. 145 (English) Rev. 3 Corr., Punta del Este, August 16, 1961, 44.

[182] Ibid., 44-45. See Department of State Bulletin, XLV (1961), 459-469.

[183] NCA, News Letter, Special Bulletin, No. 31, September 8, 1961.

agreement," would use its good offices to urge the participation of other countries and help enforce export quotas. Problems of over-production would have to be tackled, free movement of coffee promoted, a realistic system of adjustable quotas planned, and, if the United States get its way, exports of all types of coffee, "in whatever form," would need to be charged against export quotas.[184]

On May 22 the Secretary General of the United Nations formally called for a Coffee Conference to begin on July 9. The U.N. Coffee Conference was held at U.N. headquarters and turned into a seven-week marathon, July 9 to August 25, 1962. On September 28, the Conference was reconvened, and the ICA adopted as a whole. Twenty-four of the 58 delegations signed the Agreement at that time.

In the previous March the NCA Foreign Affairs Committee had met once again with Deputy Secretary Blumenthal at the State Department. The Committee came away satisfied that State views "substantially reflect the position previously expressed by the National Coffee Association."[185] Two months later the NCA Board decided to "amplify" its proposals and submitted to the State Department a list of ten recommendations. Most of these, for example, the recommendation that the Agreement should be operative for a five year period, were technical and designed to assume implementation of the six principles that the Association had already advanced. On June 28, John McKiernan reports, the State Department advised him that the NCA's "10 recommendations would be the basis for

---

[184] Excerpts from a statement by Paul Callanan, U.S. State Department, to a meeting of the Coffee Study Group, September 27, 1961 as cited in "United States Coffee Policy, Coffee Annual, 1961 (New York, George Gordon Paton, 1962), 59-60; and NCA, News Letter, Special Bulletin No. 4., September 27, 1961.

[185] NCA, News Letter, Special Bulletin No. 12, March 15, 1962.

the U.S. position in the negotiations for the new International Coffee Agreement at the United Nations Coffee Conference."[186]

The United States and the Coffee Conference (1962). The U.S. "position," at the inception of the Coffee Conference, has been described in some detail by Richard Bilder, a legal adviser to the American delegation at the Conference. This position, embodied in a formal and confidential negotiating instruction to the Delegation, contained the following essentials:

> The new long-term agreement should be based upon realistic export quotas which should not exceed the best available estimate of probable world demand. The United States should work hard for this objective, but should be careful not to inject itself in any way into the question of allocation of country quotas within this global figure.
>
> The quota system should cover all types of coffee to all destinations for all purposes, and should not leave any loopholes. Thus no 'ex-quota' shipments to 'new markets' should be permitted.
>
> The agreement probably should not contain any specific price target, in view of the negotiating and administrative difficulties in attempting to establish specific price ranges for each type of coffee, as well as the political problems specific price targets would raise. Instead prices should be generally left to the operation of market forces under the quota system. However, it should be made clear that the agreement is not intended to operate so as to bring about unwarranted price rises, and specific provisions to protect consumer countries in this respect should be included.
>
> The agreement should provide for the free movement of coffee as a non-discriminatory basis from all countries into consumption, and should seek to eliminate obstacles to trade and fiscal burdens which inhibit increasing consumption.
>
> Finally, the agreement should, as a key principle, recognize that overproduction is a root cause of the coffee problem, and provide some means for the orderly reduction of production and stocks and the

---

[186]McKiernan, Statement to the Senate Foreign Relations Committee, The International Coffee Agreement, 1962, 93.

> encouragement of economic diversification in the producing areas.[187]

"Many, but not all, of these objectives," Bilder later reflected, "were achieved."[188]

How well did United States negotiators fare? What elements of their negotiating "position" were ultimately accepted or rejected? To what extent were NCA views reflected in the U.S. position, and how did these fare in the final Coffee Agreement? What was the role of the Foreign Affairs Committee in the Coffee Conference?[189]

The U.S. delegation to the UN Coffee Conference, headed by W. Michael Blumenthal, included eleven government officials from the Departments of Agriculture, Commerce and State and eight members of the NCA's Foreign Affairs Committee.[190] To the consternation of the latter the Green Coffee Association of New York attempted at the penultimate moment to secure State Department

---

[187] Footnote 23, in Richard B. Bilder, "The International Coffee Agreement: A Case History in Negotiation," Law and Contemporary Problems, XXVIII (spring, 1963), 343. This is an excellent participant-observer account of the Conference. See also W. Michael Blumenthal's statement of the U.S. position before the conference, July 10, 1962, in Department of State Bulletin, XLVII (1962), 234.

[188] Ibid.

[189] Two excellent sources for exploring these questions are Bilder, "The International Coffee Agreement," 355-369; and George Robbins' Report to the NCA Board of Directors, October 31, 1962, as found in 'NCA Committee Report on UN Coffee Conference," op. cit., 28, 66, 68, and 70-72.

[190] For an official listing of delegation members see United Nations, United Nations Coffee Conference, 1962: Summary of Proceedings, E/Conf., 42/8 (New York: United Nations, 1962), 13-14. FAC participants were Edward Aborn, President, TENCO, Division of Coca-Cola; Arthur Anisansel, Vice-President and Director, Imperial Commodities Corporation; Peter Folger, Executive Vice-President, J.A. Folger and Co.; Reuben W. Hills, III, President, Hills Bros. Coffee Inc.; Samuel Israel, Jr., President, Leon Israel and Bros., Inc.; John F. McKiernan, President, National Coffee Association; Austin O'Brien, Partner, Byrne, Delay and Co.; and George V. Robbins, Director of Green Coffee Operations, General Foods, and Chairman of FAC.

recognition for its own ad hoc Foreign Affairs Committee to participate in the conference. The State Department declined to allow the group into the delegation but Deputy Secretary Blumenthal met with it, ironically in the company of NCA President, John McKiernan, and according to one authoritative source, pledged to seek a strong provision against producer establishment of selling offices in the consuming countries.[191]

According to George Robbins,

> The United States Government people were most appreciative of the support of the industry. They were exceedingly happy that we were there to give them advice. They saw to it that every important committee meeting had at least one industry member attending along with government people, and in certain instances on certain subjects, only industry people attended the meetings.[192]

The quota system was the major issue of the Conference, and quota allocation the most "bitterly fought" among the producers.[193] The issue on which the Conference "almost foundered, concerned the actual fixing and allocation of these quotas."[194]

The idea of an export quota system as the basis for negotiation had been accepted beforehand by virtually everyone. Coffee prices would be influenced by regulating the flow of exports into the world market. The NCA, it will be recalled, had endorsed this idea, while frequently advising the State Department against the idea of a buffer stock arrangement. Bilder explains that the buffer stock proposal had been dismissed because of the large coffee surplus and the

---

[191] Tea and Coffee Trade Journal, CXXIII (July, 1962), 58.

[192] "NCA Committee Report on UN Coffee Conference," op. cit., 281.

[193] Bilder, op. cit., 355-58.

[194] Ibid., 355.

"enormous funds" that would be required to finance a buffer stock.[195] The NCA, which lobbied strenuously against the proposal, had an additional objection in mind— that the buffer stock concept involved a closer regulation of the market than it, and especially its trader members, were prepared to accept. Under this arrangement prices would be directly influenced by the decisions of a buffer stock manager.

The two main quota issues for resolution at the Coffee Conference were: how large the overall quota should be and how this quota should be adjusted over the period of the Agreement; and secondly, the allocation of shares of this overall quota among exporter members.

The U.S. delegation, with the full endorsement of the NCA, contended for a "realistic" overall quota commensurate with projected demand, as estimated by the best possible economic analysis. The producer delegations were inclined to a determination of a "realistic" quota by simply aggregating individually-set country quotas. A final decision on this issue was postponed to the end of the Conference, when countries had finished their battle over individual country quotas. The overall quota, finally included in the Agreement itself, reflected something of a compromise between the two conceptions of how it should be set. Nonetheless, the International Coffee Council was empowered to adjust this overall quota annually and quarterly, with producer basic quotas prorated accordingly; and thus, in part, negotation on this matter was deferred.

The discussion of "adjusting" annual and quarterly overall quotas— the ICC's function most directly bearing upon the fortunes of nations and economic groups— was naturally linked to the issue of voting procedure. The NCA

---

[195] Ibid., footnote, 355.

had made it a cardinal point that the United States have "sufficient controlling vote to protect the interests of the United States consumers,"[196] or it could have added more candidly, American business interests. To this end it seems to have been generally satisfied with the U.S. delegation's insistence on a weighted voting procedure. In the approved formula consuming countries were granted 1,000 votes as a group, and producers as a group the same number. The United States and Brazil secured 400 votes each in their respective groups. For most important decisions, including adjustment of annual and quarterly quotas, two-thirds of the votes counted in the consumer and producer groups separately, would be required. The U.S. delegation was extremely satisfied with this outcome, as with just one other consumer's support, it could block any action of the Council.[197]

One amendment to the voting procedure, however, seems to have originated in FAC pressure on the American delegation. George Robbins believes the point at issue was controversial enough to have wrecked the conference.[198] The producers, he reports, were highly resistant to a proposal that would permit "a simple majority of consuming countries voting to increase the ..... quota in order to bring down price to a fair level to the consumer." According to Robbins,

> The American delegation insisted— and when I say in this case 'the American delegation,' I mean the trade members of the American delegation—

---

[196] First of six recommendations of NCA to State Department, June 27, 1961, as found in NCA, News Letter, No. 754, July 10, 1961.

[197] It was not fully anticipated that the U.S. would have a considerably weaker hand in securing "positive" action by the ICC, e.g., in raising quarterly overall quotas, within coffee years.

[198] "NCA Committee Report on UN Coffee Conference," op. cit., 70.

> that Mr. Blumenthal take the point of view that America will not sign this Agreement. We will have no part of it, unless we have a clause in it that is satisfactory to us and that, in our opinion, will protect the American consumer against any false manipulation of prices in the coffee business.[199]

Article 34(6) of the ICA satisfied FAC and the American on this point:

> If the Council finds that a sharp and unusual increase or decrease in the general level of prices is due to artificial manipulation of the coffee market through agreements among importers or exporters or both, it shall then decide by a simple majority vote on what corrective measures should be applied to readjust the total level of the quarterly export quotas in effect.[200]

All participant-observers agree that the issue of quota allocation was the most troublesome for the Conference. The Coffee Conference was like most other commodity agreement conferences that have attempted to negotiate quota systems. Final determinations about the size of the global quota, and the country allocations thereof, were postponed to the last days of the meetings. When the producer delegates finally received the proposal country quota allocations, George Robbins recalls, "it was something like a 'nuclear explosion.'"[201]

The U.S. government had anticipated this furor, and had resolved at the outset to be careful not to inject itself in any way into the allocation of quotas.[202] The American delegation managed to abide by this directive, except to the extent, if George Robbins is correct, of acting as intermediaries among the disputing producer countries. Robbins himself, as the single major buyer

---

199 Ibid.

200 Article 34(5) provides for the same procedure in the event of "marked price rises or falls occurring within brief periods."

201 "NCA Committee Report on UN Coffee Conference," op. cit., 71.

202 Bilder, op. cit., footnote 343. See his succinct account of how this issue was handled by the Conference, 356-58.

of the world, seems to have had a strong personal role in getting the producing countries to stay at the negotiating table to resolve their differences.[203]

Price goals or provisions are invariably a vital and devisive issue in commodity agreement negotiations. The central question for the Coffee Conference was whether or not, and to what extent, the Agreement should contain specific price targets, for example, price ranges within which the Coffee Council should try to regulate price movements. This issue has repeatedly confounded the negotiations for a cocoa agreement.

The U.S. delegation entered the conference, Bilder says, with the instruction that:

> The agreement probably should not contain any specific price target, in view of the negotiating and administrative difficulties in attempting to establish specific price ranges for each type of coffee, as well as the political problems specific price targets would raise. Instead, prices should be generally left to the operation of market forces under the quota system. However, it should be made clear that the agreement is not intended to operate so as to bring about unwarranted price rises, and specific provisions to protect consumer countries in this respect, should be included.[204]

It did, however, participate seriously in the deliberations of the Economic Committee No. 2 that canvassed proposals for price targets. The NCA, in any case, became anxious that the U.S. might be drawn into agreeing to stringent price goals, and on July 17 advised Deputy Secretary Blumenthal that it objected to any "pact which would guarantee prices."[205]

George Robbins, the Chairman of FAC, it was noted earlier, had broached the idea of market regulation to maintain floor and ceiling prices in

---

203 "NCA Committee Report on UN Coffee Conference," op. cit.

204 Bilder, op. cit., footnote, 343.

205 McKiernan, Statement to Senate Foreign Relations Committee, 93.

in 1958.[206] But by 1962 the mainstream of NCA views, bolstered by strong trader opinion, was still against close market regulation. FAC, therefore, added its considerable weight to the view that none should be negotiated.

There was no great likelihood, in any event, that the Conference would negotiate explicit price objectives or ranges. There was even little open debate on the issue.[207] According to Bilder, "It quickly became apparent that it was politically impossible for the importing countries to accept any provisions which would actively seek sharp increases in prices."[208]

If there was any single objective upon which all delegations could agree, it was the desirability of preventing any further <u>decline</u> of prices. This was the obvious straddle point for all views of what to do about price provisions. The producing countries were desperate for help, and the consuming countries believed that they had much to gain economically and politically, by measures to simply halt the price declines, and very little to lose by involvement. This lowest common denominator of agreement was made possible by the fact that the market had been in steady and sharp decline, and by the absence of any relief in sight.

The consensus at the time about what should be done about price goals, was expressed in Article 27(2): "the Members agree on the necessity of assuring that the general level of coffee prices does not decline below the general level of such prices in 1962." This minimalist approach deferred negotiation on what price levels should be sought.

---

206 Robbins, "Floor and Ceiling Prices," <u>op. cit.</u>

207 Bilder, <u>op. cit.</u>, 358.

208 <u>Ibid.</u>

After quota allocation the second most "bitterly fought" issue at the Coffee Conference involved Latin American efforts to secure provisions that would reduce or eliminate European excise taxes, quantitative restrictions, and import duties on their coffee.[209] The Latin countries were concerned about trade preferences given by the Common Market and individual consuming countries, notably France, to African producers.

With the strong and frequently expressed support of the NCA, the U.S. delegation sought measures that would "provide for the free movement of coffee on a non-discriminatory basis for all countries into consumption," and that would "eliminate obstacles to trade and fiscal burdens which inhibit increasing consumption."[210] Despite the joint U.S.-Latin campaign on this issue— Brazil even withdrew from the conference for several days to protest European resistance to the desired measures— the conference could only come to agreement on declarations of intent (Article 47), rather than on mandatory commitments to reduce or remove obstacles to trade.

The NCA and U.S. government officials could also agree on the desirability of having the quota system "cover all types of coffee to all destinations for all purposes."[211] They hoped particularly to prohibit "ex quota" shipments to "new markets." Producing countries wished to exempt their exports to "new markets," that is, to countries in which there was negligible coffee consumption at the time, from charge against their quotas under the ICA. Their position was that global consumption could be increased without undercutting market regulation. The U.S. delegation took the view that while

---

209 Ibid., 359; Robbins, op. cit., 66.

210 op. cit., footnote, 343.

211 Ibid.

this might be desirable, it was not practical. Such an arrangement, it was contended, would constitute a "loophole" in the Agreement. Coffee shipments to new markets could be traded back surreptitiously into the market regulated by the ICA.

The U.S. delegation reluctantly consented to producer wishes on this issue, but later felt vindicated by what it considered the abuse of the new market principle.[212]

It is obvious to any informed observer that "production control" within producing countries would be an ideal solution to market dislocation caused by overproduction. The U.S. delegation, Bilder reports, entered negotiations with the conviction that "the agreement should, as a key principle, recognize that overproduction is a root cause of the coffee problem, and provide some means for the orderly reduction of production and stocks and the encouragement of economic diversification in the producting areas."[213] The NCA, it will be recalled, had included this principle among its original six conditions for support of an agreement.[214]

The ICA (1962) ultimately included some relatively ambitious production control concepts, for example, the provision that the ICC should penalize countries which in its judgment had not adopted a program to alter their production levels to accord with Council recommended goals (Article 49, 2). Predictably, however, implementation of the production control provisions of the ICA proved half-hearted; and the issue had to be reopened, with somewhat more vigor, at the renegotiation of the Agreement.[215] Production control is difficult enough for

---

[212] Interview, Paul Callanan, July 12, 1971.

[213] Bilder, op. cit., footnote, 343.

[214] NCA, News Letter, No. 754, July 10, 1961.

[215] See Lane Vanderslice, "The International Coffee Agreement and Control of Coffee Overproduction," Unpublished Ph.D. dissertation, University of Michigan, 1971.

individual producing countries that are heavily dependent upon coffee export and whose human and other resources cannot be easily redeployed. The problem is compounded by the fact that there are over forty coffee producers whose respective decisions on production must be "coordinated" or "supranationally" directed, if global production is to be regulated properly.

The Foreign Affairs Committee agreed from the outset that consumer import quotas should be imposed upon producers that were not members of the ICA. The United States and producer view that this was necessary for effective regulation of the market prevailed over that of certain European importers that felt import restrictions on non-members would be contrary to their trade liberalization inclinations and would present burdensome administrative responsibilities. FAC also contended strongly for a rigorous system of "certificates of origin" to fortify the quota system.

Besides the issue of promotion of coffee consumption— FAC favored the decision to transfer the World Coffee Promotion Committee, then an arm of the Pan-American Coffee Bureau, to ICC jurisdiction, with funding to be provided by the producers— the Foreign Affairs Committee's last major concern was in securing a provision to prohibit producers from establishing selling offices in the consuming countries. As has been indicated, this was a matter of intense interest to trading firms of the NCA. FAC secured a much less definitive provision (Article 53, 2) on this than it would have liked. The provision did not explicitly forbid producer governments establishing selling offices in the consuming countries. Still only the U.S. delegation's strong advocacy, Robbins asserts, assured the article at all.[216]

---

[216] "NCA Committee Report on UN Coffee Conference," op. cit., 68.

On most of the major issues of the UN Coffee Conference—for example, quota system, price provisions and voting—the U.S. delegation achieved the purposes it had set for itself beforehand. In a relatively few cases, for example, regarding the new markets issue, its views were rejected; in a few others, for example, the obstacles to trade and production control issues, it secured only partial satisfaction of its goals.

It is hardly surprising that the FAC was generally content with the first International Coffee Agreement, which was open for signature from September of 1962. It had helped formulate the U.S. position before the Conference, and recognized that this, to a large degree, had been adopted.

What, in the FAC's own perspective, had it accomplished by advising the State Department in the Coffee Conference? What had been its overriding purposes? "The Committee [FAC]," former NCA President John McKiernan, has asserted, "was at the U.N. to insist that the provisions of the new Agreement would be fair and equitable to the American industry."[217] FAC proposals to the State Department before the Conference, he has observed elsewhere, "were carefully conceived so that they would require minimal sacrifice for the U.S. coffee trade and call for the least possible government intervention in the normal channels of our business."[218] Several years later McKiernan would reflect upon his Association's role in both the establishment and implementation of the ICA:

---

[217] John F. McKiernan, "One of Coffee's Most Eventful Years," Tea and Coffee Trade Journal, CXXIV (January, 1963), 26.

[218] John F. McKiernan, "The Role of the NCA," Coffee Annual, 1961 (New York: George Gordon Paton, 1962), 41.

> Our success in having the National Coffee Association's views implemented in the formulation and operation of the Agreement have made it more acceptable, more practical, more workable, and more tamper-proof than it would have been without our intervention.[219]

Certainly the industry leaders were sufficiently satisfied with the essentials of the ICA. The more skeptical trader members of the NCA, despite great dissatisfaction over the Agreement's lack of a strong prohibition against producer government selling offices in the consuming countries, went along with the leadership. Observers, in fact, were surprised at the quiet stoicism with which the traders accepted the weak and ambiguous assurances of Article 53 that traditional channels of trade would be respected.[220]

Sources of U.S. Policy Change. United States entry into the International Coffee Agreement aroused both hopes and fears that the Kennedy inauguration had marked a major transition in American policy towards commodity agreements. In retrospect, and particularly in the light of subsequent official statements and actions, the U.S. initiative for the Coffee Agreement seems more a gradual and incremental adjustment of policy, impelled by a fortuitous combination of factors, only one of which was substantial business support, than a manifestation of a bold thrust towards a global system of commodity agreements.[221]

---

219 John F. McKiernan, "First Let's See How Agreement Shapes Up," Tea and Coffee Trade Journal, CXXXII (June, 1967), 29.

220 Editorial, "NCA Faces Challenges of Declining Consumption and the Coffee Agreement," Tea and Coffee Trade Journal, CXXIV (March, 1963) 13.

221 Policy development in the Coffee Agreement case conforms closely to the incrementalist theory of how policy is normally made. According to Prof. Lindblom, "Usually—though not always—what is feasible politically is policy only incrementally, or marginally, different from existing policies." Charles E. Lindblom, The Policy-Making Process, Foundations of Modern Political Science Series (Englewood Cliffs, N.J.: Prentice-Hall, Inc., 1968), 26.

This incremental change over a five year period (1958-1962) has been characterized in an authoritative internal memorandum prepared in the State Department in 1968.[222] "Prior to 1961," the memorandum asserted, "U.S. policy

> generally stressed those measures [to deal with the 'commodity problem'] which avoided any form of interference with the free play of market forces... As a partial answer to the problem of short-term market instability, the U.S. also gave strong support to the development of a compensatory financing facility within the IMF, designed to offset, in part, unexpected and excessive short-falls in the export earnings of developing countries. It also supported the case-by-case examination of particular commodity situations in commodity study groups [e.g., the Coffee Study Group], but generally drew the line at having this activity lead to a commodity agreement...
>
> It participated in the negotiations leading to a tin agreement, but then decided against participation. It resisted proposals for agreements in other products, sometimes on good economic grounds (e.g., rubber), but sometimes, as in the case of coffee and cocoa, solely on the philosophical grounds that there should be no unnecessary interference with trade and private enterprise and that the rigidities introduced by a commodity agreement would outweigh any possible benefits.
>
> The one development which above all else forced the U.S. to reconsider this position was the deterioration in the world coffee economy... Prices fell sharply, with serious repercussions on the economies of many producing countries, and there was no prospect of early improvement, but rather a risk of further price declines as surpluses mounted. At first, under the strictures of its own policy, the U.S. encouraged an export quota scheme among producing countries despite its distaste for producer agreements. This proved ineffective in the absence of adequate enforcement procedures, and the U.S. was brought to the point where it had either to support a move to develop a really workable coffee agreement, with U.S. participation, or accept some unthinkable consequences for its economic interests and foreign policy goals in Latin America and other producing areas...

---

[222] Source withheld.

> The implication [of President Kennedy's Alliance for Progress address in March, 1961], later made explicit by U.S. spokesmen, was that the U.S. would examine with an open-mind any reasonable proposal and would have no doctrinaire or a priori opposition to any particular method of dealing with commodity market problems, meaning specifically commodity control agreements.[223]

In order to understand what role American business may have had in promoting, opposing or otherwise relating to this policy change, specifically in regard to the Coffee Agreement, it is desirable to consider, first, what major non-business factors probably contributed to the change.

A combination of external factors, at least, were significant in propelling the Eisenhower administration to "study" the problems of the coffee market, and the Kennedy administration to negotiate the Coffee Agreement. Each of these external stimuli registered upon the U.S. policy-making system with increasing intensity between 1958 and 1962, but as will be discussed below, the change of administrations itself was an autonomous factor in inducing change.

The first factor to loosen the U.S.'s ideological opposition to consumer participation in regulation of the coffee market was, undoubtedly, the severely depressed state of the coffee market during the late fifties and early sixties. "The one development," to repeat a revealing phrase in the just mentioned State Department memorandum, "which above all else [my emphasis] forced the U.S. to reconsider this position [philosophical objection to interference with trade and private enterprise] was the deterioration in the world coffee economy which occurred after 1958." "By 1959-60," the memorandum continues, "world exportable production had reached 62 million bags as against consumption (outside producing countries) of 37 million bags. Prices fell sharply, with serious

---

[223] Ibid.

repercussions on the economies of many producing countries, and there was no prospect of early improvement, but rather a risk of further price declines, as surpluses mounted."[224]

Policy-makers perceived that the coffee market was in a deep and protracted state of crisis. They felt they either had to participate in measures to bolster the market, "or accept some unthinkable consequences for its [U.S.'s] economic interests and foreign policy goals in Latin America and other coffee-producing areas."[225] And, they could pragmatically assume, the critical conditions in the coffee market were conducive to successful negotiation of a commodity agreement and to building a consensus within the United States favoring a Coffee Agreement.

Secondly, asserts a commodity expert in the State Department, a "more positive and constructive" commodity agreements position was spurred by "the emergence of new independent countries heavily dependent on commodity trade, and their insistent pressure for the cooperation of the industrialized countries to help them with their commodity problems."[226] By the turn into the sixties a large number of African and Asian states had joined the long-independent Latin countries in clamoring for world attention for their trade and other economic problems. These many new countries, bilaterally and collectively through the United Nations and regional organizations, worked assiduously to

---

[224] Ibid.

[225] Ibid.

[226] U.S., Department of State, Commodity Agreements—A Partial Answer to the Trade Problems of Developing Countries, by Henry Brodie, Department of State Publication 7935, Commercial Policy Series 200, August, 1965, 12.

establish the "legitimacy" of the often maligned "commodity agreement." UNCTAD's promotion of commodity agreements after 1964 merely gave organizational expression to an LDC preference that had been gaining force for several years, as many new LDC's entered the United Nations.[227]

LDC demands for coffee market regulation arose in the context of a great new wave of attention to commodity problems and commodity agreements. Coffee, in a sense provided a test case, and occasioned commensurate national and international discourse on the pros and cons of commodity agreements.[228] The negotiations for a coffee agreement both encouraged, and were fed by, the more ambitious demands of the LDC's for an integrated global system of commodity agreements.

According to one State Department informant, there was a marked increase in the occasions on which the U.S. was called upon to "take a position" on commodity problems and agreements from around 1958. American representatives at the U.N. and other international organizations continually called for more responsiveness to LDC appeals.[229]

The emergence of many new African states, several of which were highly dependent on coffee earnings, added to the already significant number of countries that could benefit from an agreement. Petroleum might be the most important LDC product by value; coffee was certainly the most significant in

---

[227] For a critical and not very sympathetic view of how the global view on the use of commodity agreements has evolved, under the impact of LDC pressures, see Law, op. cit., 87-102.

[228] For example, see the 11 articles in a major journal edition solely devoted to commodity agreements, Law and Contemporary Problems, XXVIII (spring 1963).

[229] Interview, Virginia McClung, July 27, 1971.

terms of numbers of countries (over thirty) that depended upon it for export earnings.

Thirdly, policy-makers perceived that the coffee crisis was especially menacing for Latin America, and that a Coffee Agreement would benefit two major South American countries (Brazil and Colombia) and several coffee-reliant Central American countries. They and the general public still thought of coffee as a distinctly "Latin" commodity, even if African coffees had since the fifties claimed a sizeable market in the United States. More importantly, for policy purposes, policy-makers recognized more immediate economic and strategic interests in Latin America than, let us say, in Africa. The Alliance for Progress was developed for Latin America, and the Coffee Agreement was a natural concomitant. Virtually every interviewee for this research emphasized that Latin America was the primary, though not exclusive, target of the Coffee Agreement. From committee hearings and floor debates, one deduces that this was an even more compelling consideration for the Congress. To a very large degree, U.S. support of the Coffee Agreement was a "regional" initiative. The backdrop for it was an historic economic and political relationship with Latin America, decades of coffee trade, a hemispheric Inter-American Coffee Agreement during World War II, and close diplomatic and organizational ties, including the Organization of American States, in which coffee trade and other economic issues were continually under consideration.

Fourthly, the Cold War was surely a galvanizing factor in U.S. policy development. President Kennedy's pre-inauguration Task Forces, it has been noted, were suffused with the idea that the United States had to prevent Communist take-over of the "inevitable and necessary Latin American social transformation." This idea was implicit in a foreign officer's assessment of why the United States had become more accommodating towards commodity agreement proposals during the sixties. Among other things, he asserts, there was "the increasing realization that the economic ups and downs caused by commodity price fluctuations inspire and nurture political unrest [my emphasis]." [230]

W. Michael Blumenthal, Deputy Assistant Secretary of State in 1961, and subsequently U.S. delegate to the UN Coffee Conference, sounded a similar refrain at the time the Coffee Agreement was being negotiated. Writing generally of commodity problems in a letter to the Wall Street Journal, Blumenthal said, "The relationship of fluctuations in commodity prices to economic development plans and, indeed, to internal political stability made the development of a positive commodity policy imperative as an integral part of our foreign economic relations." [231] Blumenthal now recalls that "Castro did concern people." "We realized from the Cuban experience that a commodity [sugar] could be vital in the life of a country, and we wanted to be sensitive to the importance of coffee to many countries." [232] Edwin Martin, Assistant Secretary of State for Economic Affairs from 1960 to 1962, similarly recalls that "There was a change of principle [regarding market regulation] toward the end of the Eisenhower regime." This change, he believes, partly reflected a reaction to Vice President Nixon's turbulent reception in Latin America and Castro's coming to power in Cuba and his growing ties with the Soviet Union. [233]

---

[230] Brodie, op. cit., 12.

[231] Letter from W. Michael Blumenthal, Wall Street Journal, November 28, 1961.

[232] Interview, W. Michael Blumenthal, October 13, 1971.

[233] Letter from Edwin Martin to author, February 11, 1972.

It was not that most policy-makers made a simple-minded connection between economic conditions, on the one hand, and potential for anti-American radicalism or Communism, on the other. Certainly few believed that the Coffee Agreement itself was going to have a profound "stabilizing" effect upon LDC economies and politics. Rather there was the more generalized and intuitive sentiment, expressed by Thomas Mann. "If you have economic chaos," he has said in reference to coffee, "you may very well be presented with difficult problems from the standpoint of national security."[234]

"National security sentiment linked readily with Latin American concerns in Coffee Agreement policy-making. The United States could help bolster coffee economies everywhere; but its immediate political referent was Latin America. The importance of the Latin American connection in coffee is underlined in an analysis by Michael Blumenthal of why the United States did not give comparable support to the idea of a cocoa agreement, negotiations for which failed in 1963. "There were political arguments in favor of a [Cocoa] Agreement but these, too, were less persuasive because Latin America was not nearly as intimately involved."[235]

A fifth "external" factor favoring U.S. commitment to negotiate a a Coffee Agreement was the relatively advanced state of producer capacity and experience in organizing among themselves for market control. For decades Brazil has demonstrated some capacity to influence market prices by unilateral measures. By the late fifties the Latin producers, and finally African producers, were able to manage relatively effective producer agreements, withholding supplies from the market on a coordinated basis.

---

[234] Interview, Thomas Mann, August 8, 1971.

[235] Letter from W. Michael Blumenthal to author, October 20, 1971.

Policy-makers were impressed that the coffee producers could discipline themselves sufficiently to make a consumer-producer agreement viable. Some businessmen even feared that the producers were developing the capacity to "control" the market, without consumer participation.

Producer efforts had also created a large fund of experience in coffee market regulation, much of which could and did serve as a basis for founding a consumer-producer agreement.

Coupled with producer capacity to organize themselves was, at least, the Latin producers' experience at lobbying with the U.S. government for action. The Latin producers barraged the United States with appeals for coffee market regulation through heads of state visits to the U.S., in numerous regional forums such as the OAS, and through every other conceivable public and private channel.[236] "Latin American governments," remembers Mann, "convinced that an agreement was vital to them, pushed hard— there was no comparable support by foreign governments for any other commodity agreement— and this support was very helpful in getting a change in United States policy." [237]

A sixth factor favoring U.S. initiatives for a Coffee Agreement was highly favorable economic policy analysis within the government. When a fundamental review of U.S. commodity agreement policy was undertaken in 1961, coffee was one of the few products singled out as being economically and technically susceptible to market control by commodity agreement. According to John Pincus, a State Department consultant who advised Deputy Assistant Secretary Blumenthal

---

[236] The Pan-American Coffee Bureau (PACB), funded by the Latin producers, has promoted coffee consumption in the United States for many years. Its paid lobbyist, Samuel E. Stavisky and Associates, Washington, D.C., campaigned for the Coffee Agreement.

[237] Letter from Thomas C. Mann to author, June 28, 1971.

on commodity agreement options at that time, only a very few LDC products (coffee, tea, cocoa, sugar and possibly bananas) adequately met the stringent economic criteria for price-regulating commodity agreements.[238] State Department officials readily accepted this contention, and for a number of other reasons, being enumerated here, set a coffee agreement as a priority.

The two domestic factors most conducive to U.S. support of the Coffee Agreement were the inauguration of John F. Kennedy, and his Alliance for Progress, and the active support of the leaders of the American Coffee industry.

It has been shown that there was an awakening interest in coffee market regulation in the last two years of the Eisenhower Administration. Theoretical and organizational groundwork for the future ICA were laid by U.S. participation in the Coffee Study Group and its quiet diplomatic promotion of several producer agreements. It cannot be certain whether or not a new Republican administration, under Richard Nixon, in 1961, would have joined the Coffee Agreement. What is certain is that the coming of the Kennedy Administration gave exceptional impetus to the producer drive to secure U.S. participation in an agreement. During the campaign John Kennedy had made Latin American policy a major campaign issue. His pre-inauguration Task Forces recommended major economic, as well as political initiatives towards Latin America, including, the consideration of "emergency strengthening of the international [coffee] agreement by applying United States (and if possible European) import restrictions to enforce the quotas."[239]

---

238 Interview, John A. Pincus, August 30, 1971. A journal article by Pincus probably reflects the general line of argument that he presented at the State Department in an advisory capacity. John A. Pincus, "What Policy for Commodities," Foreign Affairs, XLII (January, 1964), 227-241. See also John A. Pincus, "Commodity Agreements; Bonanza or Illusion," Columbia Journal of World Business, II (January, 1967), 41-50.

239 Berle Task Force Report, op. cit., 30.

While the new Administration did not decide to negotiate seriously for a Coffee Agreement until nearly seven months after its inauguration, the inner logic of the Alliance for Progress would seem to have almost dictated that it would come to this decision. An ambitious program of economic aid, it was reasoned, without commensurate efforts to deal with Latin America's trade problems, prominent among which were depressed coffee prices, would be ill-conceived. Diplomatically, the United States' "positive attitude on commodity problems" was even "a helpful factor in getting the Alliance going." [240]

Within the policy-making system itself the coming of a new Administration, at least momentarily, centralized an otherwise highly dispersed decision-making network. A commitment to reconsider the U.S. stance on commodity agreements was firmly conveyed from the White House to all relevant government departments. At a critical juncture policy-makers throughout the system were sensitized to the other factors working for a coffee agreement.

The other domestic factor that, at least, accommodated U.S. initiatives for a Coffee Agreement, and probably positively encouraged them was the support of the most influential elements of the American coffee industry, and thereby, the endorsement of the National Coffee Association. W. Michael Blumenthal is one of the few, if not the only key policy-maker in that period to believe that the NCA could not have blocked U.S. entry into the ICA—either by dissuading the Executive not to negotiate or sign the Agreement, or by effectively lobbying in Congress to reject it—if it had chosen to (which it did not). "The mood in favor of action within government," he asserts, "was too great to have been thwarted by a hostile industry." [241] Thomas Mann and Henry Brodie,

---

[240] Letter from W. Michael Blumenthal to author, October 20, 1971.

[241] Interview, W. Michael Blumenthal, October 13, 1971.

representing the more common view, contend that business support for the ICA was essential to securing Congressional support for the Agreement.[242] They imply that any Administration would have been unlikely to even negotiate an Agreement, if the industry had opposed the idea.

According to Brodie, who was one of Blumenthal's alternates at the Coffee Conference and Director of the State Department's Office of International Resources:

> The coffee case involved the unusual circumstance of having industry support. You have to have industry support to get an agreement through Congress. We at State working on the project lobbied a lot with Congress. But all along we were optimistic about getting the agreement through because the industry was with us.[243]

It cannot be established definitively whether or not the NCA could have "vetoed" the Coffee Agreement, since in fact, it did not attempt to do so.[244] The more salient point, at this juncture in the analysis, is that the NCA did support U.S. entry into the Coffee Agreement.

Some leaders in the Association, notably George Robbins of General Foods, were convinced of the desirability of consumer participation in coffee market regulation some three years before the NCA board of Directors would officially endorse U.S. entry into an appropriate agreement, and if we accept their testimony, even before the State Department was prepared to seriously contemplate the idea.

---

242 Interviews, Thomas Mann, August 20, 1971; and Henry Brodie, June 30, 1971.

243 Ibid. (Brodie).

244 The next chapter on Congress and the Coffee Agreement concludes, however, that the NCA could probably have swung Congress against the Agreement.

What emerges from a close examination of the role of business in policy-making is the conclusion that government and business leaders responded positively to external pressures for a Coffee Agreement, in about the same way, at about the same time. This can be seen more clearly by viewing the development of the U.S. policy for the Coffee Agreement from the business perspective.

The U.S. Coffee Industry and the Coffee Agreement. What stance did the American coffee industry take towards LDC appeals for coffee market regulation? Why? How did it express its views? With what impact?

A previous chapter discussed the composition of the U.S. coffee industry, and distinguished two major classes of firms: roasters and traders. Within each class, not surprisingly, the larger firms tend to have relatively larger roles in formulating what may be called industry "positions" on public issues. And the giant roasters, the foremost of which is General Foods, tend to prevail among these.

Nevertheless, regarding the coffee agreement issue in the period under study, it is clear that the "industry position," just like the "government position," had to be forged by a laborious process of consensus-building. In this process leaders of the National Coffee Association—primarily executives from the large roasting and trading firms—were most strongly committed to the desirability of an agreement, and wished to strengthen the industry hand in shaping the nature of any agreement by assuring, as much as possible, that the NCA could approach the government with a single voice.

Undoubtedly, the single most important business figure in determining the industry posture towards coffee market crisis at the turn into the sixties was George V. Robbins, the Director of Green Coffee Operations for General Foods. It is imperative, therefore, to emphasize how he perceived the situation in which the Coffee Agreement arose, and to recall from the previous narrative of events how he acted upon his perceptions.

George Robbins, according to a former Deputy Secretary of State, was a "veritable coffee potentate," and by most accounts, an executive quite willing to wield his company's enormous buying power—he personally purchased one-seventh of the world's coffee—to get his way with coffee-reliant LDCs or with roaster-reliant American traders. Robbins today thinks of himself as the "Father of the Coffee Agreement."[245]

According to Robbins, and independent analysis confirms this, he was working for more active U.S. participation in dealing with the problems of the coffee market as early as 1958. He had been an industry advisor to the American delegation to the Inter-American Coffee Organization during the forties, and felt it had been a serious mistake for the State Department to completely abandon the administrative structure of that organization in 1949. As another serious dislocation of the coffee market began to become evident after 1956, he became increasingly annoyed with what he considered the State Department's habitual indifference to Latin America, and specifically with its failure to recognize that "coffee is the life-blood of the Western Hemisphere."[246]

In 1948 Robbins had warned that the Western Hemisphere was rapidly becoming a last outpost against Stalin and Molotov. The foundation upon which "to build a perfect and lasting structure of international cooperation and good will" within the Hemisphere was he concluded, coffee.[247] Ten years later,

---

[245] Interview, George Robbins, February 25, 1971.

[246] Interview, George Robbins, August 11, 1971.

[247] Address by George V. Robbins, President, National Coffee Association, to Convention of the Tea and Coffee Association of Canada, October 26, 1948, 8-10. (Mimeograph).

Robbins recalled, he had a correspondingly strong sense of the dangers inherent in what he perceived as an imminent "collapse of the coffee market." Citing coffee foreign exchange figures for El Salvador, Guatemala, Colombia and Brazil, he contends:

> You would have had a crisis on your hands if this income had been stopped. They couldn't have bought anything anymore than we could sell them anything. Really it was quite simple. Politically, the countries would have been helpless. From a security standpoint of the United States, if Latin America had gone down the drain and the Communists taken over, they [Communists] would have been right at our back door. And this would have been an uncomfortable and unhealthy situation for the U.S.[248]

Robbins adds that he saw the Coffee Agreement "as a practical way to solidify hemispheric interests," as a "pay-as-you-go plan with certain advantages over loans."[249] Unmistakably, in his view, there was a crisis in the coffee market that could only be dealt with by international regulation.

Critics who have searched for a self-interested economic motive in General Foods' advocacy of the Coffee Agreement have fixed on the theoretically plausible argument that a giant corporation such as GF, buying and roasting large amounts of coffee, will sometimes seek to stabilize the market to reduce the risks that accompany price changes. It will wish to avoid the risks of buying large amounts of green coffee under conditions in which prices for the raw material may subsequently drop. With specific reference to roaster support for the Coffee Agreement, one trader critic has asserted, "the umbrella of price stability is a bonanza to the buyer of millions of bags of coffee a year."[250] A related argument was that General Foods and other large roasters would

---

248 Interview, George Robbins, August 11, 1971.

249 Interview, George Robbins, February 25, 1971.

250 Meono, op. cit., 63.

benefit from the Coffee Agreement for being able to more effectively plan raw material utilization, under conditions of market stability.

Robbins has conceded that his company would benefit, to a degree, from market stability, but he adamantly rejects the notion that this was, in any way, its purpose in advocating the Agreement. From a purely economic standpoint, he asserts, "I could have done more coffee business, more profitably, for the company without the Coffee Agreement." And, he continues:

> GF had a very small advantage, if any, to secure from the Coffee Agreement. With our tremendous buying power, no money problems—this is a company that never borrows—we could always take advantage in situations of distress in one country or another. This can't be done now with the Coffee Agreement. The profits I used to turn in for GF were unbelievable—tremendous—many millions of dollars net every year. I didn't want to have my hands tied and yet I felt it was good for the solidarity and soundness of the world. A man has to decide sometimes where he stands with humanity.
>
> The bigger the company the more you have to be concerned about the harm you might do to other countries or the industry. Power is a dangerous thing and you can do good or harm with it. GF is a supplier of goods to people throughout the U.S. and the world. And it wants a good name, not as one that destroys people, but as one that produces good products. We have to be careful what our image is.[251]

One point all observers, both within and outside GF, will agree upon. Neither GF nor the other large roasters would suffer any great economic disadvantages from a carefully framed agreement that would seek to prevent a "collapse of the market." Under such circumstances, roaster executives like Robbins were free to take a more detached view of the political and economic implications of market regulation. Under these circumstances too Robbins' firm leadership was all the more decisive.

---

[251] Interview, George Robbins, August 11, 1971.

The other major roasting firms seem to have accepted GF's leadership for a Coffee Agreement. Peter Folger, chief executive of Folger Coffee Company, the second largest roaster (in 1963 purchased by Proctor & Gamble) is reported to have felt at one point that the best solution for the problems of the coffee market was "to let the coffee producers go down the drain."[252] Nevertheless, during the period in which the Coffee Agreement was negotiated, he participated actively in the Foreign Affairs Committee in advising the State Department on what provisions should be contained in an agreement, the idea of which he now apparently accepted in principle. Standard Brands, the third major roaster, seems to have deferred altogether to the leadership of the other major firms in the NCA, although it opposed an Agreement.[253] Hills Bros. supported the ICA of 1962, and opposed its renewal in 1968.

In theory, commodity trading firms are expected to oppose price stabilizing commodity agreements, on the assumption that a successful agreement will negate one of the main functions they serve: risk bearing in a fluctuating market. Or as in the case of cocoa, traders may be resistant to any measure that could weaken or undermine an active futures market which they use for hedging purposes.

In the period leading up to U.S. entry into the ICA of 1962, members of the trader associations of New York, New Orleans and the Pacific coast, expressed strong reservations about any government "interference" in the free market; nevertheless, they did <u>not</u>, as they would in 1968, go on record against the Coffee Agreement. Despite deep misgivings, they acceded reluctantly to NCA endorsement of the Agreement. In 1963 the Pacific Coast Coffee Association could even manage a feeble resolution favoring the Agreement:

---

[252] Interview, A. R. Ransohoff, September 14, 1971.

[253] Interview, John McKiernan, November 23, 1971.

> Whereas, the Pacific Coast Coffee Association is in favor of measures promoting the well-being of the world coffee trade as embodied in the proposed International Coffee Agreement,
>
> Be it resolved that the Pacific Coast Coffee Association reaffirms its traditional position that the best interest of the U.S. Coffee Consumers must be protected not only in theory but in practice.[254]

Later a PCCA President would explain that his "Association initially supported the concept of the Agreement; then adopted a neutral position; then, in recent years [from 1968]... opposed continued U.S. participation in the Agreement."[255]

As the events of 1968 indicate—the three major regional associations of traders then opposed renewal of the ICA—the trader segment of the coffee industry is not likely to be able to veto NCA support of government initiatives for a coffee agreement. Although numerous, they are susceptible to pressure from the few major roasters which together process well over fifty per cent of the green coffee brought into the country. John McKiernan, former President of the NCA, hardly exaggerates in asserting that "General Foods can convince the average trader that 2 + 2 = 5."[256] Or trader views can simply be ignored.

What is interesting is that the modest and skeptical trader support for the Coffee Agreement of 1962, as contrary to theoretical expectations as that

---

[254] Resolution of the Pacific Coast Coffee Association, May 12, 1963, as cited in U.S., Congress, House, Committee on Ways and Means, Tariff and Trade Proposals, Hearings, June 12, 1970, Part XIV, 91st Cong., 2d sess., 1970, 3967.

[255] Letter from Berard to Mills, Ibid., 3964. The PCCA's positions over time corresponded to that of Hills Bros., the largest west coast roaster. Hills Bros., asserts a prominent New York trader, dominates the PCCA, by dint of its large purchases of green coffee through members of that Association. Interview, A.R. Ransohoff, September 14, 1971.

[256] Interview, John McKiernan, November 23, 1971.

may have been, was not simply due to arm-twisting by the large roasters, which did occur, or to a stoic acceptance of the "inevitable." After all, the regional trade associations did strenuously object to ICA renewal in 1968, despite NCA support of it.

Traders throughout the country also became convinced that the international coffee market was caught up in exceptional and serious economic and political circumstances. Executives of some of the larger trading firms, which admittedly were in a better position than the average small firm to ride out any adverse business effects of an agreement, and which were invariably responsive to large-roaster leadership, nevertheless, perceived their business interests in a larger economic and political framework.

Fears of Communist or "radical" exploitation of economic chaos in Latin America, in the wake of a collapse of the coffee market, among other economic difficulties, were strongly felt by many of the traders who committed themselves to the idea of an agreement. Anxiety about the political future of Brazil, in particular, was keenly felt by numerous traders. "The Communist threat was uppermost in our minds," recalls J.M. Clark, a Vice-President of Anderson, Clayton and Co. "Under Goulart Brazil was moving to the left. Economic chaos could push things further in that direction, and we had large investments down there that might be jeopardized."[257] George McEvoy, the chief coffee buyer for J. Aron, then the largest single importer of coffee in the U.S., has also said that political considerations figured strongly in his company's support for the Agreement.

---

[257] Interview, J.M. Clark, September 28, 1971. Anderson, Clayton and Co. is the largest American coffee exporter in Brazil, but has non-coffee investments in Latin America, as well.

> Brazil is the key Latin American country. You had to be an old cowhand [McEvoy had lived in Brazil] to feel and sense, under Goulart, that things were going to the left. You felt it from the guarded conversations....the Communist feelings were moving. Either a Communist or agitating party could come to power. Whenever people are hungry and they are offered hope, even the hope of bread, they are susceptible to about anything....without the Agreement prices could have gone to 5 cents [per pound]....and then no telling what would have happened. Certainly some governments would have toppled....only the uninformed could deny that the rise of Castro affected our thinking.[258]

And similarly, Sam Israel, then chief buyer for Leon Isreal and Co. of New Orleans, has asserted that concern for the political future of Brazil was important. "If Brazil is unstable, this can spread like wildfire."[259] Among the small traders, A.R. Ransohoff of New York City, has said that "the more I saw Communism in this area [Latin America], the more I became concerned about the plight of the coffee market."[260]

Among the traders the "security" argument for the ICA was most salient. They typically volunteer that they responded to State Department appeals to "help out." J.M. Clark, who asserts that he was originally opposed to an agreement, recalls having been called by fellow Texan, Thomas Mann, who made a convincing political argument for his support.[261]

---

[258] Interview, George McEvoy, September 23, 1971.

[259] Interview, Sam Israel, Jr., October 12, 1971.

[260] Interview, A.R. Ransohoff, September 14, 1971.

[261] Interview, J.M. Clark, September 28, 1971. Clark remembers that Mann also contacted Edward Aborn (Tenco), Charles Duncan (Duncan Coffee Co.), Russell Atha (Folger), and Arthur Ransohoff, among others. He recalls that "George Robbins was very convincing among businessmen."

Some also contend that there was a sincere desire to help the countries and peoples with whom their business generation had worked for so many years. Still others thought it made sound economic sense for the United States to avoid beggaring its Latin neighbors who, after all, were the best customers for American exports. Experienced coffee men also realized that a depressed market would likely be followed by coffee shortages and high prices. Further, some held, it would be better to help the LDC coffee trade than to provide outright economic aid to the faltering coffee economies.

John McKiernan, the President of the NCA during the years in which the Coffee Study Group and ICA were achieved, has provided two additional reasons for coffee industry support of the ICA, or at any rate, for his own personal advocacy of this support. First, industry support was partly a pragmatic response to State Department initiatives. "State put the gun on the table," he states, "so it behooved us to act in our own interest to try to channel events that seemed inevitable. We could have tried to block a State initiative or to have adapted to the results. We chose to work with State." [262] Furthermore, he notes, "we saw the producer organizations at work and we realized that it was becoming a practical possibility that the Latins, with a large share of the world's production, might withhold stocks effectively and put us in a bad position."

As for the government policy-makers, the increasingly serious state of the coffee market, between 1958 and 1962, was the most fundamental factor to galvanize American industry support for regulation. It also encouraged them to think that it would be feasible to develop a useful control scheme that would involve a minimal amount of government intervention in the free market.

By the mid-fifties, the National Coffee Association had long been the authoritative national trade association of the American coffee industry, its

---

[262] Interview, John McKiernan, November 23, 1971.

membership including virtually all roasters and traders in the United States. Its small professional staff in New York City, Board of Directors, and standing committees were experienced in government relations on a wide range of issues of interest to Association members, e.g., regarding provision of coffee to the armed services, shipping, tax, packaging and health standards, and so on. Except for the interlude of the Inter-American Coffee Agreement (1940-1949), however, the NCA had tended to have infrequent dealings with the Department of State, certainly on a formal basis, until the second half of the fifties. Of course, coffee businessmen, as a group, were well-travelled and hardly strangers to the politics of Latin America or to American diplomatic relations with countries in that area. During the fifties the large roasters, and some traders, were reaching out for business in Africa and acquainting themselves with the emergent new nations on that continent.

With the onset of the coffee crisis of the late fifties, it was not surprising that coffee firms, particularly the major roasters and trading firms, would want to gear up their national association to represent industry interests before the government. Generally speaking, the membership accepted its President's assessment that the Association had served the industry well for many years, and there had been strength in unity. "During its nearly 50 years of operation," President McKiernan asserted in 1959, the NCA "has been recognized as the official voice of the U.S. industry, not only in Washington, but also among government and coffee officials in the producer countries of the world." Furthermore, he declared, "the Association's record of anticipating and minimizing the adverse effects of governmental regulations has been endorsed by its members."[263]

---

[263] John F. McKiernan, "The NCA's Half-Century of Service," Coffee Annual, 1959 (New York: George Gordon Paton, 1960), 43.

Also, the large roasters like General Foods, with a certain perchant for anonymity in government relations, found the NCA a convenient and trustworthy channel through which to express their preferences concerning coffee market regulation.[264]

Nor, since interest groups tend to gravitate to the critical points of decision-making in the governmental system, was it surprising that the NCA would seek an intimate advisory relationship with the State Department, as well as step up its contacts with all of the bureaucracies that might have a say in coffee market regulation.

Nevertheless, those who would expect that business would surely "control" or "dictate" U.S. policies respecting market regulation should note that the NCA was, at first, neither certain that it would gain satisfactory access to the councils of decision-making in State nor, if it did, that it would be successful in getting its views accepted. It could expect the Department of Commerce to be relatively receptive to business views, but the State Department was an uncertain, possibly "unfriendly" bureaucracy in its eyes. As Paul Callanan, an officer in the State Department at the time confirms, the NCA initially approached the Department with great wariness, suspecting during the Kennedy administration, that the United States might enter a regulatory regime unacceptable to the industry.[265]

---

[264] The largest coffee processors all maintain government relations offices in Washington, D.C., or for some purposes retain lobbyists on an ad hoc basis. Their executives have dominated the NCA's Foreign Affairs Committee, and have not infrequently advised or lobbied with the government, independent of their representations through the NCA proper. Occasionally executives of the large coffee corporations have occupied official advisory posts in the government that have faciliated access for their companies on coffee issues, e.g., Clarence Francis' intercession for his GF colleague, George Robbins.

[265] Interview, Paul Callanan, July 12, 1971.

In fact, a close advisory relationship between the NCA and the State Department's Bureau of Economic Affairs developed rapidly and smoothly. The beginnings of the relationship were firmly founded after the creation of the NCA's Foreign Affairs Committee (FAC) in 1958. FAC members advised State in the proceedings of the Coffee Study Group and concerning increasing LDC demands for participation in market regulation. This relationship was continued and elaborated as the Kennedy Administration contemplated and then worked for the Coffee Agreement. FAC was officially invited to help the Department prepare national "positions" in the evolving negotiations, and then to participate in the American delegation to the UN Coffee Conference. Subsequently, FAC has served as the official industry advisory group for U.S. delegations to the International Coffee Council. It is no exaggeration to say that over the last fifteen years the advisory relationship has been thoroughly institutionalized.

What factors contributed to a close advisory relationship from the beginning? First, the NCA, unlike any other non-coffee interest groups, insisted upon a regular hearing for its views from State and other government officials. Besides the regional coffee traders associations, no consumer, foreign affairs, union, or other domestic interest groups demanded a hearing on the Coffee Agreement issue. In such circumstances, John Pincus, a sometime advisor to the State Department has observed, "State people get in the habit of deferring to business because it is the only active constituency."[266]

The regional coffee trade associations of New York, New Orleans and the Pacific Coast, would have liked a direct relationship with the State Department, and sometimes, as at the Coffee Conference, attempted to establish one. However, the leading members of the NCA, principally the major roasters, have been in a position to persuade or pressure these associations into chan-

[266] Interview, John Pincus, August 30, 1971.

neling most of their views on coffee issues through the NCA. Equally, or more important, the State Department has not been hospitable to formal advisory relationships with coffee interest groups other than the NCA. NCA views on coffee market regulation, in the period under study, were generally compatible with those of the Department, whereas those of the green coffee associations were either troublesome or completely incompatible. The State Department also realized that it was politically desirable and feasible to develop an exclusive formal advisory relationship with the NCA, as the broadly representative and authoritative peak association of the industry.

Secondly, State Department officials felt that close liaison with the NCA was "legitimate," that the business community had a "right" to have its views and interests accommodated in any regulation of the market. As Thomas Mann asserted strongly, "I never thought of not consulting the American coffee industry. They deserved to be heard."[267] Since the State Department, however, did not seek to develop a regular advisory relationship with any non-business groups that might have been supposed to have a substantial stake in market regulation, it must be assumed that its sense of what constituted a legitimate advisory relationship was closely linked with what it deemed a necessary advisory relationship.

Thirdly, the State Department recognized that the NCA was in a unique position to provide information and expertise in the development of a regulatory system, and that its cooperation would be desirable, if not required, for administering U.S. participation in an agreement.[268] The State Department and other government bureaucracies had relatively few commodity experts, and

---

[267] Interview, Thomas Mann, August 20, 1971.

[268] Numerous interest group studies have cited this reason for government bureaucracies opening themselves to group advice. See, for example, S.E. Finer, Anonymous Empire: A Study of the Lobby in Great Britain (London): The Pall Mall Press Limited, 1958, 30-31.

readily acknowledge their appreciation of business assistance in developing, implementing and operating the ICA. Technical expertise, even more in the intricate cocoa agreement negotiations than in the coffee negotiations, has afforded business opportunities for both access to and influence upon commodity agreement decisions.

Fourthly, and probably paramount, the State Department recognized that NCA endorsement of any Coffee Agreement it might negotiate would be highly advantageous, if not critical, for securing subsequent Senate consent to ratification and implementing legislation from both houses of Congress. And further as S. E. Finer has said of bureaucracies and interest groups, the former tend to recognize that "it is prudent to consult the affected publics in advance of final decisions." [269]

Finally, it would seem that close government-interest group relationships are more apt to flourish when both parties recognize a large degree of compatibility between their respective policy preferences. The NCA advisory relationship to the State Department arose exclusively with respect to one issue: whether or not, and on what terms there should be coffee market regulation. Rather early the two sides realized they were in sufficient agreement about fundamentals to proceed with mutual confidence and a strong sense of "joining forces" to accomplish common purposes.

Related to this, government officials and NCA leaders felt generally compatible with one another as personalities and professionals. As an alternate delegate to the Conference said, "The NCA leaders are State Department

---

[269] Ibid., 30. "Where such publics are organized," he adds, "consultation is that much the easier. It is easier still when organizations are few and highly representative." 30-31.

types." [270] That is, they tended to be internationalist in outlook and to take a broad view of their business interests. They were, said another State Department informant, more "stateman-like" in their approach to coffee problems than were the American cocoa industry leaders in the case of cocoa. [271]

NCA leaders became convinced that their relationship to the State Department was highly advantageous to the industry. NCA's "liaison" with the Department, said John McKiernan in 1966, "provides the industry with almost unlimited opportunities to make its opinion heard in Washington." [272] Even more revealingly, George Robbins, during his tenure as Chairman of the Foreign Affairs Committee, gave a candid assessment of the worth of FAC's first five years of collaboration with the State Department. In a report to the NCA Board of Directors in 1963, Robbins stated:

> The State Department has asked the Association for continued collaboration and guidance [1963]. I think if we follow the request of working with the State Department and keeping it posted on trends and situations in the coffee business, we will get along as well as possibly can be desired.

And further, with great candor,

> I can't help but feel how much better a relationship of this kind is, than one with a paid public relations man who is supposed to have great influence in Government circles. I think our type of consulting with the Government surpasses any other type that could possibly be suggested. [273]

---

[270] Interview, Paul Callanan, July 12, 1971.

[271] Interview, Edward Fried, June 24, 1971.

[272] John F. McKiernan, "State Department Cooperates with NCA," Tea and Coffee Trade Journal, CXXX (March, 1966), 19.

[273] Report from George Robbins, Chairman, Foreign Affairs Committee, to NCA Board of Directors (date in 1963 uncertain), as quoted in George Robbins, 'NCA Foreign Affairs Chairman Reports," Tea and Coffee Trade Journal, CXXV (December, 1963), 54.

Finally, what general conclusions can be drawn from the foregoing narrative, concerning the impact on policy of the NCA relationship with State? First, regarding the "decision" to enter the ICA, it is apparent that certain major business firms and the National Coffee Association positively encouraged U.S. leadership for a coffee agreement. This strongly reinforced the predisposition of the Kennedy Administration towards seeking an agreement.

Coalitions of support for coffee market regulation developed across the lines between government, on the one hand, and the coffee industry, on the other. In the first phase of policy development, to cite the most significant example, George Robbins assisted Thomas Mann in securing White House approval for U.S. entry into the Coffee Study Group. In the period after the Kennedy inauguration, industry supporters of market regulation frequently asked respected government officials such as Mann to help bring along more skeptical individuals or segments of the NCA.

During the extended period over which U.S. support for the ICA developed, spanning at least four years, business and government were, in effect, in a state of continual negotiation over whether there should be market regulation, American participation in such, and over the nature and terms of a possible regulatory regime.

It is particularly difficult, and perhaps impossible, to factor out the role and impact of business in determining the particular terms of the U.S. position on market regulation. NCA officials have been candid in admitting that they sought a useful agreement that would interfere as little as possible with the free market, and that would be temporary. All evidence points to their having conformed closely to these principles, particularly in opposing either guaranteed prices or a buffer stock.

Although there was a high degree of correspondence between NCA preferences and the ultimate U.S. position on market regulation, it could not be established to what degree business pressure was decisive. Business preferences, however, constituted one of several factors that surely guided US policy-makers towards a minimalist conception of the objectives of an agreement.

This indeed seems implicit in an observation by Richard Bilder, a legal advisor to the American delegation to the UN Coffee Conference. "While generally committed in the interest of international cooperation to attempting to assist exporting countries in achieving a workable solution to the coffee problem," he notes, "the importers [including prominently the U.S.] as a group were for the most part anxious to 'do their duty' with the assumption of as few obligations as possible." "In particular," he adds with more pointed reference to the interests of this research, "they were under the political necessity [my emphasis] of ensuring that their consuming public was not subjected to any marked increase of coffee prices, or their domestic trade to any more burdensome administrative regulations than were essential to the Agreement's operation."[274]

The next chapter explores Congressional handling of the Coffee Agreement. That inquiry suggests a major reason why most policy-makers feel that substantial business support for U.S. entry into a commodity agreement is, in Bilder's words, a "political necessity."

---

[274] Bilder, *op. cit.*, 345.

CHAPTER IV

Business, Congress and the Coffee Agreement

"When the International Coffee Agreement is negotiated with the United States, it has to be negotiated twice—first with the diplomats, and then with the Congress."[275]

This is hardly a daring proposition to anyone generally familiar with Congress's prominent role in the politics of policy-making for many other international trade issues that have both commercial and foreign policy implications. Still the Congressional politics of the Coffee Agreement remain generally obscure and need to be studied for a better understanding of factors that may or may not predispose the U.S. to commodity agreements generally.

Moreover, if Congress does have a decisive role in policy-making for commodity agreements, what are the implications of this, if any, for the relationships between business and the policy-making process?

This chapter develops the thesis that Congressional participation in policy-making for commodity agreements enhances the opportunities of certain business firms and associations to gain access to and standing with the bureaucracies that initiate commodity policies, notably in these cases, the State Department. Bureaucratic needs for business support of agreements before Congress increase the likelihood that authoritative business views will be accommodated in the early stages of policy development and of international negotiation, before Congress even enters the process.

---

[275] Interview, Nicolas Rivero, July 13, 1971.

If, however, business is not satisfied that its views have been taken into account sufficiently—for example, if it opposes a particular commodity agreement that the government has signed—it theoretically has recourse to a Congressional strategy to overturn an agreement. In either instance, the case of the Coffee Agreement would indicate, the prospects for business access to and influence on policies are heightened by the likelihood that Congressional support of commodity agreements will usually be tenuous, even under conditions that could be considered quite favorable to such agreements. Business will tend to "hold the balance" when commodity agreements go to Congress. Dominant business firms and associations will have substantial leverage to move an ambivalent and divided Congress to favor or to oppose an agreement. They will have a particularly advantageous position to block an agreement.

Congress into the Act. A logical starting point for exploring the Congressional politics of commodity agreements, and specifically how these bear upon the relationships of business to policy-making, is to consider how Congress itself became an actor in the two coffee cases, for which there is an actual legislative history. The cocoa case is considered briefly later in the chapter. Second, a simple narrative description of Congressional involvement with the coffee issues is a necessary backdrop to subsequent analysis.[276]

Third, an analysis of factors favoring or impeding Congressional support of the Coffee Agreement follows. It will be shown that despite all the factors favoring Congressional support of the Coffee Agreement—more positive factors seem to have been present than would likely obtain for agreements covering most other commodities produced primarily in the LDCs, certainly cocoa—that support has been comparatively tenuous and unenthusiastic.

---

[276] See Appendix for legislative chronology for the Coffee Agreement.

Fourth, a description and analysis of business's role in promoting the Coffee Agreement before Congress then follows naturally. The fact of business support, rather than its limited promotional activities as such, can be considered the important factor. Finally, the significance of business support for the Coffee Agreement in the Congress can better be appreciated if the soluble coffee case is highlighted. In this case business confronted the State Department with the credible threat of being able to turn Congress away from the Coffee Agreement, unless Brazil could be persuaded to make satisfactory concessions in the soluble coffee dispute.

A prominent characteristic of American national government is the existence of separate institutions that share powers in the making of certain policies.

The politics of American coffee policy has been strongly influenced by the reality of dispersed powers between the Executive and Congress. Congress has derived its authority to participate in coffee policy-making basically from its constitutional powers to grant or withhold advice and consent to treaties, and to regulate commerce. The Senate alone deliberates upon advice and consent to treaties; both Senate and House participate in the regulation of trade.

The International Coffee Agreement (1962) was a response to LDC aspirations for consumer country participation in the enforcement of mutually acceptable market control measures. The several exclusively producer agreements that preceded the ICA of 1962, and which incidentally the United States had encouraged diplomatically, had been comparatively successful attempts at international collaboration. But they had basically faltered upon the inability or unwillingness of all exporters to faithfully observe their commitments to limit exports. It was generally recognized that importer cooperation in policing export quotas was required. United States cooperation would be crucial, since the U.S. was the single most important importing country, taking about half the world's exports of coffee at the time of the Agreement.

Consumer participation in the international control of coffee was effected through a multilateral treaty negotiated under United Nations auspices. According to Richard B. Bilder, a former officer in the State Department's Office of the Legal Adviser and a member of the U.S. delegation to the Coffee Conference, close scrutiny was given beforehand to the legal implications of the final draft proposal for a coffee agreement that was presented to the UN Coffee Conference. "It became clear," he subsequently wrote, "that new legislation would be desirable before the United States joined any agreement along the lines of the one proposed, and, further, that it was impractical to attempt to secure such legislation prior to the anticipated adjournment of Congress."[277] "For these and certain other reasons, it was decided that, if the United States should join a coffee agreement, it would do so through formal treaty procedure, with the advice and consent of the Senate and concurrent passage of the necessary implementing legislation, rather than by executive agreement."[278]

Thus, both the Senate and the House had constitutionally based authority with which to help shape the course of U.S. coffee policy and the international regulation of the world coffee market. In the first instance, Senate authority could theoretically be used to reject the coffee treaty altogether. Congress could also brandish the threat of denying or withdrawing its support of an agreement to influence American and foreign diplomats who direct the operations of the International Coffee Organization. One further step removed, it could also use its authority to influence the content of a second or subsequent agreement. In some

---

[277] Bilder, op. cit., 343-344.

[278] Bilder, op. cit., 344.

instances, it could use its authority over the Coffee Agreement to wield influence over a tangential or completely unrelated issue.

There were some important restraints upon Congressional involvement in policy-making for the Coffee Agreement, as well. The initial agreement, presented to Congress as a treaty, forbade any reservations that countries might wish to register at point of ratification. The Senate, therefore, could reject the treaty altogether; but it would have to bear the onus of overturning a Presidential initiative. Similarly it was not in a position to call for revisions in the already negotiated treaty, though it would have occasion to press the administration for changes in the subsequent treaties that would be renegotiated after the first.

There are numerous trade issues concerning which Congress obviously has had more substantial leverage upon all phases of policy-making than it has had for the Coffee Agreement. In the case of the U.S. Sugar Act, for example, Congress has reserved the ultimate power to allocate shares of the U.S. sugar market to both domestic and foreign producers. Congress remains the hub of policy-making, although bureaucracies such as the Departments of Agriculture and State, respectively, assume major roles also.

In the case of the Coffee Agreement Congress began with a more peripheral position in the policy-making process, although it could exercise the prerogative of rejecting the treaty altogether. Since the ICA provides for a thorough-going "international" regime, in which, for example, export quotas are set initially and then adjusted periodically by negotiation, Congress must exert its influence indirectly, primarily through its periodic opportunities to either consider the coffee treaty itself or to provide implementing acts to enable full U.S. compliance with that treaty. As will be shown, Congress resorted to short-term implementing acts—granting enforcement authority to the President for periods shorter than the five-year life of each of the Coffee Agreements—

in order to give it more occasions to check the otherwise large degree of discretion granted the State Department.

Which committees within Congress have dealt with the Coffee Agreement? The prospects for legislation before Congress, it is generally known, depend very much on which committees gain jurisdiction, and on the predispositions of their respective chairmen and members. Different committees, by virtue of variously defined roles and composition, often bring different perspectives to the same piece of legislation.

The Senate Committee on Foreign Relations, of course, would hold hearings on the ICA, and report to the Senate concerning advice and consent to the treaty. Senator William Fulbright, chairman of the Committee, and several other internationalists in the Committee, were to spearhead a majority that would play a strong advocacy role for the ICA during its long passage through Congress.

It is probably less obvious to the average observer which committees would be assigned responsibility for considering the coffee implementing legislation. Chairman Wilbur Mills, whose Committee on Ways and Means assumed jurisdiction in the House for the legislation, acknowledged that his Committee was traditionally concerned with legislation pertaining to customs matters. He noted further that a number of committees had had jurisdiction for different "commodity agreements." "It is interesting," he said, "that the International Wheat Agreement and the implementation of it came through the Banking and Currency Committee, and that the International Sugar Agreement and its implementation came from the Committee on Agriculture of the House."[279]

---

[279] U.S., Congress, House, 88th Cong., 1st sess., Congressional Record, November 14, 1963, 20714.

Chairman Mills has managed the coffee legislation through all the vicissitudes of repeated passages through the House. His dutiful, rather than enthusiastic leadership in behalf of the Agreement, is partly reflected in a statement he made to the House in 1965:

> ...in my opinion [the coffee legislation] is an important piece of legislation, though I must say in the very beginning that it does not carry with it, perhaps, the appeal that some legislation which has come from the Committee on Ways and Means might carry with it.[280]

A close observer of Mill's handling of the coffee legislation through the years has given a more cryptic characterization of his stance. "He has supported the legislation consistently, but for all the flak he gets over it in Committee and on the Floor, he considers it a real pain."

The Senate Committee on Finance has also held jurisdiction over the coffee legislation. This is because the "committee has the responsibility for all legislation affecting tariffs and import trade."[281] Senators Harry F. Byrd and Russell Long have presided over the legislation in Committee.

Two International Coffee Agreements have been presented to the Senate for advice and consent.[282] The ICA of 1962, a five-year treaty, was sent to the Senate in October of 1962. The Senate consented to ratification the following May by a relatively narrow, but not critical margin.[283] According to the late Senator

---

[280] U.S., Congress, House, 89th Cong., 1st sess., Congressional Record, CXI, May 12, 1965, 10249.

[281] U.S., Congress, Senate Committee on Finance, History of the Committee on Finance, Senate Doc. 91-57, March 5, 1970, 91st Cong., 2nd sess., p. 8.

[282] A third Agreement (1973) does not contain the regulatory features of the first two agreements.

[283] Sixty years being required by the 2/3 rule in that vote, 69 senators voted yea, 20 voted nay. Among the 11 Senators not present to vote, a private poll indicates, 7 favored ratification and 4 opposed. Congressional Quarterly Almanac, 1963, 669.

Dirksen, however, Senate support of the ICA was in the balance as late as the morning of the final vote. He implies that last minute assurances to the Senate by President Kennedy, including the indication that the Congress would definitely be approached for implementing legislation, assuaged several skeptical Senators like himself who might otherwise have voted against ratification.[284]

The five-year International Coffee Agreement of 1968 was given consent to ratification on June 28, 1968. If anything, the passage was easier this time, with 51 of the 59 Senators present, voting favorably.

For both agreements the process of consent to ratification was conducted relatively smoothly and expeditiously. The Senate, however, insisted on several understandings with the Kennedy Administration as conditions for its consent to ratification of the first ICA (1962). Senator Aiken expressed the general position of the supporters of ratification when he stated:

> ...in view of the understanding reached with the State Department that the treaty will not be self-executing; the further understanding that the executive branch will not attempt to make U.S. participation in the agreement effective until implementing legislation is approved; and the still further understanding that the State Department agrees to make our participation in the coffee agreement a 2-year trial run, when the subject will again be referred to Congress, I believe it to be in the interest of the United States to approve the agreement today.[285]

Subsequently, there was to be confusion and rancor over whether the State Department had violated its commitment "not to attempt to make U.S. participation

---

[284] U.S., Congress, Senate, 88th Cong. 2d sess., Congressional Record, July 31, 1964, 16982.

[285] U.S., Congress, Senate, 88th Cong., 1st sess., Congressional Record, May 21, 1963, 8623.

in the agreement effective until implementing legislation is approved."[286] The most significant of these understandings, however, was the one providing for what Aiken called the "2-year trial run."

A persistent theme in the generally desultory Congressional debates over the ICA was to be the concern over the retail price effects of international regulation. The Senate was prepared to consent to the treaty as such, but insisted upon Congressional review after a two-year trial period. This initiated a pattern of short-term provisions of implementing legislation, which denied the possibility of legislation running concurrently with the five-year agreements. Just as Congress has tended to deny longer-term foreign aid appropriations, so in this case it had denied longer-term implementing legislation.

Not until October, 1963, over a year after the signing of the first ICA did the implementing legislation (H.R. 8864) actually begin its long and tortuous journey through Congress. Implementing legislation would authorize the President to regulate coffee imports into the United States in accordance with obligations assumed under the ICA. Regulation would consist primarily of requiring that all imported coffee be accompanied by certificates of origin <u>or</u> of reexport; of limiting imports

---

[286] On December 27, 1963, the Johnson Administration deposited an instrument of ratification of the ICA at the U.N. Without U.S. ratification by the end of December, the Coffee Agreement would have simply expired. Congressional opponents of the Agreement chose to interpret U.S. ratification as constituting a violation, to use Senator Aiken's phraseology, of the administration's commitment not to attempt "to make U.S. participation in the agreement effective until implementing legislation is approved." An Assistant to the President, Ralph Dungan, has recorded that he secured Senator Harry Byrd's informal approval for ratification by December 31, on the condition that he could also secure the approval of Senators Mansfield, Dirksen and Douglas, the latter of whom was an ardent opponent of the ICA. These Senators consented to immediate ratification on the condition, in Dungan's words, that "no action would be taken by the Government under the Agreement until the implementing legislation was passed." Ralph A. Dungan, Special Assistant to the President, "Memo to the Files: Re: Coffee Agreement," Unpublished White House memorandum, January 15, 1964.

of coffee from countries not members of the ICA; and of keeping certain records, statistics and other information pertinent to the enforcement of the ICA.[287]

The International Coffee Organization, established by the ICA, had already opened its London headquarters, and the American delegation, with members of the NCA's Foreign Affairs Committee serving as advisers, had just returned from the first meeting of the International Coffee Council (ICC). Unhappily for the Agreement's prospects in Congress, untimely, adverse weather in Brazil during the summer had wreaked heavy damage upon the current coffee crop. Consequently, the ensuing crop shortage, or more immediately the expectation of shortage, boosted coffee prices, just as the House was sitting down to review the proposed Coffee Act.

To complicate matters, the Coffee Council, had just decided, despite strong protestation by the American delegation, not to increase the available coffee supply (by enlarging the world export quota). An increased supply should have had the effect of dampening the trend of price increase; at least, a decision by the ICC to increase the supply would have been an earnest of good intentions, in the eyes of a skeptical Congress.

In the event, the coffee legislation got off to a slow start. It took approximately ten months, until August of 1964, for it to pass through the complete cycle of committee hearings and floor debates in both houses. In the interim the United States government ratified the Coffee Agreement (December 27, 1963) and continued to participate in, including vote in, the ICC. It could not, for lack of legislative authorization, control its imports in conformity with the ICA.

The climax of the long, first cycle of legislative consideration of the Coffee Act came as both a surprise and a shock to the advocates of the ICA. On August

---

[287] P. L. 89-23 of May 22, 1965; and P. L. 90-634 of October 24, 1968.

18, 1964, the House voted down a conference report that incorporated a Senate amendment (Dirksen) to H.R. 8864, originally passed by the House the previous November. The bill died a few weeks later at the expiration of the 88th Congress.

The first Coffee bill is among the handful of bills that Wilbur Mills, who managed H.R. 8864 on the House floor, has lost during his tenure as Chairman of Ways and Means. The House, though unenthusiastically, had passed the Coffee bill in November, 1963.[288] The bill it defeated in August of 1964 was, if anything, from the House's standpoint, an improvement on the earlier version. The Dirksen Amendment provided for U.S. withdrawal from the ICA at the behest of a joint resolution of the Congress.

The second House vote on H.R. 8864, as amended by Senator Dirksen, however, came just before the Congressional elections of 1964. A period of rising coffee prices throughout late 1963 and early 1964 created an atmosphere in which a number of northern Democrats, many of them considered "liberals" and "internationalists," would reverse their earlier votes on the Coffee bill, and vote against it.

According to close observers of Congressional affairs, a group of northern Democrats had been greatly displeased by concessions made by the Johnson administration to cattle interests in the fashioning of import quotas on beef. Beef quotas, it was expected, would result in retail price increases. Coincidentally, the Coffee bill came to a vote, just after the House had voted favorably on the beef quotas.

Many northern Democrats, thereupon, broke with the administration over the Coffee vote. They had opposed the beef quotas, and now did not want to be party

---

[288] H.R. 8864 was passed on November 14, 1963, by a margin of 181 yeas to 145 nays, with 190 Congressmen not voting. Republicans cast 118 of the nay votes and have consistently been more negative about the ICA than the Democrats. Bipartisan support of the ICA, however, has been crucial.

to another act that might have the effect of raising consumer prices—especially with elections just three months away.[289] Their votes and a slightly augmented Republican opposition sent the Coffee bill to an unexpected defeat.[290]

This defeat of the first Coffee bill demonstrated the vulnerability of this type of commodity agreement before the Congress. Basically, the House was prepared to go along with the bill, as it would prove shortly, but the margins of support were thin, unstable, and susceptible to being overturned by mild intrusions from the setting of policy-making, such as short-run market fluctuations or elections. For some months the ICO had been postponing the call for enforcement of import regulations by consuming counties, waiting for the U.S. Congress to authorize American enforcement measures. Now the ICO made a formal call for enforcement, effective as of October 1, 1964. The United States necessarily had to default temporarily upon its obligations. In the future there would be several occasions on which the lapse of implementing legislation would result in a suspension of American regulation of imports.

The House defeat of the first Coffee bill seems, in retrospect, to have been a "fluke." When the 89th Congress convened, virtually the same bill was reintroduced, this time in the Senate (S. 701). After another round of hearings and debates, in which now familiar arguments for and against the ICA were repeated, the bill was passed quickly by both houses.[291] It was signed into law as the "International Coffee Agreement Act of 1965" (P.L. 89-23) on May 22, 1965.

---

[289] This interpretation taken from Congressional Quarterly Almanac, XXI, 89th Cong., 1st sess., 1965, 484, May 12, 1965, 10255.

[290] 183 yeas, 194 nays, 58 not voting.

[291] The House passed S. 701 on May 12, 1965, by a vote of 300 yeas to 97 nays.

Nearly three years had elapsed between the time President Kennedy first sent the ICA treaty to the Senate and the date President Johnson signed the Coffee Act. It had taken approximately eighteen months to secure the implementing legislation. The Coffee Act of 1965 provided for import regulation through September 30, 1968, that is, to the expiration date of the Coffee Agreement itself. Due to the tardy adoption of the Act, it did not seem necessary to Congress to request an earlier review of U.S. participation in the Coffee organization. The Congress and the State Department would thus have a three year respite, before entering a second, and in many respects, more arduous phase in the Congressional politics of coffee.

The International Coffee Agreement of 1968 was negotiated under the auspices of the ICO, and signed by the United States on March 21, 1968. The distribution of export quotas among producers was, as usual in commodity agreement negotiations, one of the last devisive issues to be resolved.[292] The most controversial issue, however, which nearly broke up the negotiations, revolved around the United States attempts to gain acceptance of Article 44 of the draft, a provision designed primarily to end Brazil's allegedly "discriminatory" trade policies in soluble coffee trade. In the end Brazil reluctantly accepted the ICA provision; but the dispute would drag on for another three years, and become a matter of contention within Congress, and between Congress and the State Department.

The consent to ratification of the ICA (1968), and the ICA Act of 1968, were secured this time in the relatively short period of five months, although almost a month's hiatus in enforcement occurred between the expiration of the first Coffee Act and the signing of the new one. In this second passage Congress was more familiar with the legislation and its implications. Despite the continuation of opposition to the ICA, the Congress was generally content that the ICO had administered relatively "reasonable" prices. The worst fears had not been justified.

---

292 The "new producers" of Africa made a strong bid for enlarged quotas, against the opposition of Brazil and other Latin countries.

Chairman Wilbur Mills, to characterize the position of one critically decisive Congressman, was much more at ease in managing the legislation for the second agreement than for the first.[293] In the first round he had favored the Coffee bill, over the opposition of several members of his Committee on Ways and Means, but with some private reservations about the unknowns in the situation. In the case of the second Act, three years of experience under the ICA had allayed the main doubts he had had, particularly with regard to how the ICO would "regulate" prices.

The International Coffee Agreement Act of 1968 passed Congress on October 10. Although analysis of the debates, and interviews with numerous close observers, substantiate the conclusion that the second Act passed more easily (obviously more expeditiously) than the first, it is difficult to confirm this by comparing floor votes for the two acts. In addition to the normal limitations to comparing votes, there is the additional difficulty that the Act of 1968 was incorporated as an amendment, or as "Title III" of the Renegotiation Act of 1951 (H.R. 17423), then before Congress. The final vote on the amended Renegotiation Act could, and undoubtedly did, reflect any numer of political trade-offs concerning the coffee legislation itself. Still passage of the Coffee Act was hardly in doubt at this juncture.

One of the most salient elements in the coffee legislation, however, was the aforementioned short-term leash placed upon the State Department. The second Coffee Act specified that enforcement authorization would expire on December 30, 1970, two years hence. The House Ways and Means Committee had been prepared to let the implementing legislation run the full course of the ICA treaty, until 1973. The Committee recommendation for a five-year authorization, in fact, was accepted by the whole House.[294]

---

[293] Interview Harold Lamarr, January 25, 1972.

[294] U.S., Congress, House, Committee on Ways and Means, International Coffee Agreement Act of 1968, H. Rept. 1704, 90th Cong., 2d sess., July 11, 1968.

It was the Senate Committee on Finance that insisted upon the two-year limit on legislation. This is because it wished to review the performance of Administration in regard to the anti-shipping discrimination amendment that it attached to the Coffee bill. This amendment, which became Section 306 of Title III, provided that the enforcement articles of the Coffee Act "cease to apply," if the President found that measures of the Federal Maritime Commission were insufficient to end alleged discrimination against American shipping.[295] The Committee on Finance, specifically Chairman Long of Louisiana, an important center of U.S. shipping, apparently wished to use the ICA implementing legislation as a lever with which to pressure Brazil for concessions in respect to policies affecting U.S. shipping.

On several occasions certain segments of Congress have tried to hold the Coffee Agreement hostage to secure leverage on the Administration, or even on a foreign country, in respect to another issue. Brazil has been the most frequent target of this stratagem, both because it has been a major beneficiary of the Coffee Agreement and because, in a variety of economic arenas, it now has the capacity to challenge the supremacy of the industrialized countries— in shipping, instant coffee, fishing, shoe and textile manufacture, etc. The frequency of Congressional deliberation on the Coffee bill has increased the number of opportunities for Congressmen, so inclined, to use the Coffee Agreement as a lever to influence related or distant issues, where coffee producers are also concerned.

The two-year limit written into the Coffee Act of 1968 brought Congress back into the act again, just 18 months after it had completed its first cycle of deliberations. This time the Administration's simple request for extension of the

---

[295] In the 1960's Brazil stepped up its efforts to divert more of its trade, including its coffee exports, to its own ships. This was part of a wider-scale campaign by LDCs, really the more developed among these, like Brazil, to challenge the historic monopoly position in international shipping of certain industrialized countries.

Coffee Act to 1973 was swept up in the long festering dispute between the United States and Brazil over soluble coffee.

The solubles dispute was not unfamiliar to Congress, by any means. Largely at the behest of complaining businesses and the Meatcutters union, Chairman Mills of Ways and Means had privately urged the State Department to settle the solubles dispute within the context of renegotiation of the Coffee Agreement in 1968.[296] The resulting Article 44 of the new ICA received close scrutiny in the subsequent hearings and floor debates.[297] More pointedly, a new provision was added to the International Coffee Agreement Act of 1968, authorizing "the imposition of special fees or such other measures as he [the President] deems appropriate to offset discriminatory treatment by other governments in favor of the export or re-export of processed coffee." (Sec. 302, 1).

In the spring of 1970, indecision over next steps in dealing with Brazil beset both the State Department and the business community. Chairman Mills, whose Committee was once again considering the Coffee Agreement legislation, resolved to use his authority to break the diplomatic impasse. How General Foods and the Amalgamated Meatcutters joined forces to urge this course of action upon Mills is discussed in the next chapter.

Ways and Means reported out H. R. 19567 on December 1, two months after yet another lapse in the implementing legislation. During that month the legislation passed the House, Senate Finance Committee, and on the last day of the

---

296 Interview, Julius Katz, July 15, 1971.

297 Senator Albert Gore questioned the State Department closely on its "undertaking to pressure Brazil into action to stop the export of processed coffee at lower prices." U.S., Congress, Senate, Committee on Foreign Relations, International Coffee Agreement, 1968, Hearings on Executive D, 90th Cong., 2d sess., June 4 and 12, 1968, 18.

91st Congress, the Senate itself. The Act was only extended until June, for reasons discussed below.

When at long last the President reported a generally accepted settlement of the solubles dispute in April, everyone assumed that the way was clear for extension of the Coffee Act until 1973. On June 8, however, the very day the bill was granted an open rule for floor debate, news began to reach Washington of Brazilian "harrassment" of American shrimp boats within the 200-mile territorial see limit claimed by Brazil. The U.S. had been at odds with Brazil and several other countries of Latin America, especially on the Pacific coast, concerning the width of the territorial sea limits. The U.S. had recognized national jurisdiction as extending twelve miles; the several Latin countries claimed a 200-mile limit.

Unhappily for the Coffee legislation, Representative Sam Gibbons of the House Ways and Means Committee, represented the Florida constituency from which many of the shrimp boats had sailed. Gibbons prevailed upon Chairman Mills to hold the Coffee bill from the floor once again. One possible interpretation of Gibbons' action is that he was using the shrimp boat episode to help torpedo the ICA, which he had opposed on principle in Committee. It would seem instead that he had both policy and politically expedient reasons for taking the position he did. Mills' motives are also uncertain. He could have desired to use the coffee legislation as a means to pressure Brazil, regarding the issue of sea limits. A more plausible interpretation is that as manager of the Coffee bill he sensed that the confrontation with Brazil over sea limits might, at that time, endanger the normally fragile margins of support for the coffee legislation.[298]

---

[298] A Legislative Assistant to Senator Edward Kennedy indicates that he had received this interpretation from a staff member of the House Ways and Means Cor mittee. Interview, Mark Schneider, July 8, 1971.

The territorial sea limit dispute delayed the passage of the coffe legislation for months, with enforcement authorization lapsing for the third time. As a result of serious negotiations on the sea limits dispute in late October, Chairman Mills allowed the bill to come to the floor, where it passed in November. The Senate Committee on Finance, however, was in no hurry to consider the bill. It is probable, although this has not been substantiated, that Chairman Russell Long, whose Louisiana shipping and fishing constituents were keeping a watchful eye upon Brazilian positions in this situation, wished to retard the passage of the Coffee bill to pressure Brazil for accommodation on the issue of fishing in territorial waters. The bill did not clear the Committee and full Senate until March of 1972. The authorizations of this extension would carry up to September 4, 1973, the expiration date of the Coffee Agreement of 1968.

Why Congress Supported the ICA. Although Congress has generally accepted Presidential leadership for the Coffee Agreement, its support has still been less than enthusiastic, and sometimes halting. This has been the case, despite the presence of a possibly unique combination of factors favoring Congressional support. What were the major factors that prompted Congressional endorsement of the original Coffee Agreement (1962)?

First, it has been recognized before that Congress tends to defer to Presidential leadership in foreign affairs.[299] In this instance, the Senate had the alternative of denying consent to ratification, and either House, theoretically, could have denied implementing legislation. But, undoubtedly, the pressures on Congress to "go along" were built into the situation. Either the Senate or House could have refused to follow the President's lead; but they would have most likely

---

299 An authoritative study on Congress and foreign policy concludes that Congress normally assumes the role of "amending" executive initiatives in foreign policy, to the extent that it assumes any role at all. James Robinson, Congress and Foreign Policy-Making (Homewood, Ill.: Dorsey Press, 1962).

desired strong justification for having to bear the onus for overturning a treaty already painstakingly negotiated by the State Department.

In the early phases of the legislative process House speakers expressed a sense of frustration at being "railroaded" into providing legislation for a treaty to which they were wholly or partly opposed.[300]

At the same time proponents of the Coffee bill were quite prepared to invoke the principle that Congress should not lightly overturn formal commitments made by the President in treaty-making. On several occasions, and as recently as 1971, Chairman Wilbur Mills has argued this point. Arguing for extension of the Coffee Act (1968), Mills asserted:

> Let me suggest that the issue involved is whether we are going to live up to a firm commitment that this country has— and I doubt that this is the occasion that we want to run away from treaty obligations that have been agreed to by the President of the United States and confirmed by the Senate. I am not suggesting that the House should not play a part in these matters, but I am suggesting it is a pretty sensitive situation when we turn our backs on an agreement of that formality. That is one of the reasons why I am impressed with the necessity of passing this legislation.[301]

This statement and a close reading of general Congressional sentiment indicates that the Coffee treaty and legislation enjoyed a small handicap before Congress from the outset, irrespective of its merit. It cannot be assumed, however, that this was of any decisive consequence, independent of numerous other factors present.

---

[300] U.S., Congress, House, 88th Cong., 1st sess., Congressional Record, November 14, 1963, 20715.

[301] U.S. Congress, House 92nd Cong., 1st sess., Congressional Record, November 5, 1971, 10560-10561.

Secondly, despite considerable reservations about the efficacy of commodity agreements as instruments of trade or of foreign policy, key Senate and House leaders, particularly the former, were highly responsive to the appeals of the Coffee Agreement in both regional and global political terms. By 1963 the Senate, at least, was well primed to receive the ICA favorably, despite traditional American skepticism of commodity agreements.

A superficial glance at the evolution of U.S. support for the Coffee Agreement can mislead the observer into thinking that the ICA was sprung upon a relatively unsuspecting and unprepared Congress. In fact, a significant minority in the Senate had already become quite familiar with international commodity problems, particularly of Latin America. According to a member of the Senate Foreign Relations Committee staff, the Committee became interested, during the late fifties, in the problems of Latin American commodities, including coffee, concurrently with, but to a great extent, independently of bureaucracies like the State Department.[302] Thus, when President Kennedy placed priority on the achievement of a Coffee Agreement, there was already a powerful and informed constituency within the Senate prepared to lend support.

In the spring of 1958 the Committee on Foreign Relations held one of its periodic reviews of American foreign policy towards different areas of the world. "Coincidentally," Senator Wayne Morse has written, "public attention throughout the world was abruptly and sharply focused on Latin America as a result of incidents attending Vice President Nixon's visit there."[303] To the Senators this

---

[302] Interview, Senate Foreign Relations Staff Member, July 8, 1971. Name withheld upon request.

[303] Reference to demonstrations against Vice President Nixon in Venezuela during 1958. See Senator Wayne Morse, Preface, December 12, 1959, in Senate Committee on Foreign Relations, United States-Latin American Relations: Commodity Problems in Latin America, 1959.

reception was symbolic of an extreme deterioration in U.S.-Latin American relations.

One consequence of this new spasm of interest in Latin America was the Committee's commissioning of two major studies on Latin America. The study of more direct relevance to this research, prepared by International Economic Consultants, Inc., was entitled "Commodity Problems in Latin America." It is impossible to determine what impact this report may have had on the thinking of the Senate. It is notable, however, that a study on commodity trade problems was commissioned at all, and that as early as 1959 the Senate would be exposed to policy analysis that urged a less doctrinaire and more "positive" U.S. posture towards Latin appeals for discussion of commodity agreements. It is possible that one Committee member's exposure to this report was particularly important in shaping future American policy. Reportedly, Senator John F. Kennedy took a strong interest in the Foreign Relations Committee deliberations on Latin American policy. He is known to have been specifically interested in commodity trade problems, and in the Committee report on this subject.[304]

In the spring of 1958 Congress learned that President Eisenhower was willing to countenance U.S. participation in the Coffee Study Group, at least, to discuss with the producers the mounting problems of coffee surplus and declining prices. But from this time until President Kennedy's initiatives for a Coffee Agreement, Congress would not be called upon to act upon a concrete program for coffee. The willingness to "study" coffee problems was a limited concession, while the "government was still officially skeptical that commodity agreements could be generally applied."[305]

---

[304] Interview, Foreign Relations Committee staff member, July 6, 1971.

[305] Wagner, op. cit., 141.

Closer inquiry indicates that there were contacts in the 1958-1959 period between Assistant Secretary of State Thomas Mann and members of the Congress, concerning possible U.S. responses to the deteriorating coffee market. Mann discussed with certain members of Congress the desirability and feasibility of legislation to give the President "stand-by" authority to impose coffee import controls. He is also said to have promoted the idea with Dr. Milton Eisenhower, who at the time was intimately involved in the Administration's redefinition of policy towards Latin America.[306]

The State Department did not seek import control legislation. The news of the informal contacts with Congress, in fact, stirred up considerable opposition among many businessmen not yet prepared to accept market regulation. Mann and his supporters were compelled to retreat from this modest initiative.

At the turn into the sixties, Congress, as well as both the Eisenhower and Kennedy Administrations, was extremely anxious about Latin America. Fidel Castro, showing his true colors in Cuba, and establishing direct and open ties with the Soviet Union, seemed, in most legislators' perception, a great threat to the U.S. position in the Hemisphere, especially in view of the adverse economic conditions then prevailing in so many Latin countries.

Congressional perceptions of the political implications of declining coffee prices for Latin America were a major impetus to Congressional acceptance of the ICA. Proponents of the ICA treaty and implementing legislation were undoubtedly most persuaded by the argument that the ICA, in one way or another, served important foreign policy purposes of the United States. Sen. William Fulbright brought out this point clearly in the first Foreign Relations Committee hearings on the treaty.

---

[306] National Coffee Association, News Letter, Supplement to No. 632, March 20, 1959.

George McGhee, Under Secretary of State for Political Affairs, the principal witness for the ICA at these hearings, had been making a major point of how the ICA would benefit consumers by preventing coffee prices from going too high.

Sen. Fulbright, however, wished to emphasize what to him seemed the central purpose in U.S. support of the Agreement:

> Fulbright: It seems to me to make an argument that this agreement is in the interest of the consumers is something less than frank. It is really the interest of our national foreign policy, isn't it?
>
> McGhee: Yes, sir. I think the major objective is to benefit the countries concerned as an instrument of national policy.
>
> Fulbright: It is in the interest of our foreign policy like the foreign aid bill.[307]

Congress, as well as the Kennedy Administration, was concerned about possible Castro, or generally Communist inroads along the Caribbean littoral. The future of Brazil, however, was of equal or greater concern. Among the several Congressional reports on Latin America that appeared at the beginning of the Kennedy Administration, one is particularly illustrative of this concern.[308] In this report a contingent of Senators from the Foreign Relations Committee, who had visited Brazil in late 1961, pictured a country in political and economic "crisis." They said at the time of Pres. Quadros' resignation (mid-1961) there had been "widespread talk of civil war." The Senator's conclusion was that "unless decisive political action is taken in the democratic pattern to initiate deep social and economic change the probabilities are that the political situation will

---

Senate Committee on Foreign Relations, International Coffee Agreement, 1962, 66.

U.S., Congress, Senate, Committee on Foreign Relations, Brazil and United States Policies, Report of a Study Mission to Several of the American Republics, 87th Cong., 2d sess., 1962.

explode." Underlying the political crisis, the report asserted, was a long gathering economic crisis, including currency inflation and "chronic and deepening difficulties with international payments." In analyzing the roots of Brazil's financial difficulties, the Senators concluded that "the international coffee situation is a significant factor...coffee and other exchange earnings are simply not able to carry the current volume of imports."[309]

The Study Mission made reference to coffee problems, but it took no position on the then growing Latin appeals for a commodity agreement for the product. It did, however, drive home its points about the severity of Brazil's economic and political problems, and about Brazil's special place in Latin America. On the latter point, the Senators emphasized that:

> Brazil is not typical of the other Latin American countries. On the contrary, the immense proportions of that nation and its unique heritage tend to set it apart...it would be an oversimplification to say that as Brazil goes so goes Latin America. But there is no question that the future of inter-American relations will be shaped in major part by developments in Brazil, if for no other reason than that Brazil is, and will continue to be, an enormous factor in these relations.[310]

Brazil was of special importance in drawing Congressional support for the ICA. What more immediate instrument for assisting the faltering Brazil, the major exporter of the world's coffee, than the International Coffee Agreement?

Congress, in a broader view, was also highly responsive at this time to political developments in the Latin American region. Even a cursory reading of the Congressional records indicates that, so far as the Congress was concerned, the ICA was distinctly a measure to assist Latin America. The fact that a world

---

[309] Ibid.

[310] Letter of transmittal to Chairman William Fulbright, Committee on Foreign Relations, by Study Mission to Several of the American Republics, Ibid., iii.

commodity agreement would also benefit Africa and other producing areas was undoubtedly appreciated; but Latin America was unquestionably the region of primary concern.

Senator Mansfield, speaking for Senate passage of the ICA implementing legislation in 1964, expressed the strongly felt Latin-American orientation of most supporters of the Agreement:

> ...the nations which will be deeply affected by what we do or fail to do, today, are preponderantly those of Latin America. They are the nations with which our fortunes are closely linked by geography, history, economic realities, and our own policies.[311]

How did Congress conceive of the foreign policy purposes of the ICA? It is not surprising to find the proponents of the ICA resorting to quite general and, for this period of U.S. diplomatic history, quite familiar justifications for U.S. support of the Agreement.

By the early sixties the idea that Communism could and would prey upon unfulfilled economic and social aspirations in the LDCs was a widely-held assumption among members of Congress, as well as bureaucratic policy-makers. Senators Javits, Symington, Smathers, and Morse, among others, explicitly raised the spectre of Communist influence in Latin America, during the ICA debates in 1963.[312] As concern over Nazi influence in Latin America had helped launch the Inter-American Coffee Agreement in 1940, now Communism helped inspire U.S. support of the ICA.

---

[311] U.S., Congress, Senate, 88th Cong., 2d sess., Congressional Record, July 31, 1964, 16981.

[312] The anti-Communist argument was used quite sparingly in the House debates, perhaps because foreign policy aspects of the Agreement were little discussed.

Sen. Javits expressed the sentiment in the Senate when he asserted: "This agreement is so great a contribution to international stability and international peace and to the anti-Communist struggle, that we must wonder why it is opposed."[313] Sen. Humphrey expressed the point more apocalyptically:

> this is a matter of life or death, a matter of Castroism versus freedom....Castroism will spread like the plague through Latin America unless something is done about the prices of the raw materials produced there; and those prices can be stabilized only on an international basis.[314]

Other Senators were less dramatic and explicit about the political implications of ICA passage, but were nonetheless strongly convinced that they were portentous. Sen. Mansfield believed that if the ICA were rejected, "the disillusionment throughout Latin America will be severe, and the political repercussions will be on a corresponding scale."[315] Sen. Fong, on the other hand, was content with an even more ambiguous statement of the "political" purpose of the ICA: "One of the cornerstones of our foreign policy is to help the less advanced nations of the free world develop their economies in an atmosphere of freedom."[316]

A related line of argument by the proponents of ICA was that the Agreement was a natural concomitant to the more encompassing Alliance for Progress. The Kennedy Administration had undertaken a general review of commodity trade policy concurrently with the program innovations that together comprised the Alliance for Progress. By a "logic of inclusiveness," if nothing else, it would have been difficult to launch the Alliance in 1961, without considering measures

---

[313] U.S., Congress, Senate, 88th Cong., 1st sess., Congressional Record, May 20, 1963, 8552.

[314] Ibid., 8553.

[315] Ibid., 8521.

[316] Ibid., 8526

to shore up the market for Latin America's major export, coffee. Senator Mansfield was one of several Senators, in 1963 and thereafter, to point out the possible incongruity of supporting the Alliance, without complementary measures to assist the coffee trade. "The aid," he told the Senate, "which Latin America has received under the Alliance for Progress is less than the foreign exchange Latin American has lost through the fall of coffee prices."[317]

Another subsidiary argument for the ICA emphasized American economic self-interest. Latin America, specifically the coffee producing countries, it was pointed out by numerous Senators and Congressmen, was the third most important market for U.S. exports. More specifically, as Sen. Fong argued, "Fair prices for coffee are...of great benefit to U.S. employment and exports."[318]

This argument has been assiduously promoted throughout the life of the ICA by Samuel Stavisky and Associates (World Coffee Information Center), the registered foreign agent in the United States of the Pan-American Coffee Bureau. Stavisky's sleek reports, distributed throughout the country and certainly in the Congress, have specified, in the finest detail, which communities throughout the country benefit by exporting to the coffee-producing countries.[319] It cannot be established precisely how persuasive the Stavisky campaign has been with the Congress, although it is clear from Congressional debates that supporters of the ICA have drawn liberally from Stavisky information to substantiate their arguments.

---

[317]Ibid., 8521.

[318]Ibid., 8527.

[319]See World Coffee Information Center, "Coffee—Economic Impact," (Washington, D.C.: World Coffee Information Center, Pan-American Coffee Bureau, 1970). This report indicates that in 1968 coffee generated 624,000 jobs and $4.5 billion in wages and farm income in the U.S. It specifies in copious detail which states and locales exported what products to coffee-producing countries during 1968.

It is difficult to escape the conclusion then that Congressional support of the Coffee Agreement in the mid-sixties rested upon both an inclination to defer to Presidential leadership in foreign affairs, at least for this issue, and upon the conviction of key Senate and House leaders that the Agreement was more or less essential to current U.S. foreign policy designs for Latin America.

Business and Congress. A third prominent factor favoring Congressional support of the ICA was the endorsement of the authoritative National Coffee Association (NCA). NCA support of the Agreement, particularly in view of the virtually complete absence of other organized interest groups putting forth views on the Agreement, was probably pivotal to Congress' acceptance of the Agreement. This study can only attempt to demonstrate that this was probably the case, not that it was certainly so.

Before developing this line of reasoning, however, it is necessary to emphasize how little overt contact individual coffee firms or the National Coffee Association actually had with the Congress, concerning either advice and consent to the treaties of 1962 and 1968, or the passage of implementing legislation for these. Instances of significant business "lobbying" are only in evidence in and around 1970 when the soluble coffee dispute and extension of the Coffee Agreement Act of 1968 became linked in the Congressional arena.

The fact that the NCA favored the Coffee Agreement was made quite clear to Congress in more unobtrusive ways; certainly it had to be evident that the coffee industry at-large was not opposed to it. Certain coffee businessmen had helped initiate the Agreement, and the NCA was content with the arrangement that had been negotiated with its close counsel from the earliest stages. Nevertheless, it was never felt by the proponents of the ICA that active business lobbying for the ICA was needed to assure favorable Congressional disposal of the Agreement. Expressed opposition to the ICA, particularly from within the coffee industry, more evident at the time the second ICA passed through Congress, was confined largely to letters of dissent to key members of Congress.

During the first passage of the ICA treaty and legislation through Congress, John McKiernan, the President of the NCA, was a witness for the Agreement before concerned committees. Typically, McKiernan emphasized that the NCA was the major trade association of the national coffee industry, with some 300 members accounting for approximately 85% of coffee tonnage consumed in the U.S.; that until 1957-58 the Association had opposed interference in free trade in coffee (it had, however, supported the IACA in 1941); that by 1957 it had recognized the dangers to the "American way of life" posed by the imminent breakdown of the economies of the coffee producing countries; that subsequently, it had worked closely with the State Department in developing the ICA and was satisfied that its views were fully respected and even made the "basis for the U.S. position in the negotiations;" and finally that the NCA constantly served the interests both of its members and of the American consumer.[320]

At the first hearing on the Coffee Agreement held by the Senate Foreign Relations Committee, McKiernan assured Chairman Fulbright that the U.S. coffee industry overwhelmingly favored the Agreement.[321] This was generally true, although as has been indicated, the green coffee associations of New York City, New Orleans, and the Pacific Coast supported the first agreement with considerable reservation, and under pressure from the large roasters like General Foods.

---

[320] A representative statement is included in the first hearing of the Senate Foreign Relations Committee, as found in Senate Committee on Foreign Relations, International Coffee Agreement, 1962, 90-96.

[321] Ibid., 96.

In 1968 the NCA once again supported the ICA; but support among the green coffee associations had fallen away.[322]

State Department officials also took every appropriate occasion to emphasize to the Senate and to the House that the Coffee Agreement had been developed with the full cooperation and support of the National Coffee Association. Testifying for the first Coffee Agreement, George McGhee, Under Secretary of State for Political Affairs, extolled the NCA for having shown "unparalelled industrial statesmanship in coming to the conclusion... that ruinously low coffee prices in Latin America and elsewhere would not be in their best interests or the wider interests of the country at large."[323] Anthony Solomon, the Assistant Secretary of State for Economic Affairs and principal government spokesman for the second Agreement in 1968, similarly acknowledged "the constructive response of the association [NCA] membership to the important national interests at stake in the agreement."[324]

The State Department had felt from the inception of the coffee negotiations that coffee industry preferences would carry a great deal of weight in any future Congressional deliberations over whether or not there should be a coffee agreement. This was a major reason why State brought the National Coffee Association into a close advisory relationship in the early stages of negotiation, and

---

[322]The NCA did not testify for the Agreement before the Senate Foreign Relations Committee in 1968; a letter of approval from President John F. McKiernan, dated May 20, 1968, and the supporting NCA Resolution, were read into the record of the Committee hearings. Senate Committee on Foreign Relations, International Coffee Agreement, 1968, 28-29. Communiques opposing continued U.S. participation in the Coffee Agreement were received and recorded from the green coffee associations of New Orleans, New York City and the Pacific Coast, respectively. Ibid., 29-31.

[323]Senate Committee on Foreign Relations, International Coffee Agreement, 1962, 46.

[324]Senate Committee on Foreign Relations, International Coffee Agreement, 1968, 4.

why it tried to accommodate business preferences along the way, before the Agreement actually reached Congress.

Most of the key policy-makers for coffee in the period around 1962 felt that substantial coffee industry support for the Coffee Agreement was crucial to gaining Congressional acceptance. "Without business support," Thomas Mann, an early proponent of the Coffee Agreement, has stated, "the Agreement would never have passed Congress."[325] Henry Brodie, Director of the Office of International Resources in the State Department at the time the ICA was negotiated and sent to Congress, agrees:

> There has never been much enthusiasm in the United States about commodity agreements. The coffee case involved the unusual circumstance of having industry support. You have to have industry support to get an agreement through Congress. We at State working on the project lobbied a lot with Congress. But all along we were optimistic about getting the agreement through because the industry was with us.[326]

Significantly, W. Michael Blumenthal, former Deputy Assistant Secretary of State and chief U.S. negotiator of the Coffee Agreement, disagrees that the coffee industry had, in effect, veto power over the Agreement. He labored painstakingly to assure industry acceptance of the agreement; but in retrospect, he does not believe that the latter could have thwarted in Congress the momentum that had built up for the Agreement. In 1963-1965, he believes the general mood in favor of action was too great.[327]

The contrasting assessments of business' potential for thwarting the Coffee Agreement, among policy-makers themselves, caution against facile

---

325 Interview, Thomas Mann, August 20, 1971.

326 Interview, Henry Brodie, June 30, 1971.

327 Interview, W. Michael Blumenthal, October 13, 1971.

conclusions on this question. Certainly all policy-makers had a healthy respect for the coffee industry's capacity to challenge an unwanted agreement. But until there is an actual test of wills between government and business in the Congressional arena, which did not materialize in the case of coffee, it cannot be stated for certain who will prevail. In actuality both government agencies and business prefer to avoid the costly and uncertain duel in Congress and tend to seek accommodation, first, in preliminary consensus-building contacts.

The NCA could probably have overturned Congressional support of the ICA, if it had attempted to do so, despite the fact, as Blumenthal has noted, that several fortuitous factors were otherwise giving strong impetus to support the Agreement. This contention rests on three considerations: first, that initial passage of the ICA through Congress proved arduous, even with unified business support; second, that business could probably have effectively exploited the otherwise weakly expressed "consumer protection" sentiment among Congressmen; and that business could probably have swung a sufficient number of committee or floor votes to the negative column to defeat the Agreement, by effectively advancing its own claims on national policy.

The ICA treaty of 1962 barely received the two-thirds vote in the Senate required for consent; and the first implementing bill was defeated once in the House before being passed. Senate and House debates reflect more uncertainty or skepticism about this Agreement than even the committee or floor votes indicate.

Congress's central reservation about the Coffee Agreement—for many Senators and Congressmen, the central reason for opposing the ICA—concerned its possible implications for consumer coffee prices. In the early sixties the "consumer protection" movement was embryonic; and certainly no organized consumer group appeared to lobby or testify either for or against the Coffee Agreement. Still for reasons of principle, as well undoubtedly, of political expedience, both proponents and opponents of the ICA were highly skeptical, at first, of the possible consumer price impact of the Agreement.

The section of the ICA (1962) pertaining to price objectives would naturally have invited the skepticism of Congress. Articles 1 and 27 state the general objectives of "adequate supplies" of coffee at "equitable prices." The most specific of the articles on price (27) reflects the highest common denominator of agreement that diplomats of different persuasion could achieve. The negotiators had sought a target range of minimum and maximum prices, such as were proposed in the several cocoa negotiations, but could only agree on the rather open-ended and certainly ambiguous provisions of Article 27.[328]

These provisions called at once for regulation of exports that would assure the producers of progressively rising incomes from coffee exports, that would assure the consumers of equitable prices, but that most specifically of all, would assure "that the general level of coffee prices does not decline below the general level of such prices in 1962" (Art. 27, 3).

It is clear from the record that Congress had a reasonably clear and valid impression of executive pricing purposes in the ICA, and that the majority, at least, was prepared to accommodate these. Active proponents of the Agreement were assiduous in their attempts to show that the purpose was to halt further price declines, and to demonstrate how price rises would either not be likely, given the existing massive surpluses, or if they should occur, that adequate protection was available to consumers. There was clearly no sentiment

---

[328] Interview, Paul Callanan, January 26, 1972.

expressed (or indeed felt) for this Agreement as a vigorous price-raising mechanism, in the sense that some producers might want it to be.

How much "firming up" of prices might be tolerated by ICA proponents was only intimated in the debates. Sen. Wayne Morse expressed a point of view most likely shared by Congressional supporters of the ICA. "I am perfectly willing," he said, "to support a coffee agreement on the assumption, although I do not think it can be borne out by the facts, that there might be a slight increase in the cost of coffee."[329] Morse added that it would be a false sense of economy to vote down the ICA over a few cents per pound, considering how much foreign aid was being given to Latin America.

In the end, the State Department was compelled to make clear its general orientation to the question of price levels. And congressional proponents, as well as opponents, were active in amending the administration initiated coffee bill to make the State Department more closely accountable to the Congress for its coffee diplomacy. For example, Rep. Leonor Sullivan's amendment called for annual reports from the State Department that would provide full information on the operation of the agreement, especially with respect to price levels, and provide a summary of all actions taken "to protect the interests of United States consumers" (Sec. 5), and Sen. Dirksen's amendment to the ICA bill was meant to place "a weapon in the hands of Congress."[330] In the slightly altered form in which it appeared in the final Coffee Act, the Dirksen amendment (Sec. 2) provided that enforcement authorization for import regulation that would cease to apply if "the Congress by concurrent resolution determines that an unwarranted increase in the price of coffee has occurred." Some doubt was expressed by

---

[329] U.S., Congress, Senate, 89th Cong., 1st sess., Congressional Record, III, February 2, 1965, 1827.

[330] U.S., Congress, Senate, 88th Cong., 2d sess., Congressional Record, July 13, 1964, 16982.

members of Congress as to the constitutionality or wisdom of such a restraint on the President's conduct of foreign policy. But Sen. Dirksen insisted that it was the price the Administration would have to pay to secure the needed legislation at all. "I am so immodest as to say," he told the Senate, "that had that section not been in the bill, the bill probably would not be before the Senate at the present time."[331]

It can be seen in retrospect that the consumer-protection sentiment, whether principled or simply expedient, expressed in Congressional debates, amendments, and in the actual defeat of the first coffee bill in 1964, could have been considerably amplified under hypothetically different circumstances, for example, if the National Coffee Association had chosen to oppose the Coffee Agreement.

If the NCA had opposed the Agreement in Congress, it would surely have desired to give more shape and substance to the argument that the Agreement would be contrary to the "consumer interest."[332] If business "experts" had forecast that the operations of the ICA would likely compel American roasters to substantially raise their prices to the coffee consumer, it is probable that fewer Senators and Congressmen would have been willing to concede to the foreign policy and economic arguments that actually carried the Agreement.

---

[331] Ibid., 16982.

[332] When the ICA was first presented to Congress, Assistant Secretary of State Frederick C. Dutton assured consumer spokesman, Rep. Leonor K. Sullivan, that the National Coffee Association was a staunch friend of the American consumer. Letter from Frederick G. Dutton, Assistant Secretary of State, to the Hon. Leonor K. Sullivan, October 3, 1962, as reprinted in U.S., Congress, Senate, 88th Cong., 1st sess., Congressional Record, May 20, 1963, 8555.

Foreign policy arguments for commodity agreements for wholly LDC-produced commodities are probably a poor substitute for influential and supportive domestic interest groups, when the effect of such agreements may be, or may plausibly said to be, higher prices for the American consumer. This should be all the more true, if the only domestic interest groups in the policy-making arena, are opposed to a particular agreement.

The House defeat of the first Coffee bill in 1964 indicates that Congress, as a legislative body with constantly changing voter coalitions, has a low tolerance for price increases of commodity imports, where the production of such imports is almost exclusively foreign-owned. In the case of sugar, Congress has shown itself consistently willing to go against the consumer interest in lower retail sugar prices. But this, most serious studies of sugar politics conclude, is primarily due to the inordinate influence of the domestic Sugar Lobby on bureaucratic and Congressional policy-making.

The coffee industry could have been a formidable opponent to the ICA, in its own right, aside from the vulnerability of the agreement in Congress to a well organized, consumer-interest campaign. The National Coffee Association, at the inception of the ICA, was the peak association for approximately 300 roaster, trading and allied firms widely dispersed throughout the United States. The NCA, as a united front, would have had considerable potential for pressuring or persuading numerous legislators to vote against the ICA, particularly in the absence of competing interest groups of any type. As the soluble coffee case suggests, the NCA would also have been able to gain access to the key Committee chairmen. That case also suggests the possibility that business might have forged an alliance with organized labor, seeking to demonstrate that the ICA would affect employment in the industry adversely.[333] In 1958 there were an estimated 175,000 workers in the U.S. coffee industry, earning over $1 million in wages.[334]

While it remains conjectural that business could have derailed the Coffee Agreement in Congress, it is nonetheless certain that policy-makers in State and other bureaucracies were too sensitive to this possibility to fail to seek to bring business into the consensus favoring an agreement, before Congress got into the act. Most State Department interviewees confirmed this point, but were usually quick to add that bringing business into an advisory relationship with government was also meant to tap business expertise on coffee matters and to allow the industry its "legitimate" voice concerning policies affecting it. Since State, however, did not seek out the advice of other potentially interested groups, for example, consumer, labor or foreign policy groups, it can be supposed that the "legitimacy" of the coffee industry's voice was very much a function of its desire, and particularly its capacity, to command a hearing.

Congress and the Soluble Coffee Dispute. The soluble coffee and cocoa cases, discussed in the next chapters, illustrate types of relationships between business and Congress, and the official policy-making system at large, that were theoretically possible in the Coffee Agreement case (1962-1965), but which did not materialize because the National Coffee Association favored the Coffee Agreement.[335] In this section a few contrasts are drawn between the business-

---

333 The largest union of national coffee workers, the Amalgamated Meatcutters, has 5,000 coffee worker members.

334 Estimate by John McKnight Associates, as found in Table 9, World Coffee Information Center, Coffee: Economic Impact, prepared by Samuel E. Stavisky & Associates, Washington, D.C., 1970, 17.

335 The Coffee Agreement and soluble coffee cases are distinguished in this study for analytical purposes only; in reality, the soluble coffee dispute between the United States and Brazil was inextricably bound up with the negotiation and implementation of the second Coffee Agreement (1968) and the American politics of policy-making for that Agreement.

Congress nexus of the solubles dispute, which is considered in depth in the next chapter, and the corresponding relationship in the Coffee Agreement case.

In the soluble coffee case, business used the threat of intervention in Congress, or at points actually did intervene, for its own policy purposes, in ways it had not felt necessary at the inception of the Coffee Agreement itself. General Foods, initially Nestle, other major solubles producers, and even green coffee traders perceived the sharp rise of Brazilian soluble coffee imports after 1965 as a severe threat to their substantial investments and sales of the soluble product, or in the case of the traders, to their transactions in green coffee. Nor was business wholly satisfied with the results of the NCA "advisory" relationship to State that had served it so well in the instance of the Coffee Agreement.

To propel the State Department into action against Brazil, the NCA promoted the view that the ICA itself would be jeopardized, if Brazil were allowed to continue its "discriminatory" trading practices. Either the African producers would revolt, because Brazil was cutting into their green coffee exports to American solubles producers, or American business would withdraw its support from the Agreement. Although the State Department became convinced of the legitimacy of business opposition to Brazilian policy, it was the threatened collapse of the consensus supporting U.S. participation in the ICA that compelled it to overcome its ambivalence about pressing Brazil for concessions.

Overt business intervention in Congress, specifically General Foods consultation with Chairman Wilbur Mills, and the latter's response, lent credibility and substance to threats that the ICA could founder upon the solubles dispute. And periodic Congressional involvements with the Coffee Agreement implementing legislation afforded business firms and associations some timely opportunities to exert leverage on soluble coffee policies.

Congress and the Cocoa Negotiations. Despite over fifteen years of intermittent negotiations resulting in the International Cocoa Agreement of 1972, which the United States so far has refused to sign, no cocoa treaty has been sent to Congress for advice and consent, or for implementing legislation. It is probable that general American cocoa industry opposition to a cocoa agreement, which it has been made clear could and would be registered strongly with Congress, if that were necessary, has been a major factor in restraining the State Department from signing any one of several proposed agreements under negotiation. As analysis in the last chapter on the cocoa issue suggests, it has not been the only factor.

Two types of evidence support this contention: first, evidence that business has, on at least one occasion (1963), sought to line up Congressional opposition to an agreement that it feared the President was about to sign, and that it has otherwise been prepared to enter the Congressional arena to resist an unthinkable agreement; and second, and more importantly, evidence that most key policymakers would be exceedingly reluctant to send an agreement to Congress, without what one of their number has termed "substantial business support."[336] Most have felt that the odds in favor of Congressional support of a cocoa agreement, in the face of general cocoa industry opposition, would be very unfavorable.

During 1963, the year of the first of four full-dress negotiating conferences for an international cocoa agreement, the American cocoa industry became "fearful that the U.S. Government may mistake transient popularity with producing

---

[336] Interview, Paul Callanan, January 26, 1972.

countries for political advantage, and may acquiesce in an agreement."[337] Since 1956 the industry had had a formalized advisory relationship with the State Department in the numerous meetings of the Cocoa Study Group; but feeling that the government might now yield to producer pressures for an "unreasonable" agreement, it declared that the "U.S. industry would have no alternative but to oppose ratification of the agreement, with all of the undesirable foreign policy implications that this might produce."[338]

Anxiety about the possibility of the U.S. signing an "unrealistic" cocoa agreement at the Geneva Conference in September of 1963 prompted the industry to seek the representational services of the Washington law firm of Clifford, Warnke, Glass, McIlwaine, and Finney. The Clifford firm, primarily at the initiative of Thomas D. Finney, Jr., a partner, who has handled the cocoa account through the years, conveyed the industry position on the current draft cocoa agreement to members of the Congress and undertook discussions with representatives that might be amenable to challenge any cocoa threaty that should be sent to Congress. Finney and company argued that an agreement was really not needed, but further, if there had to be one, that it should not interfere with the successful operation of the free market or retard the growth of consumption.[339]

It is not certain what, if any, impact the industry overtures to Congress had, either on Congress itself, or on the State Department. In any event, within

---

[337] Myer Rashish, "The Proposed International Cocoa Agreement," Unpublished Background Paper issued in behalf of the New York Cocoa Exchange, the Cocoa Merchants' Association of America, Inc., the Chocolate Manufacturers Association of the United States of America, and the National Confectioners' Association of the United States, Inc., August 1963, 2. This paper, which was distributed in Congress in the fall of 1963, was issued by the Washington law firm of Clifford, Warnke, Glass, McIlwaine and Finney.

[338] _Ibid._, 2.

[339] _Ibid._, 17.

the month of September, the Geneva negotiations failed to produce a cocoa agreement.

A close reading of the Congressional hearings and debates in this period renders no particular evidence that any Senators or Congressmen had been rallied to the industry side through lobbying. It was not really until 1964 that Senate critics of the Coffee Agreement began to warn of a possible cocoa agreement. Sen. Carlson, a persistent critic of the ICA, had been told at the first Committee on Foreign Relations hearing on the latter in March of 1963 that a cocoa agreement "was coming up for consideration;"[340] but he and Senator Douglas did not really speak out forcefully against the idea of a cocoa agreement until over a year later.

During the Senate debates on the coffee legislation during the summer of 1964 Senator Carlson lamented the fact that the UNCTAD meeting of the previous February, which he had attended, had been dominated by the sentiment that there should be a "global price program for commodities."[341] He asserted that the Senate could expect other agreements to follow, if a precedent were established in coffee, and then, he added,

> I can state categorically that the cocoa agreement would have been here today had it not been for some opposition to the coffee agreement.[342]

Carlson apparently assumed, or had insider's knowledge to that effect, that minority opposition to the Coffee Agreement had dampened State Department enthusiasm for negotiating a cocoa agreement during the previous fall.

---

[340] Senate Committee on Foreign Relations, International Coffee Agreement, 1962, 57.

[341] U.S., Congress, Senate, 88th Con., 2d sess., Congressional Record, July 31, 1964, 16959.

[342] Ibid., 16972.

Senator Paul Douglas also warned that "Behind coffee is cocoa." Contending that Senate support of the Coffee Agreement might encourage the State Department to send a cocoa agreement to Congress, he exlaimed that:

> The cry will be that we [the Congress] must agree to an international cocoa treaty on cocoa in order to boost up Ghana and possibly Angola and to keep Angola and Portuguese Africa out of the hands of the Communists."[343]

It can only be conjectured what would have happened, if a cocoa agreement had been sent to Congress in the period under study. A plausible hypothesis is that a cocoa agreement would have had tougher going than the ICA had. Among other reasons, the ICA had triggered policy-maker, including Congressional concerns about economic and political conditions in Latin America. It is highly improbable that a cocoa agreement, oriented primarily to African producers, would have elicited the same crucial degree of Congressional support. Also the cocoa market had not experienced a protracted period of very low (or high) prices such as the coffee market did over the extended period in which the Agreement was planned, negotiated, and ultimately passed through Congress. It, therefore, would have been more difficult to convince Congress of the "need" for an agreement, especially if it is assumed that the cocoa industry would have been contending strongly that it was not needed. Ironically, the same characteristic of the cocoa market that invited regulation— price fluctuation— probably conduced to unstable diplomatic and political conditions in which to negotiate an agreement with the U.S. and to gain Congressional support.

A crucial contrast between cocoa agreement prospects before Congress and those for the Coffee Agreement would have been the contrasting positions of

---

Ibid., 16972.

the cocoa and coffee industries respectively. If a prospective cocoa agreement did not have much political impetus behind it, in the first place, it would have been all the more vulnerable to cocoa industry opposition.

It is clear that most bureaucratic policy-makers in the period under study were convinced that it would be exceedingly difficult to secure Congressional support for a cocoa agreement, in the face of unified industry opposition. There were varying views as to whether this would be possible. Paul Callanan, Chief of the Tropical Products Division in the State Department during the period of the first three cocoa conferences (1963, 1966 and 1967), believes that a cocoa agreement could not have been cleared through Congress without "substantial" support from important sectors of the cocoa industry, especially the chocolate manufacturers. Since this support had not been forthcoming, he observes, "What's the use in knocking our brains out for an Agreement and then have the Senate veto it?"[344]

Another key policy-maker of that period is inclined to the more general view that "You have to have trade support to get any commodity agreement through Congress." "In all honesty," he has observed, "we were not all that serious about the 1963 cocoa negotiations. We had to bend over backwards to the cocoa trade [which opposed an agreement]."[345] Jerome Jacobson, the Deputy Assistant Secretary of State who headed the U.S. delegation to the 1963 conference, has stated that "George Ball [then Under Secretary of State for Economic Affairs] did not want to make the cocoa industry unhappy, and placed great restraints upon the delegation to the cocoa conference." Still on the basis of his preliminary explorations with "ten or eleven" Senators in 1963, "he contends that a determined effort

---

344 Interview, Paul Callanan, January 26, 1972.

345 Source withheld.

by the administration could have carried a cocoa agreement in Congress."[346]

Charles York, Paul Callanan's successor as Chief of the Tropical Products Division in State, doubts that the "cocoa industry could overturn a well conceived cocoa agreement promoted strongly by the government."[347] And in 1971 a State Department source expressed the view that:

> Allegations that the U.S. industry has played a major role in the shaping of U.S. Government policy on this subject [cocoa negotiations] are incorrect, and are not borne out by the record.

And continuing,

> We do not view the attitude of the U.S. industry as an obstacle to the conclusion of, or to Congressional acceptance of [emphasize mine] an effective and reasonable Agreement.[348]

Whatever view various participant-observers may have held of the cocoa industry's potential to block a cocoa agreement in Congress, it seems clear that there has never been any strong inclination to test this potential. W. Michael Blumenthal's recollections of policy-maker attitudes towards cocoa agreement negotiations in 1963 are probably indicative of general attitudes in subsequent years. He recalls that "George Ball and most of us were less sympathetic toward a cocoa agreement [than a Coffee Agreement]" for several reasons, but including the reason that "neither he nor anyone else was that anxious to take on the industry [known to oppose an agreement] and the Congress."[349] If for other reasons there had been strong policy-maker sentiment for a cocoa agreement, the battle with the cocoa industry might have been joined, and perhaps won. But in the absence of such sentiment, the cocoa industry has

---

[346] Interview, Jerome Jacobson, July 12, 1971. Still Jacobson believes that the United States could not have met Ghanaian expectations, in any event.

[347] Interview, Charles York, July 2, 1971.

[348] Source withheld.

[349] Letter from W. Michael Blumenthal to author, October 20, 1971.

been in a strategic position to tip the scales of bureaucratic policy-making against U.S. support for a cocoa agreement.

An Observation on Three Cases. The coffee and cocoa industries have shown a distinct preference for policy advocacy through unobtrusive, "advisory" relations with the State Department, and secondarily with other bureaucracies. But potential or actual Congressional participation in policy-making for the issues has helped them to secure standing with the executive branch and afforded them an alternative channel of access to policy-making when they have not felt satisfied with bureaucratic responses.

Much previous research has indicated that bureaucracies often feel pressure to accommodate interest group points of view before such groups challenge their consensus-building efforts in Congress. For the issues under study, the considerable pressure on the State Department to accommodate industry views has been very much a function of the difficulties of securing and sustaining Congressional support for commodity agreements as such. Since commodity agreements for foreign-owned production are likely to be particularly vulnerable in Congress, the pressure on State to assure business support is all the greater.

Congressional participation, thus, reinforces a conservative bias in U.S. policy-making towards commodity agreements. It affords direct opportunities for business opponents to undertake blocking measures against agreements presented to Congress; and more importantly in these cases, it increases the risks for the State Department of disregarding industry objections to all or part of an agreement.

CHAPTER V

United States and Brazil: American Business and the Soluble Coffee Dispute

LDCs tend to view industrialized countries as either indifferent or hostile to their efforts to process and export indigenous primary products. Such was the case between 1966 and 1971 when the United States put pressure on Brazil to abandon an export system that had enabled Brazil to capture, in a short period of time, a substantial share of the American market for soluble coffee.

A spokesman for Brazil in the soluble coffee dispute observed that at the very time President Lyndon Johnson was endorsing the Declaration of Presidents at Punta del Este in April of 1967— the Declaration encouraged LDCs to promote industrialization of agricultural production and exports of processed agricultural products— the State Department was launching a campaign to thwart imports into the United States from Brazil's newly expanded soluble coffee industry. "What," asked this spokesman rhetorically, "could explain the paradox of the United States opposing Brazilian soluble coffee imports, while professing support for LDC industrialization?"[349] Quite clearly, he concluded, the State Department

[349] The "spokesman" cited is the Washington public relations firm of Samuel E. Stavisky & Associates, Inc., which for several years has represented the Pan-American Coffee Bureau in the U.S., and more recently, the Brazilian Soluble Coffee Industry (Sindicato da Industria de Cafe). In 1967-69 Stavisky was retained by Sindicato, at an estimated cost of $75,000 in fees and expenses, to "undertake at once a vigorous campaign in defense of the free and unhampered import of Brazilian soluble coffee into the United States." Letter indicating services to be rendered, from Samuel E. Stavisky, President, to Jose Luis de Freitas Valle, President, Associacao Profissional de Industria de Cafe Soluvel, July 18, 1967, as found in Attachment 1, Exhibit B, Registration Statement under Foreign Agents Registration Act of 1938, Registration No. 1531, August, 1967, U.S. Department of Justice, Washington, D.C.

was "under the impression it must serve the interests of the U.S. coffee trade... rather than the policy of the U.S. Government [referring to declared policy of supporting LDC industrialization]."[350]

To the consternation of State Department policy-makers the view that the Department was beholden to business interests or simply wed to a narrowly "protectionist" policy towards Brazilian soluble coffee imports became widely accepted. The New York Times criticized the State Department for showing "immense sensitivity to protectionist forces on Capitol Hill but little for the deep feelings of poorer countries about industrial development."[351] And the Wall Street Journal attacked the Department for contravening sound free trade principles, and as being misguided by the determination "to protect U.S. processors of instant coffee."[352]

It is now possible to see the evolution of U.S. policy in the soluble coffee dispute with Brazil in the somewhat brighter light of retrospection, and to appraise the business role in policy-making more dispassionately than policy-makers, foreign agents or editorialists were able or willing to do during the dispute.

Business and the Evolution of U.S. Soluble Coffee Policy.

Brazil and several central American countries actively explored prospects for exporting soluble coffee to the lucrative U.S. market in the mid-1950's, ten years before Brazil made a serious bid for a market share.

---

350 Samuel E. Stavisky & Associates, Inc., "Background Memorandum," Mimeograph release for Brazilian Soluble Coffee Industry, Sao Paulo, November, 1967, 2.

351 Editorial, New York Times, February 6, 1968, 42.

352 Editorial, Wall Street Journal, February 26, 1968, 16.

Intimations of a future confrontation between the U.S. and Brazil over soluble trade are found as early as 1955. By that year the U.S. soluble coffee industry was already becoming restive over the possibilities of large scale soluble imports from Latin America; and the National Coffee Association (NCA) formed a standing Soluble Coffee Committee to monitor developments in this sphere that might affect the national industry.[353] In early 1956 the NCA Board passed a resolution expressing its opposition to "any form of subsidies which would give soluble coffee manufacturers in producing nations a special and unfair advantage over U.S. soluble manufacturers.[354] The Board was acting upon its Soluble Coffee Committee's conclusion that "a producer of soluble coffee located abroad could not presently export soluble coffee into the U.S.A. at significant or material advantage over a producer of soluble coffee located in this country," that is, unless he were somehow "subsidized" by his government. [emphasis mine].[355]

A year later the Pacific Coast Coffee Association (PCCA), whose members were increasingly anxious over soluble imports into west coast ports from El Salvador and Mexico, resolved that the NCA should keep the soluble imports situation under close surveillance.[356] In late October the NCA Soluble Coffee Committee again reported to the Board that the U.S. industry would suffer, if

---

353 Edward Aborn, President of Tenco, now a Coca-Cola subsidiary, was made chairman of the committee, and served the Association as a soluble coffee expert during the ensuing fifteen years. Interview, Edward Aborn, October 4, 1971.

354 National Coffee Association, News Letter, No. 468, February 3, 1956.

355 Ibid.

356 NCA, News Letter, No. 539, June 7, 1957.

foreign producers were permitted the benefits of preferential treatment, e.g., tax incentives or privileged access to raw materials, not available to American producers.[357]

In the late fifties the International Coffee Agreement had not yet been negotiated, and more importantly, there was for the U.S. industry more a threat of solubles imports than an actual deluge. The reaction of business to this threat, however, presaged what was to come later when Brazil tried to crash the American market. The primary concern in 1957, it should be emphasized, was the challenge of Mexican and Central American imports.

The Soluble Coffee Committee of the NCA Board recommended that the Association undertake informal talks with these soluble exporting countries towards assuring that they take all steps necessary to prevent "uneven competition" between their exported raw and soluble coffee.[358] The sense of this recommendation was to eliminate those government measures which would give national producers (including foreign investors) financial or raw material advantages that would not be enjoyed by soluble producers in the United States. The NCA followed this recommendation and through private diplomacy persuaded the Central American countries, and even Mexico, to yield to the complaints of the American industry.[359]

During the late fifties the American coffee industry was also exercised by Brazil's experimentation with incentives for soluble coffee export, more

---

[357] NCA, News Letter, November 8, 1957.

[358] Ibid.

[359] Interview, Edward Aborn, October 4, 1971.

because of the possibility of major Brazilian competition than because of the negligible extent of imports into the U.S. at that time. Brazil had not yet begun its ambitious promotion of national solubles production. During October of 1958, Renato Costa Lima, President of the Brazilian Coffee Institute, acknowledged that "the National Coffee Association has actively protested the favorable treatment given by Brazil to instant coffee exports.[360] Shortly thereafter Brazilian exchange rates were revised to remove the incentives being given soluble exports.[361]

It is conceivable that major confrontation over solubles trade could have developed between Brazil and the United States, even had there been no International Coffee Agreement. Sam Israel Jr., a prominent New Orleans coffee trader and leader in the NCA, is sure that this was inevitable. Paradoxically, he believes, Brazil's use of the ICA as a foil for the development of a "subsidy" system for soluble coffee exports gave American business the levers with which to neutralize this system. "All hell would have broken loose," he says, if there had been no Agreement with which to counter a Brazilian subsidy program for solubles.[362]

In 1960 the Brazilian federal government decided to promote the expansion of its national soluble coffee industry and to prepare for a major export program. There were several reasons for this decision.[363] Brazil subsequently emphasized that its primary objective was to recover its market position in

---

[360] NCA, News Letter, No. 612, October 31, 1958.

[361] NCA, News Letter, No. 617, December 4, 1958.

[362] Interview, Sam Israel, Jr., October 12, 1971.

[363] For a general discussion of these reasons see Arthur J. Cordell, "The Brazilian Soluble Problem: A Review," The Quarterly Review of Economics and Business, IX (spring, 1969), 29-32.

the United States which had been steadily eroded by American purchases of African robusta for soluble production.[364]

Incentives were given for factory construction to national and foreign investors alike; and over the next seven years several new plants were brought into production. No American corporation responded to early Brazilian efforts to secure American investment in this enterprise.[365] Nestle, the multinational corporation, which had been producing soluble coffee in Brazil since 1948, was the only "foreign" corporation to participate in the expansion of soluble production and export.

In 1965 exports to the United States from Brazil's enlarged soluble industry began to expand dramatically. Within three years its share of the U.S. soluble coffee market jumped from one per cent (1965) to fourteen per cent (1967), precipitating the confrontation between Brazil and the United States. Brazilian soluble was marketed exclusively through American companies that either blended the product with their own or simply packaged it under their own labels. Small or medium-sized roasters (for example, Hills Bros. or MJB) and chain food stores were quick to seize the opportunity of lower cost supplies; but eventually even the major American producers did so, with General Foods becoming the major importer of Brazilian soluble.

---

364 See Samuel Stavisky & Associates, Inc.,"A Situation Report: U.S. Switches Tactics in Battle to Ban Brazil's Instant Coffee." Mimeograph issued for Brazilian Soluble Coffee Industry, December 29, 1967, 1.

365 Since the late fifties Brazil has tried, relatively unsuccessfully, to lure American investment to its soluble industry. Brazil's effort to secure General Foods investment failed.

Everyone could agree on the reason for Brazil's success in the American market—it was providing a high quality product at substantially lower prices than could be met by American processors. According to one authorative estimate (1969) substitution of Brazilian powder for the Brazilian portion of a standard instant blend could result in a cost savings of 3 cents on the finished pound. Greater savings could be reaped by packaging a wholly Brazilian powder.[366]

How could Brazilian producers undersell their American competitors? It is generally agreed that this was made possible by a shrewdly conceived arrangement whereby domestic soluble producers were exempted from export duties ("contributions") that were charged on green coffee exports, and allowed supplies of low cost beans of good quality which were not made available to foreign soluble plants.

American producers, on the other hand, were not only denied access to the low cost beans going to the Brazilian companies, but they had to purchase their raw materials at international market prices supported by the Coffee Agreement, and in the case of Brazilian milds, at prices reflecting Brazil's export duties on green coffee. In addition, the quota and price support features of the Coffee Agreement prevented American companies from securing competitively low-priced beans in the necessary quantities from African sources. These "facts" about the Brazilian scheme were never particularly disputed. The implications of the scheme, its "legitimacy," and its effects were heatedly disputed.

---

[366] Cordell, op. cit., 32-33.

If the Brazilian challenge had arisen in a different time or, at least, when there was no operative Coffee Agreement, the form and possibly the outcome of the struggle between the United States and Brazil might have been different. It may have been fortuitous for the American soluble industry that there was a Coffee Agreement at the time of the solubles dispute. For as Brazil could capitalize on the existence of the Agreement to fashion a subsidy-like system to promote its exports to the United States, so the American industry could use the Agreement as a lever to secure governmental measures against Brazilian imports.[367]

The National Coffee Association and the regional trade associations became alarmed at the rapid rise of Brazilian imports in 1966, and indignant that Brazil should "exploit" the Coffee Agreement. From early in the year until the late spring of 1970, they constantly pressed the U.S. government for action against Brazil. In June of 1966, at the direction of the NCA Board, John McKiernan wrote to Edward R. Fried, Deputy Assistant Secretary of State for International Resources and Food Policy, "to solicit the Government's support in attempting to eliminate the unfair advantage presently being afforded to producers of instant coffee in Brazil."[368] A similar letter was sent to the Deputy Assistant Secretary of Commerce. In September, apparently uncertain that State would take immediate and vigorous action, or any at all, McKiernan sent

---

367 Sam Israel has made this point. Israel believes that the Congress of the late sixties would have been very unsympathetic to appeals for protective tariffs against soluble imports. Interview, Sam Israel, Jr., October 12, 1971.

368 Letter to State Department, as reproduced in NCA, News Letter, No. 1011, June 13, 1966, 1.

similar appeals to the Trade Information Office of the Special Representative for Trade Negotiations, and to the U.S. Tariff Commission.[369]

By October the NCA Board was showing distinct impatience with what it considered State's tardiness in acting on its appeals. In a letter, this time to Donald Palmer, Deputy Assistant Secretary for Latin American Affairs, the NCA Board Chairman conveyed a sharply worded resolution which threatened that recourse to Congress would be taken, if urgent measures were not taken to stop Brazil's discriminatory trade in soluble coffee.[370] The resolution reminded the State Department that the coffee industry had cooperated with the "Government as patriotic Americans in the...efforts to aid the coffee producing countries" and complained that the "spirit of this effort" was being violated by one or more producers engaged in discriminatory trade in soluble coffee. At least one of the regional associations, the Green Coffee Association of New Orleans, sent a similar resolution to the State Department, threatening Congressional action.[371]

The Department of State appears not to have settled down to serious consideration of the solubles issue until early 1967. By this time the pattern of

---

[369] In 1964 Congress had amended the Tariff Act of 1930 to exclude instant coffee from its list of dutiable imports. Until that time the U.S. Commissioner of Customs had defined instant coffee as subject to a 3 cents per pound import duty, within the meaning of the Act. On the advice of the State Department and other departments Congress assumed that removal of the duty would have only slight economic significance for American industry and labor, but that it would benefit the United States internationally by aiding the Alliance for Progress and Latin American economic growth. See statement by Rep. Wilbur Mills in U.S., Congress, House, 88th Cong., 2d sess., Congressional Record, May 27, 1967, 12044. Just two years before, the Brazilian onslaught in the U.S. market, the NCA unwittingly acquiesced in the removal of the tariff.

[370] NCA, News Letter, No. 1030, October 24, 1966.

[371] NCA, News Letter, No. 1035, Nov. 28, 1966.

increasing Brazilian imports was undeniable and officers in State began to sense that Brazil's policy might really jeopardize the Coffee Agreement, and certainly the crucial support of the American industry for it.

While the NCA and regional coffee associations were making their appeals for action, the two leading instant coffee corporations in the United States, General Foods and Nestle (US), together accounting for approximately 65 per cent of the U.S. solubles market, were lobbying with State for action privately. Edward Fried, then Deputy Assistant Secretary of State, would later recall that the industry's primary role in this period was to "flag" the danger Brazilian soluble export policy posed for the Coffee Agreement. The State Department, he believes, would have come to the position it did anyway, but not so quickly, had it not been for business remonstrations.[372]

For the first four years of the solubles dispute Nestle (US), was in the forefront among opponents of Brazilian imports. Nestle, a General Foods coffee executive remembers, until its volte face in 1970, constantly prodded G.F. for more decisive action to stop the imports.[373] In March of 1967 Nestle's Director of coffee and cocoa purchasing was active in trying to persuade the appropriate offices of State's Bureau of Economic Affairs that they should act against Brazil's export policy. The main thrust of Nestle's argument was that this policy threatened the important objectives of the Coffee Agreement. Among other things, it argued that Brazilian imports going to the private label companies

---

372 Interview, Edward Fried, June 24, 1971.

373 Interview, Frederick Otterbein, September 22, 1971.

were forcing the brand-name companies to seek "economies at the expense of consumption (promotion instead of advertising; short-cuts on quality, etc.) thus ultimately depressing green coffee prices through lack of demand." Furthermore, it contended, robusta producing countries would be encouraged to imitate Brazilian practice, to establish their own soluble processing industries at the expense of heavy subsidization and loss of foreign exchange earnings.[374]

The Department of State seems to have been persuaded by Nestle's general line of argument, if not all its particulars. In the following May Edward Fried, Deputy Assistant Secretary of State, gave the first public indication of State's inclination to act against Brazilian imports, in a speech to the Pacific Coast Coffee Association. Fried said:

> I believe no producing country can rightfully expect to use the price stability that the Agreement brings to its green coffee sales in order to build a coffee processing industry that competes unfairly with its best customers, the users of green coffee...Not only is such action intolerable on grounds of self-interest, but it touches off a self-defeating chain of events in other producing countries.[375]

Fried's rationale would be elaborated later by a written State Department response to a question put by Senator Wayne Morse in 1968 to then Assistant Secretary of State for Economic Affairs, Anthony Solomon:

> We have objected to Brazilian Government policies which favor the export of soluble coffee over the export of green coffee, largely because of the unfair competition to our domestic processors of coffee and the danger they represent to the future of the ICA itself.

---

374 Source withheld.

375 Extract of a speech by Edward Fried, as found verbatim in "Agreement is Still Part of U.S. Policy," Tea and Coffee Trade Journal, CXXXII (June, 1967), 26.

> One of the important objectives of the International Coffee Agreement is to maintain coffee prices at stable levels by limiting coffee supplies through a quota system. In the absence of an Agreement American processors could have met competition from Brazilian instant coffee if they chose, by turning to lower quality and lower cost green beans from Africa and Asian producers. However, they were not free to do so; the African and Asian suppliers are limited by tight export quotas and naturally enough these regions prefer to sell their higher quality and higher priced beans. The United States helps to enforce export quotas by limiting coffee imports to those covered by quotas. Thus, unless Brazil's policy of not applying the same tax on soluble coffee as they did on green coffee exports was changed, we would be in the anomalous position of telling our producers that they could not be defended against unfair and damaging competitive practices, which were made possible by the operations of the Coffee Agreement.[376]

Sometime in early 1967 the Department of State initiated bilateral talks with Brazil concerning industry complaints. Meanwhile the Amalgamated Meatcutters and Butcher Workmen (AFL-CIO), like the adversely affected businesses, was becoming increasingly restive about the slow response of the State Department to its appeals against Brazilian imports. This union had organized a large percentage of the national coffee workers in the late forties; and at the time of this dispute had some 5,000 coffee members, a relatively few of which were workers in the highly automated instant coffee segment of the industry. Contrary to the reports of several observers at the time, the Amalgamated Meatcutters played a more autonomous and significant role in the solubles dispute than is generally known.[377]

---

376 Memorandum from Anthony Solomon to Senator Wayne Morse, as cited in Senate Committee on Foreign Relations, International Coffee Agreement, 1968, 56.

377 Accounts at the time tended to treat the Amalgamated Meatcutters as a "company union" of General Foods, following the bidding of GF in efforts to influence government policy. Arnold Mayer, a lobbyist for the Union in Washington, believes that his union, if anything, played a more persistent and decisive role in getting State to act against Brazil, than did GF. "Our purpose," he said, "was to protect the few but lucrative contracts our Union had in the soluble coffee industry." Finally he lamented the "typical unresponsiveness" to labor union concerns exhibited by the State Department in the dispute. Interview, Arnold Mayer, July 30, 1971.

In September of 1966 the Union had appeared before the U.S. Tariff Commission to complain of the displacement of workers by the unfair trade practices of Brazil. In this same period New Jersey Union officials were briefing Congressional hopefuls on the threat to New Jersey workers from Brazilian soluble imports. In June of 1967 Representative Dominick Daniels (D - N.J.) introduced a bill to impose import duties on Brazilian soluble imports.[378] An official of the Amalgamated Meatcutters has explained that Daniels acted at the request of his union. "We were never optimistic that this bill would get anywhere, but as part of our early strategy, we hoped to scare the State Department into action."[379] The bill was defeated.

By mid-1967 several parties recognized that the imminent renegotiation of the Coffee Agreement would surely consider the issue of trade of soluble coffee under the Agreement. The Amalgamated Meatcutters and General Foods, at least, wanted to be sure that the occasion was used to settle the solubles dispute on terms favorable to them. To this end Arnold Mayer of the Meatcutters, James Andrews, President of the Maxwell Division of General Foods, and Rep. Daniels had a private meeting during the summer with Chairman Wilbur Mills, whose House Ways and Means had jurisdiction over Coffee Agreement legislation. Chairman Mills seems to have been easily and genuinely convinced of the merits of the general argument presented by the country's largest solubles producer and major union of coffee workers.

The main consequence of this meeting was that Mills wrote to Secretary of State Dean Rusk, urging that the solubles dispute be settled in the context of negotiations for the second ICA. Julius Katz, a senior commodities officer in the Bureau of Economic Affairs at that time recalls that Chairman Mills had

---

[378] H.R. 11275.

[379] Interview, Arnold Mayer, July 30, 1971

urged such an approach. "Implicit in Mill's suggestion was the feeling that the solubles dispute had to be settled before another Agreement could secure Congressional support.[380]

If the State Department were not already convinced that the solubles issue needed to be settled in the renegotiation of the Coffee Agreement, Mills' communique surely made this clear.

The first ICA had had little to say about international regulation of trade of soluble or other "processed" coffee. Importantly, however, it defined soluble coffee as "coffee," within the regulatory jurisdiction of the Agreement, and specified a "conversion rate" at which soluble exports would be charged to export quotas.[381] This provision acknowledged that prices for green coffee in international trade could be affected by exports of processed coffee from the bean producing countries. Otherwise, as the chief of the American delegation to the 1962 Coffee Conference recalls, the framers of the first treaty certainly did not anticipate the difficulties that arose over soluble trade, and felt no necessity for more elaborate treaty provisions on the subject.[382]

At the fall meeting (1967) of the International Coffee Council (ICC) in London the American delegation advanced several proposals for an appropriate amendment to the second ICA that would forbid Brazil's "discriminatory" trade practices. Brazil strenuously resisted these proposals, and the ICC became deadlocked. Upon adjournemt, a special ICO mission was sent to Washington and Rio to seek a compromise on the issue, which remained the last obstacle to the negotiation of the second Coffee Agreement.

---

380 Interview, Julius Katz, July 15, 1971.

381 Article 2, g provided that one pound of soluble should be charged as three pounds of green coffee against national quotas.

382 Interview, W. Michael Blumenthal, October 13, 1971.

Reluctantly Brazil finally yielded to the inclusion of provisions in what became "Chapter IX - Processed Coffee," or "Article 44" of the Coffee Agreement of 1968. The United States achieved its primary objective in paragraph one of the Article which established an obligation on the part of each member not to discriminate in favor of processed as compared with green coffee in applying governmental measures, affecting exports and re-exports of coffee to another member. The Article also provided an arbitration procedure for determing the presence and extent of "discrimination," and specified the circumstances under which a complaining member could take countermeasures against it.

Brazil was exceedingly unhappy about Article 44, and only after strenuous diplomatic resistance, accepted it.[383] A prominent Brazilian policy-maker later recalled that the United States secured the requisite support for Article 44 by threatening to scuttle the whole Coffee Agreement. According to George Maciel, "the other [producing] countries realized that the coffee agreement was much more in their own interest than the interest of Brazil, as might have been the position [for Brazil itself] in 1962. And one by one they started pressing Brazil to accept some kind of compromise with the United States to save the Agreement."[384]

---

[383]Edward Aborn, the President of Tenco, a New Jersey instant coffee processing subsidiary of Coca-Cola, recalls that during the negotiations he was personally warned by the Brazilian government that it would revoke a recently approved price increase for the Coca-Cola soft drink in Brazil, unless Tenco stopped pressing the U.S. government for measures against Brazilian instant coffee. Coca-Cola heeded this warning and withdrew from its active role in the NCA against Brazilian imports. Interview, Edward Aborn, October 4, 1971.

[384]Statement by George Maciel, as found in International Coffee Organization, Arbitration Panel, op. cit., 19.

To the surprise of American diplomats African robusta-producing members of the ICO maintained a studied silence throughout the solubles dispute, and only unobtrusively supported Article 44, when it might have been expected they would have advocated it eagerly and openly. The Deputy Assistant Secretary of State at the time, Edward Fried, remains somewhat puzzled by the failure of the African countries to work diplomatically with the United States against Brazil's policy, inasmuch as it was generally recognized that Brazilian success in the American market would tend to displace purchases of African robusta.

Albert Prosterman, a long-time American adviser to African coffee-producing countries, has offered a convincing explanation of African behavior. The African countries, he insists, recognized that their immediate economic interest lay in countering Brazil's solubles export program; at the same time, they were unwilling to actively and openly oppose a fellow LDCs efforts to industrialize its agricultural sector.[385] Parenthetically, at the same time coffee negotiators were seized with the issue of soluble coffee, the American and Netherlands delegations to the U.N. Cocoa Conference (1967) in Geneva were proposing an Article 44-type provision for the cocoa treaty under consideration.[386] Expressing the sentiment of the cocoa producing countries towards this proposal, the Nigerian delegate declared that the proposed new article should be entitled "Action to dismantle cocoa processing industries in cocoa producing countries."[387]

---

385 Prosterman's Washington firm had advised the countries of the Inter-African Coffee Organization for over ten years, and now urged them to actively work for Article 44. He recalls that this is one of the few instances in which his African clients ever declined to take his advice. Interview, Albert M. Prosterman, January 24, 1972.

386 U.N., Conference on Trade and Development, Summary Records of Executive Committee, Tenth Meeting, December 15, 1967, TD/Cocoa, 2/EX/Sr. 1-13, 90-98.

387 *Ibid.*, 93.

Brazil's reluctant acceptance of Article 44, though it did not resolve the solubles dispute, did prevent U.S. abandonment of the Coffee Agreement. The second Coffee Act passed Congress relatively easily. At the time Chairman Wilbur Mills asked Anthony Solomon, Assistant Secretary of State for Economic Affairs, whether he expected Brazil to comply with Article 44. Solomon replied that he anticipated compliance, but thought there might be some differences over the extent of discrimination to be corrected.[388] Solomon was correct in anticipating the latter difference, but did not foresee that the dispute was only entering a new phase.

During 1968 Brazil refused to change its solubles export policy, and so at the end of the year the United States resorted to the complaint procedure under Article 44. In the following February an ICO arbitration panel of three men heard oral testimony for the United States and Brazil concerning the latter's complaint of "discrimination."[389] The arbitration did not resolve the dispute, though it might have tipped the balance, to some degree, towards a negotiated settlement. As might have been predicted, the Brazilian panelist rendered an opinion passionately invoking "equity" in the treatment of industrializing counties, and finding no violation of Article 44.[390] The U.S. panelist, on the other

---

388 U.S., Congress, House, Committee on Ways and Means, International Coffee Agreement, 13.

389 Arbitration panelists were Paulo Egydio Martins, a former Brazilian Minister of Commerce and Industry; David Herwitz, a Harvard law professor; and Bengt Odevall, a former Swedish consular officer in Minnesota and afterwards an ambassador to Brazil.

390 International Coffee Organization, "Findings of Arbitration Panel Established Under the Provisions of Article 44," Doc. ED-297/69 (E), March 3, 1969, as reprinted in "International Coffee Arbitration of Brazil-United States Dispute in Processed Coffee February 28, 1969," International Legal Materials, VIII (1969), 576.

hand, found "discriminatory treatment" in violation of Article 44 and was "satisfied that authorizing the United States to take appropriate measures to remedy the situation under Article 44(3) unless Brazil does so itself represents satisfactory remedy in the circumstances."[391]

Mr. Odevall, the chairman and the deciding voice in the arbitration, concluded "that the United States is entitled to take...action pursuant to paragraph 3 of Article 44, while having due regard for provisions of paragraph 4 of this Article."[392] However, with studied ambiguity, Odevall did not explicitly recognize "discriminatory" treatment by Brazil. Furthermore, he was unwilling to have the panel consider the extent of discrimination. The American panelist himself acknowledged the difficulties of quantifying the extent of discrimination, but he believed that could have been done had his colleagues been willing, which they were not.

Odevall later told one of the Brazilian participants in the proceedings that "Brazil at first will not like my opinion; but I am confident that as time passes she will come to appreciate it."[393] By this he apparently meant that while his opinion lent some legitimacy to reasonable countermeasures that the United States might take, it was by no means a decisive affirmation of the U.S. position. In any event, Brazil, according to an internal State Department memorandum, continued to argue "that the decision was invalid because a majority did not expressly find 'discriminatory treatment' nor measure its extent."

---

[391] Ibid., 566.

[392] Ibid., 565. Paragraph 4 states the principle that members should give due regard to the need of developing countries to industrialize and export manufactured products.

[393] Interview, George Maciel, July 16, 1971.

The arbitration, however, was probably a factor in bringing diplomatic progress and in shifting the dispute to a different focus. For months the dispute had centered upon whether discriminatory treatment existed at all and on whether restraints should be put upon Brazilian solubles exports, by one means or another. But within two months after the arbitration, Brazil indicated its readiness to accommodate U.S. concerns, to a small degree anyway.

On April 30, 1969, after intensive negotiations, the U.S. and Brazil announced a one-year agreement on solubles trade. The essence of the agreement was that Brazil would impose an export tax of 13 cents per pound on its solubles exports to the United States. It was agreed that the two countries would meet on or about January 15th of the following year to seek agreement on any further measures to be taken. Finally it was agreed that:

> In the event that no agreement is reached on these further measures by March 1, 1970, the United States reserves its right to impose measures it deems appropriate to correct the present undesirable situation. In the view of the United States Government, this would involve taking steps to insure that a total tax burden of 30 cents per pound is levied on Brazilian soluble coffee by May 1, 1970.[394]

Subsequently, differences within and between the two countries would center upon what "total tax burden" Brazil would need to bear to "equalize" trading opportunities between American and Brazilian solubles producers. The reader will surmise that this calculation would be highly technical, only susceptible to subjective determination, and certainly subject to conflicting viewpoints, based partly on conflicting interests. Hence, the issue would be fundamentally political.

---

394 See diplomatic notes between William Belton (U.S.) and Jose de Maghaes Pinto (Brazil), as reprinted in International Legal Materials, VIII (1968), 579.

As the 1969 solubles agreement indicated, the State Department had determined that a total tax burden of 30 cents per pound should be the longer-run target. The Department pledged itself in writing to this target, in response to "our industry's demand for an unequivocal commitment."[395] For many months industry advisers had been offering varying estimates of what had to be done to equalize competition; but the "30 cent solution" was quite subjectively derived. It was based partly on economic analysis and partly on purely political calculations of what minimum imposition on Brazil would assuage the Meatcutters Union and businesses whose support was deemed critical. "We are publicly committed," State officials acknowledged among themselves, "to imposing an import fee, which when taken with the Brazilian export tax, will yield a total burden of 30 cents. Should we fail to carry out this commitment, we will jeopardize the support of our domestic industry for the Coffee Agreement."[396]

How were the solubles dispute and support for the Coffee Agreement linked? When the one year solubles agreement expired, Brazil refused to increase its export tax on soluble beyond 13 cents; and despite the protestations of the American embassy in Brazil, which thought that the 13 cent measure was sufficient, the State Department held to the position that something more had to be done. Another stalemate in the negotiations could have developed.

Congress, by dint of its timely involvement with the implementing legislation for the Coffee Agreement, however, had a central role in precipitating resolution of the dispute. Its reentry into the policy-making arena for soluble coffee was also fortuitous for the opponents of Brazilian imports. Congress, it will be recalled, had only provided implementing legislation for the second ICA,

---

[395] Source withheld.

[396] Ibid.

covering the two year period up to October 1, 1970. Thus, in the preceding April, the month in which the solubles agreement with Brazil expired, the State Department had to introduce appropriate legislation in the House for the extension of the ICA Act of 1968.

For the next several months the bill was lodged in the House Committee on Ways and Means. Before hearings on the bill in late spring, however, a rather surprising turn of events occurred within the National Coffee Association. On May 1, 1970, the NCA Board of Directors, which until that time had continuously called for stronger measures against Brazilian imports, reversed itself sharply. Noting that considerable progress had been made in correcting previous inequities, and the changing economies of soluble production in Brazil, the NCA Board resolved:

> To express its opposition to increases in the Brazilian export tax on soluble coffee into the United States and/or the institution of a duty in the United States on imports of soluble coffee from Brazil.[397]

Nestle (US), reversing its own previous position, led the coup against established NCA policy. According to Edward Aborn, Nestle presented the resolution unexpectedly at the end of the board meeting, and had quietly mustered support from a sufficient number of pliant member traders and "undecideds" to gain a majority. He and Coca-Cola's representative on the Board felt they could not speak out openly against the Nestle motion or vote against it, for fear of government reprisals against Coca-Cola operations in Brazil.[398]

---

[397] Resolution of the NCA Board of Directors, May 1, 1970, as reprinted verbatim in NCA Special Bulletin, No. 173, May 4, 1970. There were 10 votes for, 7 against and 4 abstentions.

[398] Interview, Edward Aborn, October 4, 1971.

Frederick Otterbein, the General Foods Vice President on the Board, believes the vote was a momentary aberration, due to his "not keeping the guys in line." Nestle, he admits, had taken him by surprise.[399] Later he assured the State Department that he could get the resolution reversed, if that were desirable for policy purposes; but he was told that this would only complicate matters.[400]

The State Department felt that the NCA had "pulled the rug from under its feet."[401] The new NCA resolution called into question State's advocacy of the "30 cent solution." If the NCA no longer favored more concessions by Brazil, why should the State Department? Brazil and other critics were quick to ask the question, and to provide their own answer. It had to be assumed, Brazil now argued, that State was beholden to General Foods, whose position had just been overturned in the NCA Board.[402]

Officially the State Department declared that "NCA or business preferences are not controlling in the making of American policy."[403] From its perspective, however, the political realities were little changed. It was probably true that General Foods could have reversed the NCA Board decision. A U.S. policy for soluble coffee that would not satisfy General Foods would not, in the end, satisfy the NCA or Wilbur Mills. The Amalgamated Meatcutters, furthermore,

---

399 Interview, Frederick Otterbein, September 22, 1971.

400 Interview, Julius Katz, July 15, 1971.

401 Ibid.

402 Samuel E. Stavisky & Associates, the Washington public relations firm representing the Brazilian soluble coffee industry, had all along been emphasizing the surreptitious role of General Foods in distorting U.S. policy towards Brazil.

403 Interview, Julius Katz, July 15, 1971.

were already committed to the 30 cent solution.[404] More importantly Chairman Mills was already thinking in terms of this solution.

General Foods, however, was uncertain what the State Department would do next. For in May or June (1970) it joined the Amalgamated Meatcutters in another private conference with Chairman Wilbur Mills and this time, Rep. John W. Byrnes, the minority leader of Ways and Means. General Foods was represented by James Andrews, President of its Maxwell House Division, and by Frederick Otterbein, Vice-President for Green Coffee Operations. Leon B. Schachter, Vice-President and Director of the Washington office of the Amalgamated Meatcutters, attended with his deputy, Arnold Mayer. One or more Ways and Means staff members were present.[405]

General Foods and the Meatcutters emphasized to the Committee leaders that Brazil still retained a marked advantage in the solubles trade, which represented a clear and present threat to U.S. instant coffee producers and workers. They also complained of the State Department's unwillingness, or at least, of its slowness to act decisively against Brazil. According to Arnold Mayer of the Amalgamated Meatcutters, Chairman Mills himself expressed exasperation at the failure of the State Department to resolve this dispute. In Mayer's words, Mills indicated that State was "toying with the Congress," and not pressing hard enough for a settlement.[406]

In June Chairman Mills expressed similar concerns personally to Julius Katz, the Deputy Assistant Secretary of State. Also his Committee heard brief testimony and received written statements on the Coffee Agreement and the solubles dispute, in the context of a major series of hearings on trade and tariff

---

404 Interview, Arnold Mayer, July 30, 1971.

405 Ibid.

406 Ibid.

proposals. In one such statement, Leon B. Schachter, Vice-President of the Amalgamated Meatcutters, declared that the "present American production of soluble or instant coffee is threatened with extinction."[407] Observing that Wilbur Mills and his Committee had earlier (1967-68) been instrumental in "accelerating" negotiations between the U.S. and Brazil,[408] he said that his Union had "little hope that the State Department will take decisive action to solve this situation without being pushed into action by this Committee."[409]

Chairman Mills did push. In mid-July his Committee decided not to report out the extension bill for the Coffee Act, until Brazil was prepared to abide by Article 44 of the Agreement. The Committee vote did not come at the most propitious moment, from the standpoint of Coffee Act clearance, irrespective of the Committee's growing pique with Brazil. First, the aforementioned June trade hearings had issued in a number of protectionist decisions. At the time the Committee was deciding to defer clearance of the Coffee Act, it was also voting for mandatory import quotas on textiles and shoes, and for a general quota provision that would help U.S. products experiencing a "disruptive" challenge from competitive imports. Under certain circumstances, the President would be obliged to impose import quotas.

Also in recent months there had been a sharp rise in green coffee prices from which the U.S. would seek relief at the August session of the ICC. Since, however, a consistent theme in Congressional criticism of the ICA had been that it could be detrimental to consumers, a period of high prices strengthened the hand of the Coffee Agreement critics, some of them in the Committee, and

---

[407] Statement by Leon B. Schachter, as found in Committee on Ways and Means, Tariff and Trade Proposals, Hearings, op. cit., 3961.

[408] Ibid.

[409] Ibid., 3963.

generally exacerbated strong feelings about what was considered Brazil's ungrateful disregard for the ICA in the solubles dispute.

The Coffee Act was allowed to expire on September 30, and American regulation of imports to lapse. In the fall Mills indicated to the State Department that he would countenance short-term extension of the implementing legislation, if State and Brazil were to show some progress towards a settlement of the solubles dispute. In December, stating that he was pleased with the ICC decisions on green coffee in August, Mills had his Committee report out the Coffee bill.

The Committee report stated "that Brazil should take action to end the discrimination and fulfill its obligations under the International Coffee Agreement."[410] It said that the Committee had amended the Act to give the President the necessary authority to impose "special fees or such other measures as he deems appropriate to offset discriminatory treatment by other governments in favor of the export or reexport of processed coffee." (Sec. 302, 1, C).[411] Finally the report rued the "previous delays" in getting a settlement and this time "requested" that the President report back to Congress by the subsequent April 1, indicating satisfactory corrective measures, either by Brazil or by the President unilaterally. Failing such measures, the report declared, the Committee would not consider implementing legislation for the Coffee Agreement

---

[410] U.S., Congress, House, Committee on Ways and Means, International Coffee Act, Report to accompany H.R. 19567, No. 91-1641, December 1, 1970, 91st Cong., 2d sess., 1970, 5.

[411] The report makes clear that the Committee had embraced the idea of the "30 cent solution" or some comparable solution to correct the situation. Ibid., 5.

again. It was recommended that the Coffee Act be extended only through June 30, 1971.

Before the 91st Congress expired at the end of December, the Coffee bill passed the House, the Senate Finance Committee, and the Senate itself. In the Senate Sen. Edward Kennedy spoke for passage of the bill, but lamented the fact that the Committee on Ways and Means was threatening the existence of the ICA by its demands on Brazil in the soluble coffee dispute. Observing incorrectly that General Foods was the "only coffee company that has demanded an increase in Brazil's export tax," he questioned whether the Congress should adopt this company's position "to the disadvantage of the American consumer."[412]

But Sen. Kennedy's was a solitary and not very persistent voice on this issue. The more influential voice, as events would prove, had been heard when Chairman Mills spoke on the subject before the House several days earlier:

> ...I am getting sick and tired of us trying to help countries throughout the world by these types of arrangements [ICA] and assuming a responsibility in connection with it, and then the minute we get the ink dry on the agreement they do something in turn to violate the agreement. [Brazil's soluble coffee policy][413]

Developments on the diplomatic front followed quickly in early 1971. Negotiations previously had focused on tax or tariff solutions. Eventually discussions returned to an early Brazilian proposal that reportedly had been rejected by the United States as undesirable for anti-trust reasons.[414]

---

412 U.S., Congress, Senate, 91st Cong., 2d sess., Congressional Record, December 31, 1970, 21680. Kennedy also asked that the NCA resolution in May, expressing satisfaction with current Brazilian measures, be entered into the record.

413 U.S., Congress, House, 91st Cong., 2d sess., Congressional Record, December 18, 1970, 12088.

414 Interview, George Maciel, July 16, 1971.

In this phase the National Coffee Association, as an entity, withheld advice on particular proposals, as it was recognized that it would be difficult to develop an association consensus for any single proposal.

The open threat by the House Ways and Means Committee seems to have been taken seriously. By the April 1st deadline the President was able to report to the Ways and Means Committee that in March an agreement had been reached which "eliminates an issue which has strained our relations with Brazil for several years."[415] "In essence," Secretary of State Rogers explained:

> the agreement will enable American manufacturers of soluble coffee to purchase an appropriate quantity of Brazilian coffee suitable for processing upon which no Brazilian contribution quota will be imposed. Sales of this special allocation coffee will be conducted through normal trade channels. Brazil will sell the coffee to individual United States firms which will receive an entitlement proportionate to their historical shares of soluble coffee production.
>
> The quantity of coffee to be sold each year under this arrangement will be 560,000 bags of 60 kilos each. The quantity may be renegotiated after the first year should levels of U.S. imports of Brazilian soluble coffee increase or decrease by more than 15 percent.
>
> Simultaneously with the effectiveness of this agreement, the Brazilian export tax of 13 cents per pound on soluble coffee will be removed.

And finally,

> Our agreement with Brazil will continue in force as long as the United States continues to implement the International Coffee Agreement, which expires on September 30, 1973.[416]

---

[415]Letter from William P. Rogers, Secretary of State, to President Richard M. Nixon, March 30, 1971, as reproduced in U.S., Congress, House, Committee on Ways and Means, Continuation of the International Coffee Agreement Act of 1968, Report to accompany H.R. 8293 Rpt. No. 92-242, 92nd Cong., 1st sess., June 2, 1971, 7.

[416]Ibid. Brazil renounced the solubles agreement in 1973 when the Coffee Council failed to agree on quotas, and in anticipation of the suspension of the ICA's regulatory features in October.

The primary beneficiaries of the new agreement, everyone could see, and some would complain, were the major producers of soluble coffee in the United States over the previous years, that is, General Foods, Nestle (US), and Folger. General Foods alone would get roughly half the Brazilian allocation of tax-free green coffee, because for several years it had produced that percentage of soluble manufactured within the United States. Not all business firms, of course, were content with the settlement; but these obviously had little standing to register their opposition effectively in the political arena. Hills Bros. of San Francisco, the most persistent and ardent opponent of restrictions on Brazilian solubles imports, was particularly disadvantaged by the Agreement, since it had processed very little soluble coffee in the past.

The State Department was content that the agreement was "satisfactory to all major [emphasis mine] interests concerned."[417] House Ways and Means, in reporting favorably on solubles settlement and in recommending that the Coffee Act now be extended to 1973, dismissed the complaints against the settlement rather summarily:

> The Committee has received a number of complaints about the United States-Brazilian agreement, mostly from small roasters and coffee importers and brokers who by and large were benefitted by the competitive situation that existed prior to the accord. None of these coffee processors produces soluble coffee in the United States. The committee is satisfied that the Agreement on soluble coffee is of interest to the U.S. coffee trade as a whole and can result in lower price to soluble coffee consumers in this country.[418]

With the solubles dispute settled, at least for the time being, it now seemed certain that the ICA Act would be readily extended by Congress. However, on the day (June 8) the Act was being considered for a rule by the House,

---

[417] Ibid., 8.

[418] Committee on Ways and Means, Continuation of the International Coffee Agreement, Report, op. cit., 9.

reports reached Congress that Brazil had been "harrassing" U.S. shrimp boats within its 200-mile territorial sea. Brazil had recently joined other Latin American countries in claiming a 200-mile limit. Again implementing legislation for the ill-starred Coffee Agreement was held up, pending some diplomatic progress towards settlement of the new dispute over territorial sea limits. On July 1st, the existing Coffee Act expired. The irony, of course, was that the solubles agreement with Brazil was suspended at the moment the Act lapsed, because its continuation, by agreement, was contingent on continuing U.S. implementation of the Coffee Agreement. The ICA Act did not clear Congress until March of 1972. Meanwhile General Foods and other firms with a stake in the new solubles agreement had reversed fields and were calling for Congressional passage of the ICA Act.

Business and Policy-Making: Relationships and Influence. Unquestionably the major soluble producers in the United States, General Foods and Nestle (US), were the most active and influential business firms in the solubles dispute, the former as it turned out, more so than the latter. General Foods felt it had too large a stake in newly constructed solubles plant capacity, not to mention its sizeable investment in the development of freeze-dry technology, to permit the Brazilian onslaught to go unchallenged. Brazil's attempt to entice GF into plant investment there were considered seriously, but rejected. Nor was the GF management overly concerned with the warnings of its International Division that Brazil might take reprisals against existing GF investment in Brazil, if GF were to take a hard line on Brazilian solubles imports into the United States. Its soluble coffee interests were considered more substantial.[419]

---

[419] Interview, Frederick Otterbein, September 22, 1971.

General Foods imported Brazilian solubles and became the primary importer— in "self-defense"— but it was also the major, if at times reluctant opponent of Brazilian imports. Several participant-observers have commented upon the rather surprising timidity with which GF, at times, advanced its claims on U.S. policy. Arnold Mayer of the Amalgamated Meatcutters believes that GF was exceedingly sensitive to charges of holding a monopoly position in the solubles market, and asserts that his Union had to constantly nudge the company into action.[420] GF sought a low profile in its dealings with the policy-makers, but as the previous narrative indicated, it was prepared to act decisively at crucial junctures in policy development.

Nestle (US) was a more ardent opponent of Brazilian imports, until May of 1970, although as early as the mid-sixties it was importing substantial amounts of soluble from its fraternal company in Brazil. How is Nestle's <u>volte face</u> of 1970 to be explained? This research has produced no conclusive evidence of why Nestle (US) first opposed the imports and then, in a break with the other major opponents, accepted the terms of the 1969 U.S. - Brazilian agreement. Nestle's Director of Purchasing during the solubles dispute has explained that his company's change of political stance in 1970 was due to the conviction, based on close study of the effects of Brazil's imposition of the 13 cent export tax, that this latter tax had indeed neutralized the unfair advantage that Brazilian exporters were getting before the tax.[421] Other business interviewees find this a completely unconvincing explanation.[422] Edward Aborn, professing no certain

---

[420] Interview, Arnold Mayer, July 30, 1971.

[421] Interview, Johann Scheu, September 24, 1971. The U.S. Embassy in Brazil reached a similar conclusion in January of 1970, when asked by the State Department to give its views on the efficacy of the 13 cent export tax.

[422] Interviews, J.M. Clark, September 28, 1971; and Edward Aborn, October 4, 1971.

knowledge of Nestle motivation, has speculated that Nestle (US) may have been positioning itself in 1970 for importing large quantities of soluble coffee from Nestle (Brazil), in which case, it would have seen considerable advantage in ending NCA efforts to place greater restrictions on solubles imports. [423]

Also it would seem plausible that the reversal of the Nestle (US) position could have had something to do with Nestle Alimentana's calculations of the multinational company's larger interests. As Coca-Cola and General Foods were subjected to pressure by Brazil through their Brazilian holdings, so it would seem quite possible that Nestle Alimentana was under pressure to overrule the U.S. company. Certainly Nestle Alimentana does, from time to time, experience the tensions of reconciling its supranational interests with the policies of its national affiliates which tend to act upon more parochial perceptions of their self-interest.

It is known, for example, that on occasion in the early phases of the international cocoa negotiations the policy preferences of the corporate leadership of Nestle (US) were at a variance with those of the leadership in Nestle Alimentana. The American executives tended to oppose the very idea of commodity agreements; but sometimes they were directed to follow Vevey's preference for a more accommodating position in the cocoa negotiations. Nestle Alimentana executives, of course, had to take a broader view of the multinational corporation's interest, accommodating a wider range of conflicting pressures, including LDC pressures to a greater extent, than any single national affiliate had to do. Greater accommodation towards the idea of commodity agreements would presumably have been a gesture to the LDCs in which there were Nestle Alimentana holdings, or in relation to which it otherwise wished to gain favor. [424]

---

[423] Ibid., (Aborn).

[424] These observations on Nestle as a multinational corporation derived from a Joint Interview, James Buckley and Johann J. Scheu, September 24, 1971.

The third and fourth ranking U.S. producers of soluble coffee, Folger (Proctor and Gamble) and Standard Brands, did not play a visible role in lobbying with the government for action on solubles; but they did align themselves with General Foods in the NCA.

Hills Bros. of San Francisco was the most vocal advocate of unrestricted Brazilian imports, among the small and medium-sized marketers of instant coffee. As its President, Reuben Hills, wrote the Assistant Secretary of State for Economic Affairs, "the availability of Brazilian instant under present conditions [1968] has made it possible for small and medium-sized marketers of instant coffee to offer their customers a better product at a competitive price," that is, to compete with the giant coffee corporations like GF. Hills, as early as 1968, called on State to "reconsider its position on the Brazilian question." He pointed out that this position was "inconsistent with the principle of aiding developing countries as expressed in the Aliance for Progress."[425] Hills Bros., it will be recalled, had closed its own solubles plant in the mid-sixties and imported and packaged a wholly Brazilian product under its own label. Its economic interest in a continued flow of Brazilian imports was evident.

Brazilian imports, it has been generally recognized, were most significant for tipping the scales of competition between the "private label" companies and the giant American producers. Nestle acknowledged as much when it complained to State that the "private label trade" was favored by Brazilian imports, but "doing least for consumption and product improvement."[426] Large food chains like A & P certainly sought to capitalize on the situation by putting their

---

[425] Letter from Reuben Hills, President of Hills Bros., to Anthony Solomon, Assistant Secretary of State for Economic Affairs, January 30, 1968, as printed in an editorial, Tea and Coffee Trade Journal, CXXXIV (March, 1968), 55.

[426] Source withheld.

own labels on Brazilian soluble. A & P, in fact, discontinued its purchases from the major "private label supplier" in the United States, Tenco. So far as this research could determine, however, the private label companies, though they stood to gain handsomely from continued Brazilian imports, did not choose to lobby strenuously, if at all, for their position. It is possible that the relative returns from coffee, in their overall income picture, were insufficiently significant to propel them into the policy-making arena against the industry giants.

Tenco deserves mention as a private label supplier that was considerably disadvantaged by Brazilian imports. In the face of these the company had to idle part of its plant capacity and lay off some 40-50 of its 600 employees. Ultimately 30-40% of its own national sales consisted of imported Brazilian imports.[427] Until early 1968 its respected President, Ed Aborn, was in the forefront of NCA efforts to gain government assistance against Brazilian policy. After that time, he himself has acknowledged, he and the parent Coca-Cola Co. retreated from this activity, due to Brazilian threats of reprisal against Coca-Cola soft drink operations in Brazil.[428] An alternative explanation for the Coca-Cola/Tenco retreat from opposition to Brazilian imports is that Coca-Cola purchased Brazil's Frusol solubles producing plant in 1968, about the time it decided to ease off its activities against Brazilian imports. Perhaps Coca-Cola was positioning itself to export coffee back into the United States. In any event, Tenco's role in the coffee industry was not particularly decisive in the final outcome of the solubles dispute.

Most of the national green coffee traders remained opposed to Brazilian solubles imports throughout the dispute, though some gradually began to participate in the trade of Brazilian soluble coffee itself. Characteristically vocal about

---

[427] Interview, Ed Aborn, October 4, 1971.

[428] Ibid.

Brazil's exploitation of the Coffee Agreement, the traders as a group were otherwise unhappy with the Coffee Agreement at the time it came up for renewal in 1968. And this new source of dissatisfaction helped propel their regional trade associations into active opposition to further U.S. participation in the Agreement. George McEvoy of J. Aron & Co., and during the period of the dispute, a Chairman of the NCA, asserts that he had been one of the strongest opponents of Brazilian policy. If allowed to subsidize their processed coffee exports to the United States (regular or instant coffee), he contends, there would be little to stop the LDCs from getting a decisive competitive advantage. "They could even afford to air freight their products to the U.S."[429] The overriding consideration for green coffee traders throughout the dispute was that imports of processed coffee products would displace corresponding amounts of green coffee trade.

It is difficult to escape the conclusion that business opponents of Brazilian solubles policy would have been satisfied with little less than sufficient measures to keep Brazilian imports at a minimum. Despite NCA and State Department rhetoric to the effect that American solubles producers were "willing to meet any kind of fair, unsubsidized competition from whatever source,"[430] it was generally recognized in the industry that Brazilian or other LDC solubles producers could not compete in the U.S. market without some special dispensation from their respective governments that would be labelled as "unfair" in the U.S.

During the five year dispute the NCA and the two major solubles producers, GF and Nestle, dominated the channels of access into the Office of

---

[429] Interview, George McEvoy, September 23, 1971.

[430] Observation by Edward Fried in speech to PCCA, May 15, 1967, as found in "Agreement is Still Part of U.S. Policy," op. cit., 26.

International Resources and Food Policy within State, although other groups were not necessarily denied access or failed to use it.[431] This office, it was noted earlier, is formally charged to "maintain liaison with industry groups concerned with the implications of international trade in tropical products." By the time the solubles dispute erupted, in fact, the NCA was in the eighth year of a rather formalized advisory relationship with the State Department. The NCA Foreign Affairs Committee, it was indicated in the previous chapter, had continually advised the Department in the negotiation and operation of the Coffee Agreement. In the course of this relationship communications between industry and State were frequent and unencumbered.

In the solubles dispute, the Deputy Assistant Secretary of State at the time remembers, the NCA influenced State, at least, to the extent of signalling the "problem" and getting State to act upon it earlier than it would otherwise have done.[432] He and his colleagues were persuaded that Brazil's policy was a menace to the ICA in that it would depress demand for green coffee, and consequently prices, and that sooner or later African or other producer opposition and countermeasures would destroy the Coffee Agreement. This argument had to be, and was accepted on the strength of its high plausibility, for the consequences foreseen never materialized. When asked by Senator Morse in 1968 whether U.S. action against Brazil's policy was taken because that policy was "doing damage to the International Coffee Agreement," Deputy Assistant Secretary of State Katz replied, "Senator, I cannot honestly say that it had yet gotten to the point where it did damage, but there was strong feeling on the part of the other countries that

---

[431] Leaders of the Amalgamated Meatcutters, however, feel that the State Department is constitutionally unresponsive to labor concerns. Arnold Mayer, their lobbyist in Washington, complains that State was specifically indifferent to labor complaints in this dispute, and this was a major reason for the Union's turning to the more receptive House Committee on Ways and Means. Interview, Arnold Mayer, July 30, 1971.

[432] Interview, Edward Fried, June 24, 1971.

if it grew it could damage the agreement."[433] On that occasion Katz underlined the conviction of the State Department that other producers "certainly supported our action," specifically citing Colombia and Guatemala.[434]

The key State Department officials were also genuinely convinced that Brazil's policy was "unfair" to an American industry that had supported the Coffee Agreement, partly for Brazil's benefit. Furthermore, they tended to view the Brazilians as experienced and shrewd, and not to be allowed quarter, as if they were of the poorest and most vulnerable of the LDCs.

Government bureaucracies often turn to interest groups for expertise on matters that are subject to policy development. This had certainly been one major reason for State's inviting the NCA to advise it on Coffee Agreement issues. There is evidence that the NCA and companies like Nestle moved quickly to provide expertise concerning the solubles dispute, or in the shape of things, partisan analysis. Nestle, for example, provided rather copious analysis of the implications of Brazilian policy; and it seems clear that the Department was receptive to Nestle arguments. At the same time, some key State officials came to believe that Brazilian policy was partly inspired by the fact that senior military officers in the government had investments in the solubles industry.[435]

Secondly, the NCA and major solubles companies had a major role in shaping policy-maker perceptions of what would be acceptable terms of settlement in the dispute. It proved impossible to trace the precise origins of either the "30 cent solution" or of the terms of the final settlement in 1971. The central

---

433 Senate Committee on Foreign Relations, International Coffee Agreement, 1968, 52.

434 Ibid., 53.

435 Interview, Edward Fried, June 24, 1971.

elements of the latter, however, were proposed early in the dispute by Brazil, but at first rejected by the U.S. The precise origin of the "30 cent solution" is even more elusive. Still it is clear from the data gathered from interviews and State Department documents that the figure evolved out of a Department consensus of what would be minimally acceptable to the NCA, based presumably upon many conversations with businessmen and their official pronouncements. When the Brazilians would not accept this as a basis for negotiation, and given the pressures for a settlement of some kind from Congress, the negotiators reverted to the proposal that was finally adopted.

The question of what measures should be taken beyond the 1969 agreement (13 cent export tax) between the two countries split not only the industry ranks, but brought the only major fissure among policy-makers in the State Department. A Deputy Director of the Office of Brazilian Affairs recalls that there were several heated sessions between his Office and the Office of International Resources and Food Policy over whether or not more concessions should be expected of Brazil. "We insisted," he said, "that the Economics Bureau could easily hurt our relations with Brazil without otherwise accomplishing restraints on her imports." "They thought we were parochial-minded and only taking into account our client's interests."[436] Finally, he states, "Our consensus focused on what minimum we could ask of Brazil while still preserving the Agreement."[437]

Despite the purported "consensus," the "minimum" to be expected of Brazil remained an increase of Brazil's export tax, or in the end, the demanding

---

[436] Several interviews reflected the familiar observation about foreign affairs bureaucracies that differences of perspective and orientation characterize area and functional desks respectively. Interviewees in the area desks tend to see the Office of International Resources as somewhat indulgent towards American business, while officers in the latter complain of "clientitis" among desk officers, that is, excessive zeal in behalf of the countries with which they deal.

[437] Interview, Richard E. Lippincott, July 28, 1971.

terms of the agreement achieved. Still, according to George Maciel, a decidedly pro-Brazil observer, the intercession of the Office of Brazilian Affairs had been advantageous to Brazil.[438]

Finally business, or more pointedly, General Foods in collaboration with the Amalgamated Meatcutters, indirectedly forced a settlement favorable to itself by enlisting the assistance of the sympathetic House Ways and Means Committee. The Bureau of Economic Affairs, despite its several reasons for believing in the merits of the General Foods case—considerations of "equity" and so on—was not enthusiastic about exerting pressure on Brazil for concessions. After 1969 there was conflict within State over how much pressure should be put on Brazil. Business and labor had all along been restive over State's slowness and indecisiveness in acting against Brazil. A resort to Congress was a rather obvious fall-back measure, and as early as 1967 or 1968, General Foods, at least, was using this lever.

The NCA proper, although it very early threatened resort to Congress, never seems to have acted upon this threat. During 1968 it and major producing firms declined the invitation of the Senate Foreign Relations Committee to testify for their position, presumably on the grounds that they would be vulnerable to charges of protectionism.[439] Significantly, after the NCA's reversal of its position on Brazilian solubles in 1970, the Association still did not lobby with Congress.

---

[438] Interview, George Maciel, July 16, 1971.

[439] Senator Albert Gore, even in the absence of business witnesses, was strongly critical of State Department efforts on behalf of business. "The purpose," he declared, "which the U.S. Government for some strange reason sought was to make the soluble coffee from Brazil competitive with the prices established by the coffee trust in the United States." U.S., Congress, Senate, Committee on Foreign Relations, International Coffee Agreement, 1968, 45.

Before and after this time it was General Foods, in collaboration with the Amalgamated Meatcutters, that opted to instigate Congressional pressure on the State Department.

In the coffee and cocoa agreement cases the point is made that actual or potential Congressional participation in policy-making affords business and other interest groups additional opportunities to influence bureaucratic behavior. The solubles case illustrates this point concretely and vividly.

"The urgency of the solubles issue," a State Department officer has noted, "was almost solely a function of the fragility of the consensus supporting the Coffee Agreement."[440] The ICA, it was shown earlier, had never excited great enthusiasm in Congress, and indeed Chairman Wilbur Mills had had to exert considerable effort to fend off conservative opponents. When in 1970 the Congress was again called on to extend the ICA Act the moment was particularly propitious for successful interest group intervention. At this time Congress was becoming increasingly favorable to measures to protect purportedly disadvantaged American industries for a variety of products. Also the crucial legislator, Chairman Mills, was growing personally impatient with what he perceived as Brazil's disregard for American magnanimity in supporting the Coffee Agreement.

State Department officials had very early recognized the dangers to the consensus within the American policy-making system favoring the Coffee Agreement.[441] While those in the Bureau of Economics were strongly convinced of the merits of the industry case against Brazil's imports, they were for policy purposes all the more impressed by the possibility that business disaffection from the ICA could undermine tenuous Congressional support for the Agreement.

---

[440] Interview, Richard Lippincott, July 28, 1971.

[441] Interview, Edward Fried, June 24, 1971.

They were not eager to challenge Brazilian efforts to "industrialize" coffee; but they felt that the circumstances of this effort placed them in a double-bind. Believing they were compelled to make a choice between preserving the Coffee Agreement and allowing Brazilian imports to come into the country unimpeded, they opted for the former. In the latter stages of the dispute, key officials were all the more certain that their range of choice was limited. To Julius Katz, who became Deputy Assistant Secretary of State in 1969, the "issue" was quite simply a "political issue," involving whether or not the Coffee Agreement could be preserved.[442]

General Foods' capacity to move events toward a settlement rested heavily upon a fortuitous combination of factors— Congressional participation in policy-making at critical junctures; the State Department's priority on preserving the Coffee Agreement; and Brazil's undoubted susceptibility to pressures from other coffee producing countries that feared American disaffection from the Coffee Agreement and competition from Brazilian solubles itself. Its predominance in the solubles industry and its preeminence in the NCA, not to mention its alliance with the Amalgamated Meatcutters, favored its getting its way.

The case-study, however, does not support the conclusion that General Foods' success was foreordained by a "client" relationship with the State Department; nor did GF "dictate" State Department policy. If the Brazilian challenge had arisen outside the context of a Coffee Agreement—which, contrary to business protestations, is not unthinkable— the nature and outcome of the dispute might have been considerably different. It would have been much more difficult for soluble producers to secure State Department or Congressional support for

---

442 Interview, Julius Katz, July 15, 1971.

tariffs or other import restrictions than it was to gain their sympathy for diplomatic action in the context of the Coffee Agreement, which, it could be argued, Brazil had transgressed.

CHAPTER VI

American Business and the Cocoa Negotiations

The quest for an international cocoa agreement, that would embrace all major producing and consuming countries, is a minor epic in the diplomatic history of the last fifteen years. Under the aegis of the FAO and UNCTAD, respectively, there have been no fewer than four full-dress conferences in Geneva and New York to negotiate an agreement (1963, 1966, 1967 and 1972), and almost countless preparatory consultations since 1956. Not until the 1972 Geneva conference was the first International Cocoa Agreement actually achieved; and even this Agreement seemed unlikely to come into force, until West Germany, an initial holdout with the United States, changed its position and signed the Agreement. The Cocoa Agreement came into force provisionally during the summer of 1973, and the London-based Cocoa Organization was founded.

The new Cocoa Agreement combines export control and buffer stock mechanisms to regulate the market, and its membership represents 70 percent of the world's consumption and 90 percent of its production. Significantly, the United States has refused to sign the Agreement. It remains to be seen whether the pact can survive, let alone flourish, without the participation of the single most important consuming nation, or whether or not the U.S. will ultimately accede to pressure to join the Agreement.

Reviewing the history of abortive cocoa agreement negotiations up to 1972, the LDC observer was apt to fault the United States, and secondarily other consuming countries, for the failure to "organize" the cocoa market. He was also likely to assert that the American cocoa industry was, to a large degree, accountable for what was perceived as a conservative or distinctly negative bias in U.S. policy towards LDC proposals for a cocoa agreement. Now that the Common market countries have opted to support the Cocoa Agreement of 1972, despite American opposition, it is likely that U.S. policy, and alleged industry influence thereon, will be all the more the object of LDC criticism. This chapter assesses the validity of LDC claims about business influence on U.S. cocoa agreement policy, in a ten year perspective.

The frequency of LDC charges that the American cocoa industry has had a decisively negative influence on U.S. policy towards cocoa agreement proposals, prompted a State Department officer, as recently as 1971, to assure his colleagues in an internal Department memorandum that "Allegations that the U.S. industry has played a major role in the shaping of U.S. Government policy on this subject [cocoa agreement negotiations] are incorrect, and are not borne out by the record. "We do not view," he added, "the attitude of the U.S. industry as an obstacle to the conclusion of, or to Congressional acceptance of, an effective and reasonable Agreement."[443]

On the basis of this research, it is possible to understand the occasionally expressed consternation of U.S. government officials at charges that their reservations about cocoa market regulation have been primarily, or even exclusively due to the restraining hand of the domestic cocoa industry. Again, as in the case of coffee, it is clear that several factors, for example, perceived economic conditions in the cocoa market, help account for U.S. positions in cocoa diplomacy during these years. The mono-causal explanations, including the assertion that the State Department marches to the drum of the American cocoa industry, do not hold up.

---

[443] Source withheld.

On the other hand, this research tends to contradict the confident assurances of the aforementioned State Department officer that the domestic industry has had no "major role in the shaping of U.S. Government policy." In different phases of the long cocoa negotiations, government officials have viewed industry attitudes as an "obstacle," if not necessarily an insuperable obstacle, to securing Congressional approval to any agreement that might be presented to Congress. Without other strongly compelling reasons for entering an agreement, they have tended to be reluctant to negotiate an agreement that might encounter industry opposition in Congress.

Analysis of the business-government relationships in policy-making for cocoa must proceed at a fairly high level of abstraction. The cocoa negotiations span a long period of time and four American presidencies. They have been so extensive and intricate, as to defy the most modest efforts to reconstruct their evolution. It would be even more difficult to reconstruct all the twists and turns of governmental policies, for the U.S. alone, but certainly for all the major governments concerned. The difficulty of analysis is compounded when one attempts to trace the evolution of government policies, or of industry positions, regarding all the specific terms of numerous agreements that have been proposed.

At the risk of gross oversimplification, this study focuses on what seems to have been the general orientation of the United States over the years, concerning the question of whether there should be a cocoa agreement at all, and if so, on what terms. Secondly, it considers the U.S. approach to the most important and divisive issue—price objectives in proposed cocoa agreements. In this context, it should be possible to be relatively precise about the nature and impact of the cocoa industry relationships to policy-making.

Cocoa Negotiations Reviewed. Other studies have surveyed the evolution of cocoa negotiations up, at least, to 1967.[444] Ironically, cocoa was first placed on the agenda of international organization, when two major consuming countries, Belgium and Switzerland, appealed in 1956 to the United Nations Economic and Social Council and OEEC, respectively, for study of the world cocoa market. Their initiatives, though prompted by a period of very high cocoa prices in 1954 which they believed attributable to Gold Coast Marketing Board policies, led shortly thereafter to the founding of the Cocoa Study Group, under the Food and Agricultural Organization.

By the time, however, representatives of 24 nations, including the United States, met in November to organize the new study group, a new trend of declining prices was in the making.

In the period since 1956 the impetus for commodity agreement negotiations has invariably derived from a phase of declining or "low" prices. Also since that year, development-minded, cocoa producing nations, most of which are African countries that came to independence in 1957-1960, have seized the initiative for cocoa market regulation. In 1964 the LDC-oriented United Nations Conference on Trade and Development took over direction of the cocoa negotiations from FAO, and inspired by the achievement of the Coffee Agreement two years earlier, set a cocoa agreement as a goal of highest priority. Cocoa was an immediate and obvious candidate for market regulation, since there had been several years of preparatory negotiations and since prices were at an historic

---

[444] For a detailed study of negotiations from the late fifties through the abortive 1963 and 1966 Cocoa Conferences see Wayne A. Schutjer and Edward Jide Ayo, Negotiating a World Cocoa Agreement: Analysis and Prospects, Bulletin 744, October 1967 (University Park, Pennsylvania: The Pennsylvania State University, College of Agriculture, Agricultural Experiment Station, 1967).

low at the time UNCTAD came on the scene. But UNCTAD leaders were also intent that a cocoa agreement should be a step in the direction of a more comprehensive system of commodity agreements for numerous commodities.[445]

The FAO Study Group was established in 1956 to provide a forum for consultation and for the dissemination of accurate information on supply and demand conditions. At the first meeting of the Group in Brussels, for the primary purpose of organization, a Nigerian delegate's assertion that the time had come for international regulation of the cocoa market was greeted unenthusiastically, even by other producer delegations.

At the Ibadan meeting of the Group in September of 1957, however, the idea of a stabilization agreement was discussed openly, and thereafter, would continually be at the center of international discussions of the cocoa market. Most of the major issues of market regulation that would be aired repeatedly in subsequent meetings were introduced at Ibadan. Delegates rejected the idea of a closely regulated market that would require <u>export</u> controls, and concentrated instead upon a buffer stock arrangement that would be employed to brake price movements above or below a negotiated range. The meeting became deadlocked over producer-consumer disagreement over who should bear the substantial costs of a buffer stock. The consuming countries indicated they would expect the producers to finance the stock, and through all the years of negotiations have never abandoned this position. The most substantive action of the Ibadan meeting was to establish a small working group with the mandate of devising a scheme for market regulation.

Eight industry leaders accompanied the U.S. delegation to the Ibadan meeting. Alwyn Fischel, a cocoa trader with the firm of A.C. Israel & Co.,

---

[445] Interview, Raul Prebisch, April 20, 1971.

and then a major spokesman for the industry, recalls that he urged the Study Group to acknowledge the effectiveness of the cocoa exchanges in helping the market to adjust to periods of heavy cocoa production.[446] This has been a constant theme of the American cocoa industry, which, strongly committed to the use of cocoa exchange as the linchpin of a free market for cocoa, has insisted that no system of market regulation compromise the operations of these exchanges.

Four more Study Groups sessions were held in the years leading up to the first Cocoa Conference (1963). For the most part these sessions concentrated upon numerous proposals for regulatory regimes, and tended to skirt the devisive issue of price objectives.

At Hamburg (1958) discussion focused upon buffer stock proposals, and at subsequent sessions on either export or sales quota systems, sometimes in combination with a buffer stock.[447] A relatively stable and sound market in the crop year 1958-1959 momentarily deflated the efforts for market regulation—again producer advocates of regulation tend to retreat when the market is strong—but in 1960 prices were once again weak and unstable.

Declining cocoa prices between 1960 and 1963 coincided with the coming of the Kennedy Administration, and as previous chapters have indicated, a greater willingness in Washington to consider proposals for commodity market

---

[446] Interview, Alwyn Fischel, March 29, 1972.

[447] Some experts believe that only a sales quota regime, possibly in conjunction with a buffer stock, can effectively regulate the cocoa market. A high percentage of cocoa transactions are based on "forward" sales, several months in advance of actual delivery. The contention is that "sales," and not exports of actual cocoa, must be regulated. The Cocoa Agreement of 1972 contains provision for export quotas.

regulation on their merits, on a case-by-case basis. The Kennedy Administration, in fact, set first priority on dealing with the problems of the coffee market; but an European observer is probably correct that the change of administrations, in addition to conditions in the market, gave fresh impetus to the otherwise languishing cocoa negotiations.[448]

In May of 1962 four African countries and Brazil began to concert their efforts in the Cocoa Producers Alliance (CPA).[449] That same month at the Montreux session of the Cocoa Study Group, a working party was instructed to develop a draft cocoa agreement for a formal negotiating conference. The draft from this group was presented to the sixth and final session of the Coffee Study Group at Port-of-Spain, Trinidad, in March of 1963.

The Port-of-Spain conference approved a negotiable draft, with the consent of all major producers and consumers, and called on the United Nations to convene a formal Cocoa Conference to consider it. The draft called for a sales quota system administered by an International Cocoa Council, but for no buffer stock. It also contained a formula for establishing a range of maximum and minimum prices, between which the Cocoa Council would attempt to regulate prices prices by the imposition of sales quotas, and an 'intervention" price at which quotas would be imposed. The key provision was that at the lower limits of a negotiated price range producers would restrict their sales, according to agreed quotas. Importantly, the draft did not contain specific price figures, only a formula that would apply when those were determined by negotiation.

---

[448] Marcel Oechslin, Formation des prix du Cacao et possibilité de leur stabilisation, (Zürich: Glättli, 1965), 101.

[449] Ghana, Nigeria, Ivory Coast, Cameroon and Brazil.

At Port-of-Spain the producers continued to decline to negotiate the issue of specific price ranges for regulation; however, the United States, which had pressed for an exploratory discussion of prices, came away satisfied that other major consumers were agreed with it on what minimum price should be defended.

The first U.N. Cocoa Conference (September 26-October 24, 1963), the U.S. Government believed, was convened in the belief that a "solid basis existed for the negotiation of a comprehensive international cocoa agreement."[450] This belief, the U.S. delegates later reported, quickly proved to be "erroneous."[451] In the event, the producing nations called for support of cocoa prices at a minimum price of 31.25 cents per pound, or finally for an intervention price of no less than 27 cents (the prevailing price at the time of the conference was 25 cents). The consumers proposed a minimum of 18 cents, but most, excepting the U.S., were finally prepared to consider an intervention price of 20 cents.

From the very outset, the American delegates contended, the consuming countries were "stunned" by the producer conception of price objectives for the agreement. In their view, the producer advocacy of "an international effort to raise average [cocoa] returns substantially above what normal market forces would dictate was entirely contrary to the basis on which the present draft agreement [1963] was developed.[452] "Consumers indicated," the U.S. delegates reported, that "they were not prepared to subscribe to the notion that

---

[450] U.S., Department of State, "Report of the United States Delegation to the United Nations Cocoa Conference, September 26-October 24, 1963," Unpublished report submitted to the Secretary of State by the U.S. delegate, Jerome Jacobson, 1963, 5.

[451] Ibid.

[452] Ibid.

the Agreement be used as a device to transfer resources from the consuming countries to the producing countries." Further, "the propriety and feasibility of using an international cocoa agreement for this purpose had never been discussed in the long preparatory meetings leading up to this Conference." "The draft agreement," they concluded, "had been conceived by all the participants as essentially a standby agreement to prevent a ruinous price collapse in the event of another sudden upsurge in production such as occurred in 1960-61."[453]

The gruelling negotiations of this first U.N. Cocoa Conference continued for a month; but the "wide gap between producers and consumers on the price issue cast a general pall on the work of the other [Conference] committees."[454] "None of the other major issues," the American delegates reported, "were resolved--the structure of the organization, the distribution of votes, the quota mechanism, measures to expand consumption, financing of stocks, etc."[455]

The controversy over price ranges for market regulation, evidenced at that Conference, has been a hardy perennial of all subsequent cocoa negotiations. This controversy, most observers believe, has reflected a more fundamental cleavage, at least, until the 1972 Cocoa Agreement, between consumers and producers over the legitimate purposes of a commodity agreement.

Tony Killick, the British economist and cocoa trade expert, has asserted that "It is possible to explain the failure of the 1963 conference as the

---

[453] Ibid., 5-6.

[454] Ibid., 7.

[455] Ibid.

result of a disagreement between the producers and the consumers as to the proper purpose of an International Cocoa Agreement."[456] This, he points out, expressed itself in the manner in which the two sides sought to justify their divergent views on what price ranges should be contained in an agreement.

"An International Cocoa Agreement can only be meaningful for us," the producers asserted after the collapse of the Conference, "if it helps to avoid extremes of high and low prices on the cocoa market, if it is designed to stabilise and gradually expand [emphasis mine] the foreign exchange earnings of exporters, and if it is able to re-establish their terms of trade at a more reasonable level than they have been in the recent past."[457] In reply, Jerome Jacobson, Deputy Secretary of State, expressed the more conservative attitude of the consumers towards the purpose of an agreement. An agreement, he said, should provide a "means of insuring producers against very serious losses in their foreign exchange earnings if we should again enter a period where substantial surpluses were built up."[458]

Killick is, undoubtedly, correct that attempts to negotiate a cocoa agreement depend fundamentally upon compatible views of an agreement's basic function. He is possibly correct that the producers could have secured an agreement in 1963, if they had been willing to accept a pact, conceived simply to protect against serious price lows and general instability of prices.[459]

---

[456] Killick, in A Study of Contemporary Ghana, Chapter 11, 383.

[457] Final Joint Statement by the Delegations of the Producing Countries, October 24, 1963, as found in U.S. Department of State, "Report on the United Nations Cocoa Conference," Annex B, 1.

[458] Final Joint Statement, by the Delegations of Importing Countries, October 24, 1963, as found in Ibid., Annex C, 2.

[459] Killick, op. cit., 385.

It should be recalled that the Coffee Agreement was achieved in 1962, when consumers and producers agreed simply upon the imperative of keeping coffee prices from dropping below their 1962 level. Producers were in dire enough circumstances to accept this minimalist definition of price objectives; and the consumer preference for limited intervention in the market could be easily accommodated.

After the abortive 1963 Conference cocoa prices continued to fall. In March of 1965 they reached a post-WWII low. During 1964-65, producer organizational efforts to shore up the market proceeded on several fronts. The Cocoa Producers Alliance implemented their own export quota agreement, but this collapsed quickly, as one or more of the participants broke ranks and exceeded their quotas.

Nine months after its inception UNCTAD moved to resume serious negotiations for an agreement, and set up a working group to prepare the way. Meanwhile President Kwame Nkrumah of Ghana urged that developed countries of the Commonwealth respond to the economic plight of the cocoa producers, and in September of 1965 actually proposed a Commonwealth control and compensatory finance scheme. His call for British and French leadership to assist the cocoa producers foreshadowed the Cocoa Agreement of 1973, when major importers of the Common Market formed the central bloc of consumer support for an Agreement, over the objections of the United States.

The second U.N. Cocoa Conference was held at United Nations headquarters in May and June of 1966. The draft text for negotiation proposed a price range of about ten cents, again without specifying the upper and lower price limits; and it provided for a sales quota system, as well as for the first time, a buffer stock mechanism to supplement the quota arrangements.

Thirty-nine consuming and producing countries once again labored mightily for one month to bring forth a cocoa agreement. But again, despite considerable progress on many issues, they were stymied on the question of what the minimum price of the range for regulations should be. This time, however, the extent of the difference between the consumers and producers was considerably less than it had been in 1963. The consuming countries initially favored an 18 cent minimum, but as in 1963, some such as Great Britain and France, were prepared to go to 19 cents, or if one source is correct, to 20 cents.[460] The United States, despite some wavering, held adamently to the 18 cent figure. The producing countries initially asked a minimum of 21 to 22 cents per pound, and were prepared to accept 19 cents, or certainly 20 cents.[461]

According to Frederick Arkhurst, Ghana's chief delegate to the Conference, the disagreement over minimum price "which brought this conference to an unsuccessful conclusion is not so much between producers and consumers as between the United States delegation and all other delegations." He intimated that the U.S. position, in turn, was heavily influenced by American industry advisers at the Conference.[462]

The advisers themselves remember the 1966 Conference as the one occasion on which their consensus on the cocoa agreement talks nearly suffered

---

460 "New York Talks Break Down," West Africa, (July 2, 1966), 749.

461 Julian Hemphill, Hershey Chocolate Corporation, who attended the conference, indicates that UNCTAD Secretary-General Raul Prebisch had persuaded the producers to accept 19 cents, but that the United States, under strong industry pressure, would not accept this figure. Interview, Julian Hemphill, February 9, 1972.

462 "New York Talks Break Down," op. cit., 749.

a serious, and for them, disastrous breakdown. For reasons not altogether clear, Julian Hemphill, the Hershey executive and leader of the industry advisers, was prepared at one point to accept a 19 cent minimum price, and to lead the industry in support of an agreement—a phenomenal turn of events considering Hershey's normal opposition to market regulation. Hemphill himself concedes that this was the case, and explains that he and the industry's Washington lobbyist, Thomas Finney, concluding that the U.S. government was about to commit itself to an agreement anyway, wished to secure the most satisfactory compromise terms possible.[463] Hemphill's position precipitated immediate resistance from the other industry advisers. With the help of Nestle (US), not represented at this particular Conference, they persuaded the top managers of Hershey Corp. to disown Hemphill's acquiesence in an agreement. The successful coup by junior members of the industry delegation forced Hemphill to retreat from his position, and was probably pivotal in holding the U.S. delegation to its initial position favoring an 18 cent minimum price.

Despite crucial differences over the price issue, substantial agreement was achieved at the Conference on several other issues.[464] This progress, in addition to the ostensibly narrowing range of differences over minimum price, encouraged the participating countries to pass a resolution calling for a resumption of the Conference before the end of 1966.

Although events moved more slowly than many had hoped, intense diplomatic preparations over the following months led to a third Cocoa Conference at the end of 1967. Meanwhile diplomatic conditions favorable to an agreement were being rapidly undercut by a new phase of dramatically rising prices (1965–68).

---

[463] Interview, Raul Prebisch, April 20, 1971.

[464] For a list of points of agreement, see Schutjer and Ayo, op. cit., 34.

After the 1966 Conference Ghana, the leading producer, and the United States, the leading consumer, entered into bilateral talks (May-June, 1967) to find a basis for agreement that would be negotiable in a full Conference.[465] UNCTAD Secretary-General Raul Prebisch personally aided these talks. Frederick Arkhurst, leader of the official Ghanaian delegation to Washington, recalls that his primary mission was to get the U.S. to accept the idea of a 20 cent minimum price for regulation, the very price minimum that it had rejected a year before. He reports that surprisingly Assistant Secretary of State, Anthony Solomon, accepted this minimum, and that this paved the way to a bilateral "Memorandum of Agreement" on all major provisions that should be contained in a future cocoa agreement.[466]

It has proven impossible to corroborate Arkhurst's further contention that the U.S. subsequently reneged on its commitment to a 20 cent minimum—"maybe because the industry intervened again"—even though in later years it was inclined again to a lower minimum. For in October of 1967, at cocoa consultations in Geneva, it joined thirteen other countries in a public Memorandum of Agreement, based on the bilateral pact with Ghana. The Geneva Memorandum, as expanded into a "Package Deal" in June, a State Department memorandum indicates, provided for a target price range of 20 to 29 cents, a sales quota system to defend the minimum price, and a buffer stock to defend both the minimum and maximum prices.[467]

The failure of the third U.N. Cocoa Conference in Geneva at the end of 1967, West Africa reported, came as some surprise, inasmuch as a firm

---

465 Interview, Raul Prebisch, April 20, 1971.

466 Interview, Frederick Arkhurst, March 26, 1971. Report corroberated by Prebisch in Interview, April 20, 1971.

467 Source withheld.

consensus on all vital issues had been achieved in preceding consultations.[468] The reasons for the failure appear more obscure than for the earlier conferences. One view is that minimum price was again the sticking point. Brazil's position that the agreed 20 cent minimum should not include freight and insurance charges, was not acceptable to the United States and other consuming countries.[469] Another view is that the Ivory Coast and France, which had already expressed reservations about the "Package Deal," were disinclined to have an agreement at all, even though they challenged seemingly minor points in the draft agreement.[470] Raul Prebisch has expressed a third view, that rising prices at the time greatly dampened producer enthusiasm for an agreement, and that this, coupled with normal consumer skepticism, removed the pressures for compromise. Favorable market conditions, he asserts, disupted the "solid fraternity of producers."[471]

During 1969 cocoa prices reached their highest level in years. Not unpredictably, the producing countries at the continuing Geneva consultations contended for higher price targets for market regulation. Or more to the point, they were not enthusiastic about market regulation at all. In June of 1969 Brazil proposed a price minimum (25 cents) that surprised even the other producers. Late in the year, however, prices dipped downwards once again. This set the scene for the fourth and productive Conference of September-October, 1972.

---

468 "Cocoa Talks Collapse Again," West Africa, LI (December 30, 1967), 1675.

469 Ibid. Also see: "Cocoa: Twelve Years in Search of a World Pact," West Africa, LII (July 13, 1968), 813.

470 Interview, Julian Hemphill, February 10, 1972.

471 Interview, Raul Prebisch, April 20, 1971.

At this Conference, nearly a decade after the first of its kind, the first International Cocoa Agreement was successfully negotiated. What might have been an occasion for great celebration, however, was marred by the refusal of the United States, and temporarily, West Germany, to sign the Agreement.

The pivotal difference in this Conference was that the major European consuming countries— West Germany has subsequently signed the Agreement— were prepared to submerge any doubts they may have had about the terms of the Agreement, and to act independently of the United States. The role of the European countries in the last decade of cocoa negotiations invites independent study. At different points in this period one or more European countries has been more sanguine about the idea of an agreement than the United States has ever been. It is probable, as many observers and diplomats believe, that British and European ties with Africa, originating in the colonial period, have fostered greater sympathies for an Agreement to regulate the trade of a product largely produced on that continent, much as U.S.-Latin American ties certainly helped to foster the Coffee Agreement.

Nonetheless, the United States was and remains opposed to the new Agreement. It holds that the pact is generally unwieldy and unworkable, that the export quota mechanism is inappropriate, and above all, that the minimum price of 23 cents set for regulation is unacceptable. Nor have the political dynamics of policy-making for this phase of cocoa agreement negotiations, it will be shown in subsequent pages, been much different than in previous phases.

It remains to be seen whether the new International Cocoa Organization, headquartered in London, can function effectively, or at all, so long as the United States, which accounts for about 25% of world imports, remains outside. Certainly in the short-run, since prices in 1973 moved above the top of the range for regulation, due to a cocoa shortage and heavy speculation, the Cocoa Organization has begun operations under relatively adverse conditions.

The United States and the Cocoa Negotiations. As in the case of coffee, it is important to characterize what the official U.S. orientation to the cocoa negotiations has been, and the several factors that probably have accounted for it. This will place in perspective the nature and impact of the cocoa industry role in policy-making.

It would be incorrect to say that the United States has been opposed, in principle, to a cocoa agreement, during the years under study. It is doubtful that the government would have maintained a charade of negotiating an agreement for so long, without some degree of interest in securing what it would consider a "reasonable" agreement. Furthermore, there is positive evidence that, at least in certain phases, it has acted upon the assumption that such an agreement should be sought, and might practically be achieved. For example, in the period of 1966-1967 key officers in the State Department's Bureau of Economic Affairs worked intensively for an agreement, and expecting that one was imminent, advised the Secretary of State that approval to negotiate for an agreement should be given in the anticipation that considerable political effort would have to be expended to secure Congressional acceptance.[472]

The U.S. is opposed to the Cocoa Agreement of 1972, has generally been opposed to the producers' conception of an agreement, and as a logical extension of the latter, has frequently opposed particular terms of proposals advanced by the producers, notably the minimum prices at which producers have desired market support.

---

[472] Interview, Paul Callanan, January 26, 1972. Anthony M. Solomon, Assistant Secretary of State for Economic Affairs in the mid-sixties, has asserted: "I pressed hard for a properly functioning international cocoa agreement." Letter from Anthony M. Solomon to author, April 6, 1972.

There has been a consistent theme in U.S. policy positions throughout the years that has frequently put the United States at odds with the producers. This is that the free market system is basically sound and viable for cocoa trade. Any cocoa agreement, consequently, should be conceived as an "insurance" scheme, one that protects against the worst extremes of price movement, particularly low prices, while interfering as little as possible with the workings of the free market. The U.S. position has really not changed, in this respect, since 1963 when State Department officials were quite explicit in their views about the purposes of the agreement then under negotiation. Speaking for the consuming countries, Jerome Jacobson, the U.S. delegate to the Cocoa Conference, asserted that the consumers looked upon commodity agreements "as a means of insuring producers against very serious losses in their foreign exchange earnings."[473] In other words, Jacobson later reported to the Secretary of State, "The draft agreement [1963] had been conceived...as essentially a standby agreement to prevent a ruinous price collapse."[474]

U.S. officials also indicated in this period that any market regulation should "recognize the essential role of private trade in moving increasing quantities of cocoa into consumption."[475] Or as W. Michael Blumenthal, Deputy Assistant Secretary of State, asserted, "An agreement, properly timed and

---

473 Final Joint Statement by the Delegations of Importing Countries, October 24, 1963, as found in U.S., Department of State, "Report on the United Nations Cocoa Conference," Annex C, 2.

474 "Report on the United Nations Cocoa Conference," 5-6.

475 Statement by Henry Brodie, U.S. delegate to the Committee on Commodity Problems of the FAO Study Group, Provisional Summary Record of the Sixth and Final Meeting, March 29, 1963, as found in "The Proposed International Cocoa Agreement," Appendix B, 22.

administered, can help stabilize export incomes of producing countries at reasonable levels and encourage the growth of markets through traditional channels of trade and the free enterprise system."[476]

The circumstances surrounding the U.S. decision to enter the FAO Cocoa Study Group in 1956 are more obscure than those attending U.S. entry into the Coffee Study Group the next year. This decision, ironically, seems to have been taken with less reservation and fanfare than that for the Coffee Group. Possibly the Eisenhower Administration expected less pressure for a commodity agreement in the cocoa forum than it did in its coffee counterpart. Some such reasoning would have to explain why it readily entered the Cocoa Group, but more hesitantly joined the Coffee Group.

Thomas Mann, the Assistant Secretary of State for Economic Affairs in the mid-fifties when proposals for cocoa market regulation first appeared, has only vague recollections of government thinking on these proposals at the time. Essentially, however, he remembers that the idea of U.S. support for a cocoa agreement was a "non-starter." Bureaucratic initiatives, such as he took for the Coffee Agreement, he recalls, are based upon some prior calculation of their changes of being accepted within the policy-making system. He doubts that there was much chance then of securing support for a cocoa agreement, or for that matter, that a cocoa agreement would have been viable.[477]

Michael Blumenthal, former Deputy Assistant Secretary of State, has a more vivid memory of how the issue of cocoa market regulation was treated in the early part of the Kennedy Administration. In the State Department's systematic study of prospects for commodity market regulation, conducted by

---

476 Letter from W. Michael Blumenthal to Julian Hemphill, Hershey Chocolate Corporation, April 12, 1963, as found in Rashish, "The Proposed International Cocoa Agreement," Appendix C, 24.

477 Interview, Thomas Mann, August 20, 1971.

Blumenthal's Office in 1961, it was decided that cocoa was one of the few products that might warrant a commodity agreement. But for a variety of economic and political reasons, discussed earlier, immediate priority was placed upon dealing with the problems of the coffee market.[478]

Even then, Blumenthal acknowledges, "George Ball [Kennedy's Under Secretary of State for Economic Affirs] and most of us were less sympathetic toward a cocoa agreement [than a Coffee Agreement]." In the first instance, he explains, the "economic rationale was never as clearcut as for coffee." Unlike coffee, cocoa could not be easily stored and withheld from the market as quota types of agreement would require. Secondly, "cocoa production takes place in some of the least of the less developed countries and there was grave doubt that the minimum discipline required to operate an agreement would be forthcoming." Third, most of the cocoa producers enjoyed preferential prices in the consumer markets of Europe, and were being substantially helped in that framework. Fourth, Blumenthal remembers there was a feeling within the government that in this period cocoa prices were at "quite satisfactory levels." Finally, he says, "the cocoa industry made a great point of the price sensitivity of cocoa products while it appears that the demand for coffee is really more inelastic." He implies that the government shared this industry viewpoint.[479]

"There were political arguments in favor of an Agreement," he adds, presumably referring to the opportunities to bolster the cocoa-producing countries economically and politically, to secure diplomatic favor with them, and to accommodate UNCTAD purposes, "but these, too, were less persuasive because Latin America was not nearly so intimately involved," as in the Coffee Agreement. Furthermore, many fewer countries would benefit from a cocoa agreement than would from the Coffee Agreement."

---

[478] Interview, W. Michael Blumenthal, October 13, 1971.

[479] Letter from W. Michael Blumenthal to author, October 20, 1971.

Furthermore, "many fewer countries would benefit from a cocoa agreement than would from the Coffee Agreement."[480]

Blumenthal also recalls that internal political factors further dampened any enthusiasm the Administration might have had for a cocoa agreement. The domestic industry was opposed to an agreement, and policy-makers anticipated difficulties of securing the requisite Senate consent to ratification and Congressional implementing legislation. By 1963, he also adds, "the enthusiasm [for policy initiatives] of the first couple of years of the Kennedy Administration had waned."[481]

In neither economic nor political terms, Blumenthal concludes, was the "urgency" of the cocoa market situation clearly enough established to inspire strong initiatives for a cocoa agreement. The United States would negotiate in good faith for a reasonable agreement (meaning one that would attempt to insure against extreme prices), but without great enthusiasm.[482]

One member of the U.S. delegation to the Cocoa Conference in 1963 contends that the delegation's negotiating instructions placed "impossible restraints" upon it. "We said we would be interested in an agreement," he remembers, "but we had to be overly careful." "Our position was quite conservative, and in all honesty, we were not that sincere about the negotiations. We had to bend over backwards to the cocoa industry."[483]

Jerome Jacobson, the U.S. delegate to the Conference, has similar recollections. He describes George Ball as having been "opposed" to a cocoa

---

[480] Ibid.

[481] Ibid.

[482] Ibid.

[483] Source withheld.

agreement, or at least, as having been unwilling to make reasonable concessions on the crucial minimum price issue. When negotiations shifted to the question of "intervention price," the price at which quotas would come into effect automatically, the most Ball would concede was a 19 cent trigger price, instead of the 18 cent price that the U.S. had advocated as a minimum price. Jacobson believes that consumers and producers would never have come together at this Conference, but also that the U.S. need not have isolated itself from the several major consumers which were prepared to accept even a 20 cent intervention price. "George Ball," Jacobson concludes, "simply did not want to make the American cocoa industry unhappy."[484]

According to Anthony Solomon, former Assistant Secretary of State for Economic Affairs, "we came very close to agreement with the cocoa producing countries" in the period of the 1966 and 1967 conferences.[485] At the 1966 Conference in New York City the outcome was very uncertain until the final moment of failure. A United Nations official recalls, in fact, that there were strong differences within the American official delegation over whether it should press ahead to agreement, or as happened, withdraw.[486] At this time the industry position was distinctly pivotal. If Julian Hemphill's (Hershey) momentary conversion to support the terms of the agreement then under discussion—especially a 19 cent minimum price which producers were prepared to accept—had prevailed, there would likely have been an agreement. In the event, industry resistance tipped the delicate scales of U.S. policy-making against an agreement.

The U.S.-Ghanaian "Memorandum of Agreement," reached in subsequent months, did not hold up at the Cocoa Conference of 1967. Reflecting upon this outcome, Anthony Solomon has emphasized that "cocoa exporting countries

---

484 Interview, Jerome Jacobson, July 22, 1971.

485 Letter from Anthony M. Solomon to author, April 6, 1972.

486 Source withheld.

unfortunately took a short-term view in that their interest in an agreement declined when the prices turned high." "This over the long-run," he adds, "was as important as industry opposition in explaining failure to reach final agreement."[487]

After the abortive Geneva negotiations of 1969 and 1970, when Brazil led the producers in calling for a range of price support totally unacceptable to the United States, the U.S. in 1971 took the new and controversial position that the whole question of cocoa market regulation should be examined anew, and that the "Package Deal" and draft agreement which had been designed for the second half of the sixties should be abandoned as bases for negotiation in the 1970's. In the State Department's view, as expressed in an internal Department memorandum, that agreement had been designed in the mistaken expectation, after the 1964-1965 "crisis of oversupply," that there would be a "persistent and massive oversupply of cocoa," such as had developed in the coffee market at the beginning of the sixties. Since a massive oversupply had not materialized, indeed quite the contrary, producers and consumers should redefine the problems with which international regulation should deal in the seventies, and develop appropriate control mechanisms for those.[488]

Entering the seventies, the U.S. posture towards proposals for a cocoa agreement was little different than it had been a decade earlier, except perhaps that it was even more cautious. In this period the domestic political climate was considerably less conducive to U.S. entry into a cocoa agreement than it had been in 1963, or possibly in any period between. Senior government officials were preoccupied with disengagement from Vietnam, and they were fighting a rearguard

---

[487] Letter from Anthony M. Solomon to author, April 6, 1972. Solomon believes that the cocoa businessmen could have been convinced to "go along" with a reasonable agreement, "although they would have done so with reluctance."

[488] Source withheld.

action to protect a small and dwindling foreign aid program. Of more direct relevance to the cocoa negotiations, the country was besieged with balance of payments difficulties and rampant inflation. By 1972 even the relatively successful Coffee Agreement, for so long the model for producer aspirations, was in difficulty. U.S. policy-makers, to some small degree anyway, were perplexed by the conflicting pressures to control prices <u>within</u> the country, on the one hand, and those from the coffee producers to support price-raising measures, on the other. This was hardly the time for expecting that the United States would be eager for a cocoa agreement, particularly for one as ambitious as emerged from the 1972 Cocoa Conference.

In summary, it can be concluded that the U.S. government's orientation towards proposals for a cocoa agreement, irrespective of industry views, has been decidedly reserved and skeptical, though not so negative as some producer critics have contended. The sources of this posture of reserve and skepticism would have weighed heavily on government decisions, even in the hypothetical absence of cocoa industry opposition to an agreement.

<u>Sources of U.S. Cocoa Policy</u>. Briefly, what have been these sources of reserve? And what contrasts can be drawn with the Coffee Agreement case? First, a severe and <u>protracted</u> period of low prices has never developed in the cocoa market, as it did in coffee. The severe low prices of 1964-1965 impelled countries to negotiate seriously for an agreement, but prices turned upwards almost immediately. Whereas conditions in the coffee market in 1958-1962 stabilized the conditions of negotiation and favored concessions of principle, especially by the producers, no fully comparable conditions have obtained in the cocoa market. U.S. policy-makers could somewhat justifiably persist in the view that there was no "clearcut economic rationale" for an agreement.[489]

---

[489] Letter from W. Michael Blumenthal to author, October 20, 1971.

Second, in policy-maker perceptions the cocoa negotiations have consistently posed the theoretical and practical question of whether an agreement should primarily be designed to deal with extreme and temporary dislocations of the free market, or on the other hand, whether it should be conceived to raise and maintain prices above their natural trend. The United States has consistently advanced the former conception, and has repeatedly balked at producer proposals that seem to reflect the more ambitious alternative. Generally speaking, U.S. policy-makers have felt that the free market could function satisfactorily, with only modest help from a regulatory regime. At the same time, they believe, as a former Assistant Secretary of State has said, that other governments, notably producer governments, tend to disregard "the philosophy of our Congress which would only go along with an international commodity agreement if it were soundly designed to reduce extreme price fluctuations and that the Congress would not accept it as a disguised form of Aid." [490]

In the coffee case this "philosophical" issue was not directly joined at the inception of the ICA. Participating governments perceived a common interest in simply preventing a collapse of the market.

Parenthetically, some U.S. policy-makers have urged producer diplomats to settle for a more modestly conceived agreement in the first instance, and then work for its elaboration in the context of an established cocoa organization.[491] They have admonished them to respect Congressional resistance to ambitious price-raising schemes, as exhibited in Congressional criticism of even the modestly conceived Coffee Agreement.

---

490 Letter from Anthony M. Solomon to author, April 6, 1972. In this view, a commodity agreement would constitute "foreign aid" to the extent that it raised prices above their presumed trend.

491 Source withheld.

Third, U.S. policy-makers have tended to doubt either the inclination or the capacity of the major cocoa producers to hold up their side of an effective regulatory arrangement. During the 1960's several second rank producers, for example, Ivory Coast and Brazil, were eager to increase their respective shares of the world market. Similarly the fledgling Cocoa Producers Alliance (CPA), established in 1962, has only gradually exhibited any degree of capacity to concert the efforts of its membership. Ghana and the other African producers have been so heavily reliant upon cocoa exports that they have often found it difficult to regulate the timing and volume of their sales, especially in concert with one another. The disinterested observer can understand the U.S. policy-maker's skepticism concerning producer capacities to help regulate the market. Similarly, he recognizes that the producers are only gradually developing the capacity to pressure the United States and the American consuming industry by concerted action in the market.

In the case of coffee, the producers, under strong Brazilian leadership, had already demonstrated both an inclination and a capacity to act unilaterally to regulate the market, and this was clearly one of several factors that prompted the U.S. to accept the desirability and feasibility of a global agreement.

Fourth, the cocoa negotiations have never elicited the intense political responses that the demands for the Coffee Agreement did. While it is undoubtedly true that the U.S.'s willingness to repeatedly negotiate for an agreement has been due to some of the same political considerations that account for its entry into the ICA—for example, the desire to bolster LDC economies and political systems and to accommodate UNCTAD pressures—strongly compelling political motives have simply not been present, such as they were for the Coffee Agreement. In 1961-1962, a former Deputy Assistant Secretary of State has remarked, "coffee was hot politically."[492] Over thirty LDCs would benefit by an agreement,

---

[492] Interview, W. Michael Blumenthal, October 13, 1971.

and several of these were important Latin American countries. Cold War motives, linked specifically with Latin American concerns, and Kennedy initiatives for the Alliance, helped propel the U.S. into the Coffee Agreement.

In policy-maker perceptions the misfortunes of the cocoa market have been of considerably less political consequence for the U.S. Officials readily acknowledge their tendency to defer to European "responsibility" for the African producers of the product. And, for the most part, they seem not to have felt that there has been any close connection between American positions on cocoa agreement proposals and desired political outcomes, either within the producing countries, or between the United States and those countries.

Finally, there is an important sense in which policy-maker experience of the Coffee Agreement has tended to further dampen U.S. interest in signing a cocoa agreement. Securing and maintaining Congressional support of the ICA over the period of a decade has been a difficult, uncertain and resource-consuming task for three consecutive administrations. This experience has tended to reinforce the bureaucrats' skepticism that they could secure Congressional support for a cocoa agreement, especially one more complex and ambitious than the ICA.

Although the Coffee Agreement has been relatively successful in stabilizing prices and in tempering extreme price movements, it is not the type of international enterprise that inspires great enthusiasm or sense of achievement among policy-makers. It has not been able to deal effectively with one of its fundamental purposes: to regulate coffee production. And finally after ten years the regulatory features of the ICA were suspended in 1973. The Coffee Agreement experience has tended to reinforce the U.S. policy-makers' conviction that commodity agreements are "standby" and temporary measures that can serve as "crutches" to aid seriously dislocated markets for some, and really only very few products.

That experience seems not to have encouraged them to believe that an extensive system of commodity agreements, on a permanent basis, is either desirable or feasible.

In conclusion, several factors have combined to foster an official posture of caution and skepticism towards cocoa agreement proposals. The next section discusses how the American cocoa industry has helped shape and reinforce this posture.

The U.S. Cocoa Industry and American Cocoa Policy. What general posture has the cocoa industry taken through the years of cocoa negotiations? How, if at all, has it sought to impress its views upon the government? With what impact? What conditions have or have not favored industry influence on national policy?

The U.S. cocoa industry, it has been said, consists primarily of three groups of firms that perceive themselves as having common, overlapping, and to some degree, divergent interests in the cocoa agreement negotiations: confectioners, chocolate manufacturers and merchants. The latter two groups have played the most prominent role in the politics of cocoa, although the confectioners could be expected to become more active, if an agreement were ever signed by the United States. Hershey Corporation, as the major grinder of cocoa beans in the country, is the single, most powerful firm within the councils of the industry, and the leader of the Chocolate Manufacturers Association. Nestle (US) and General Foods also have been major firms in the latter Association, and in the industry at large, although during the early sixties GE withdrew from the Association out of concern that the chocolate manufacturers might be subjected to anti-trust prosecution.

Three large trading firms—A.C. Israel, Gill & Duffus (the American branch of the British firm), and J. Aron—have been accounting for over half of all cocoa imported into the U.S. through middlemen. Three other firms—General Cocoa, Holco and Lonray—together have regularly imported another 20-30 percent of the annual U.S. imports handled by traders. These six firms and not more than twenty other trading firms express their common interests within the industry and to the government through the Cocoa Merchants Association of America.

The U.S. cocoa industry is substantially smaller and considerably more concentrated than its coffee counterpart. While the trading and processing of coffee are geographically extensive, cocoa bean trade and processing are heavily concentrated in Pennsylvania and New York. Pennsylvania is the nation's cocoa product manufacturing center, accounting for over three-fourths of the value of national production. New York City is the national cocoa bean trading center, and the port of entry for virtually all cocoa imported into the country. Confection manufacture, wholesaling and retailing, of course, are more widely dispersed throughout the country.

New York City has been the hub of industry "policy-making" for cocoa. There representatives of all major cocoa trading and manufacturing firms are in continual and close contact with one another, either in the course of business transactions or through associational activities. Contact is facilitated and intensified through the organization and regular trading operations of the New York Cocoa Exchange in the Wall Street area. All cocoa trading and manufacturing firms, and other firms, corporations and individuals with an interest in cocoa trade, for example, the futures dealers such as Bache & Co. or Merrill Lynch, are "members" of the Cocoa Exchange.[493] As such they participate in the

---

[493] As of January 1, 1969, there were 133 firms, corporations, or individuals with "membership" in the Exchange. New York Cocoa Exchange, Inc., "Firms, Corporations and Individuals Represented in Membership," Charter By-Laws and Rules, 1970, XIII-XXII.

business transactions of the Exchange, but also in the management of its affairs through elected officers, a Board of Managers, and some fourteen committees, one of which is the "Special Committee on Government Matters."

Industry "positions" on commodity agreement proposals over the years have been worked out in the largely obscure interplay among key business leaders and their firms, among the three associations of chocolate manufacturers, merchants and confectioners (National Confectioners Association of the United States), respectively, and within the policy-making councils of the New York Cocoa Exchange, the only comprehensively representative body of cocoa firms. While the three aforementioned associations have expressed somewhat distinctive points of view on cocoa agreement proposals, the industry has maintained a high degree of consensus concerning what should be done about these proposals. Indeed this ongoing consensus has been a constant source of strength for the industry in its relations with the official policy-makers. This consensus, of course, has been faciliated by the fact that all industry leaders have been in close business and social contact that facilitates informal decision-making.

Over the last fifteen years a relatively small group of cocoa businessmen, distinguished undoubtedly by their leadership abilities, but certainly by their affiliations with the firms that trade or process the most cocoa, have been largely responsible for forging and expressing industry views in the cocoa negotiations. During the last decade Julian Hemphill, the Director of Cocoa Purchasing for Hershey Corporation, has been the premier cocoa businessman. His views regarding cocoa proposals have not invariably been accepted, but for the most part they have been highly respected.[494]

---

[494] Among other important industry leaders in the cocoa negotiations have been Johann Scheu, Nestle (US); Alwyn Fischel and Adrian C. Israel, A.C. Israel and Company; Issac and William Witkin, General Cocoa; Thomas B. Aitken, Gill & Duffus; Martin Coyne, J. Aron & Co.; Henry Blommer, Blommer Chocolate Co.; Walter J. Perkins, Curacao Trading Co.; Louis H. Truebner, Truebner Co.; and E. D. Becker, Mars, Inc.

If the cocoa industry has maintained a common front in the protracted cocoa negotiations, it is not because individual firms or their associations have always collaborated in their approaches to national policy-making. According to Paul Callanan, a former State Department commodities expert, it was not until the late fifties, when cocoa market regulation began to be discussed seriously, that cocoa businessmen sought to convey to government their views regarding a foreign policy issue in any systematic and concerted manner. Previously individual cocoa firms or associations tended to approach government departments, most often the Department of Commerce, on issues of importance to them, independently of one another.[495]

However, as a crisis in the coffee market prompted the National Coffee Association to establish a special Foreign Affairs Committee to provide liaison with the government in the coffee negotiations, so in analogous, but different fashion, the perceived "threat" of cocoa market regulation galvanized the three American cocoa associations to present a united organizational front to the government. Although the National Confectioners Association, except for the period around the 1963 Cocoa Conference, has tended to remain aloof from the collaborative industry approach to the government for the cocoa agreement issue, the manufacturers and merchants associations, as well as the New York Cocoa Exchange have developed a system of joint representation to government. This representation, consisting of either the chief officers of these bodies or their appointed surrogates, has become the basis of a quasi-institutionalized industry advisory system linked to the State Department. The latter, in the late fifties, unobtrusively wrested the advisory relationship away from the Department of Commerce by convincing junior commerce officials that government meetings with business representatives should be held at the Department of State.[496]

---

495 Interview, Paul Callanan, January 26, 1972.

496 Ibid.

From the inception of the FAO-UNCTAD sponsorship of cocoa talks (1956) American cocoa businessmen have regularly served as "advisers" to U.S. official delegations. Eight industry advisors, for example, attended the Ibadan meeting of the Cocoa Study Group (1957), and subsequently, small or large groups of businessmen have attended virtually all consultations and conferences on cocoa.

In the early years of the talks industry leaders openly expressed their opposition to market regulation, in language, which from the perspective even of the sixties, would seem stridently "free enterprise" in character. These leaders were also candid about their perceptions of the implications of market regulation for the existing way of "doing business" in the United States. "We are of the firm belief," the President of the New York Cocoa Exchange declared in 1957, "that the establishment of any form of price control, quota system or quantity allocation would result in the breakdown of the traditional avenues of trade [private merchanting, commodity exchange, etc.] as they presently exist." "Experience has proven," he added, "that the present procedures of distribution involved in the crucible of free competiton permit the survival of only the most efficient methods, and ruthlessly eliminate waste and extravagance. There are countless examples of the chaotic conditions which follow interference by governments."[497]

In 1958 the President of the Exchange, Louis Truebner, warned members of the Exchange that their Board should "remain on the alert to prevent any attempt at imposing international regulations or agreements which...are contrary to enduring aims of a trade connected with 'economic growth' under a free enterprise system." "Any form of international controls, price or quota

---

[497] Statement by President, New York Cocoa Exchange (Alwyn Fischel), as found in New York Cocoa Exchange, Inc., <u>Report of the Board of Managers</u>, 1958, 6.

schemes," he asserted, "can only be considered injurious to the interests of the cocoa and chocolate industry of the world." [498]

At the end of the Eisenhower Administration, it has been said, there was little official inclination to become involved in cocoa market regulation, in any event, and strongly expressed industry opposition reinforced this posture. At the Hamburg meeting of the Study Group in 1958, the United States, as well as Great Britain, expressed opposition to proposals for market stabilization then before the Group.

The advent of the Kennedy Administration, as well as propitious market conditions, brought, at least, a slight shift of official U.S. policy as early as April of 1961. At the fourth session of the Cocoa Study Group in Accra, despite the protestations of its industry advisors, the U.S. delegation acceded to consumer leadership from France, Switzerland and Great Britain, and announced that it was now prepared to seriously consider proposals for market regulation.[499] This change of position opened the way to the preparation of the draft agreement, approved at Port-of-Spain in 1963, and considered at the first abortive Cocoa Conference later in the year.

It also stirred anxiety within the industry that the government might yield to producer political pressures and attempt to sign and pass an agreement through Congress, over industry opposition. This precipitated an outpouring of public statements against market regulation and more importantly, a more concerted and systematic effort by the industry to secure leverage upon the policy-making

---

[498] Statement by President, New York Cocoa Exchange (Louis H. Truebner), as found in New York Cocoa Exchange, Inc., Report of the Board of Managers, 1958, 6.

[499] A Swiss observer has attributed this shift of U.S. policy to "political reasons." Oeschlin, op. cit., 100.

process. To the Board of Managers of the New York Cocoa Exchange, "the future of a free market in cocoa" appeared "beclouded by the impending possibility of an international cocoa agreement."[500]

Shortly after the Accra meeting, at which the U.S. announced its willingness to consider market regulation, the several industry associations jointly circulated a position paper, "Realism in Cocoa Stabilization," opposing current proposals for an agreement, and characterizing the draft agreement under discussion as "unworkable and impractical." It would, concluded the paper, assure curtailment of consumption and product-substitution in the longer run, and surely undercut the short-term objective of higher producer revenues.[501] In early 1963 the Board of Managers of the New York Cocoa Exchange declared that "the cocoa industry is firmly opposed to international control, price or quota schemes."[502]

According to one business informant, however, the cocoa industry felt it had "to take out insurance" against an agreement.[503] The industry had never been as confident of its capacity to gain access to and influence government, as has been the coffee industry, but it was especially dubious in the early sixties of the efficacy of its advisory relationship with the State Department.

To augment this relationship, and at the suggestion of Adrian Israel, chief executive of A. C. Israel & Co., the major segments of the industry decided to retain the services of the prestigious Washington law firm of Clifford, Warnke, Glass,

---

[500]New York Cocoa Exchange, Inc., Report of the Board of Managers, 1962, 3.

[501]"Realism in Cocoa Stabilization," 1961, as cited in Oeschlin, op. cit., 102.

[502]New York Cocoa Exchange, Inc., Report of the Board of Managers, 1963, 3.

[503]Source withheld.

McIlwaine and Finney. The Clifford firm, recalls Alwyn Fischel, was retained to "secure an ear in government."

The Clifford law firm seems to have been retained sometime during the crop year 1962-1963, when the industry was most anxious that the State Department was on the precipice of entering an agreement, and continued, at least, until 1971-1972, when Hershey withdrew financial support for the services. The Chocolate Manufacturers Association, The Cocoa Merchants Association, and the New York Cocoa Exchange, Inc., have shared the substantial costs of these services.[504]

One of the partners of the Clifford firm, Thomas D. Finney, Jr., has handled the cocoa industry account through the years. Finney, a former Administrative Assistant to Senator Mike Monroney, had served as a senior staff man for George Ball's pre-Kennedy inaugural Task Force on Foreign Economic Policy (1960-61), before joining the Clifford law firm. This personal acquaintance with George Ball, who served as Under Secretary of State for Economic Affairs at the

---

[504]Until 1971 the Manufacturers defrayed one-half of these costs, and the Merchants and the Exchange, one fourth each. Interview, Julian Hemphill, February 9, 1972. It is estimated, on the basis of this formula, and of expenditure reports of the New York Cocoa Exchange Board of Managers (see Report of the Board of Managers for the years 1962 through 1970), that the U.S. Cocoa industry paid the Clifford firm a sum of either $95,438 or $381,752 between 1962 and 1970. The higher figure is likely, unless the expenditure reports of the Exchange reflect the shares of the manufacturers and merchants associations, respectively, as well as those of the Exchange itself. Data on actual expenditures, as contained in "Estimates of Revenue and Expenses" in each Report, has been extrapolated from a line item entitled "Consultant," or for 1965, "Consultant and UNCTAD Matters." It is assumed that the "Consultant" is the Clifford firm. Importantly the Exchange's outlay for the consultant was greatest in each of the years in which there was a U.N. Cocoa Conference (1963, 1966, and 1967), and considerably less in each of the other years. For crop year, 1962-1963, the outlay was $25,000; for 1966-1967, $12,500; and for 1967-1968, $25,225. If, as is probable, outlays by the manufacturers and merchants are not subsumed under these figures, the formula provided by Hemphill would suggest that these figures can be quadrupled to ascertain the total amounts paid by the cocoa industry to the Clifford firm.

time of the 1963 Cocoa Conference, surely facilitated Finney's personal lobbying against a cocoa agreement with Ball and other key State Department officers at the time of the latter conference, whether or not it accorded a basis for actual influence.[505]

Finney considers his representation of the cocoa industry as completely compatible with his own personal convictions about cocoa market regulation.[506] While believing that the commodity trade problems of the LDCs deserve the concern of the United States, he believes that commodity agreements as such tend to be economically unsound and politically expedient instruments of U.S. foreign policy. "It has troubled me conceptually," he says, "that trade restrictionism, as practiced in commodity agreements, has occupied the center of attention." And further:

> You have the paradox of the U.S. government saying that commodity trade is vitally important to underdeveloped countries; and yet it insists in the instance of cocoa on asking a small segment of our society to bear the burden of aiding the trade in cocoa. If it were so important, you would think that we could have a more equitable way of sharing the burdens of aiding trade of the underdeveloped countries.

Finney's "complaint" against the State Department is that it often takes an overly conservative view of what is "saleable" to Congress, and therefore, opts for policy measures that are vastly less suitable than ones that would confront basic issues directly. In this vein, he contends, the State Department has participated in discussions for a trade restrictive cocoa commodity agreement

---

[505] Jerome Jacobson, Deputy Assistant Secretary of State in 1963 and U.S. delegate to the Conference, believes that Ball was impressed by Finney's arguments against an agreement, and certainly by the fact that Finney's efforts signified that the industry would strongly resist any agreement that might be negotiated. Interview, Jerome Jacobson, July 12, 1971.

[506] Interview, Thomas Finney, January 27, 1972.

when it should have promoted, with ardent political commitment, supplementary (or compensatory) financing arrangements for LDC cocoa trade.[507]

During the late sixties Finney persuaded the cocoa industry of the wisdom of promoting a compensatory finance arrangement for the cocoa trade. He and the industry leaders unsuccessfully attempted to persuade the State Department, and even the UNCTAD Secretary-General, of the superiority of this approach to that of the typical quota systems under discussion in the cocoa negotiations.

Besides more broadly theoretical objections to proposals for a cocoa agreement, Finney is also convinced that free trade mechanisms have operated more effectively, even for the producers, than did those of the coffee market. For one thing, he insists, the traditional channels of trade have been reasonably effective at "clearing the market." No overwhelming and continuous surpluses have developed, and consumption has expanded gradually.

The Clifford firm was engaged in either 1962 or early 1963, as the cocoa industry became increasingly anxious over the apparent inclination of the Kennedy Administration to negotiate seriously for an agreement. During early 1963 it took two types of lobbying action to discourage the government from signing an agreement. On the one hand, it made high level contact with officers of the State Department, and secondarily at Commerce; on the other, it began to identify and "educate" Congressmen and Senators who might be enlisted to oppose any agreement that should be sent to Congress.

---

507 Under proposed supplementary financing schemes Developed Countries would make up shortfalls of LDC revenue from commodity exports when prices fall below certain negotiated levels. Such aid would be channeled through international banking groups like IBRD, and be funded by foreign aid appropriations of the Developed Countries. The typical compensatory scheme, such as has now been initiated in IMF, provides for temporary "loans" or monetary rights for LDCs that experience short-term foreign exchange difficulties due to low commodity export prices.

Shortly before the Conference (1963), Finney released a "Background Paper" in behalf of the industry, including in this instance, the National Confectioners' Association. This paper, which was widely disseminated among members of Congress and some bureaucrats, presented most of the basic arguments against an agreement that have been heard from the industry over subsequent years. It also enumerated the minimal terms the United States should insist upon, if it felt it must enter an agreement.

Asserting that the current interest in a cocoa agreement was due to pressure from the cocoa producers to increase their export earnings, and their hope of capitalizing upon the momentum generated by the successful negotiation of the Coffee Agreement (1962), the Background Paper declared that there was no economic need or justification for an agreement.[508] But, continued the industry brief, "we approach the negotiating conference fearful the U.S. Government may mistake transient popularity with producing countries for political advantage, and may acquiesce in an agreement, the provisions of which will be so unrealistic in terms of the economics of cocoa as to produce series long-term injury to both consumers and the cocoa producing countries."[509] If this should occur, the paper warned, "the U.S. industry would have no alternative but to oppose ratification of the agreement, with all of the undesirable foreign policy implications that this might produce."[510]

Why did the industry believe there was no economic justification for an agreement, and indeed that one could be injurious? The paper contended, first, that the draft agreement was based on the false impression that producer export

---

508 Rashish, "The Proposed International Cocoa Agreement," 1-2; and 12.

509 *Ibid.*, 1.

510 *Ibid.*

earnings from cocoa had been as unstable and "low" as cocoa prices. Even FAO studies indicated, it said, an opposite conclusion. Cocoa earnings had been relatively more stable than prices, and had trended upwards since World War II. Increased consumption, in periods of low price, had tended to stabilize and even raise cocoa export earnings.[511]

Secondly, "the present marketing arrangements encourage the expanded consumption which is the essential long term basis of the economic development of the producing countries. The draft cocoa agreement would substitute an elaborate system of sales and price manipulation which could destroy the present market system."[512]

If producers were successful in their objective of raising prices above natural market levels, there would be a "curtailment of consumption, the substitution of other ingredients in food products and the reduction of advertising and other activities designed to stimulate consumer demand." An FAO study was cited as evidence that cocoa, especially cocoa butter, was vulnerable, under high price conditions, to product substitution.[513]

Third, a sales quota system to raise prices would involve the retention and storage of stocks, necessarily in the temperate climates of the consuming countries, and "for the first time at the expense of the underdeveloped countries." The producers, as well as the draft Agreement, clearly underestimated the cost of storage operations.[514] Parenthetically, the cocoa industry has always prided itself upon the effectiveness and efficiency with which existing mechanisms have cleared the market, even in conditions of surplus.

---

[511] Ibid., 6-10.

[512] Ibid., 10.

[513] Ibid., 16.

[514] Ibid., 15.

Finally, the paper attempted to show the emptiness of the analogy drawn between the cocoa and coffee market situations, in the latter of which an Agreement had been negotiated.[515] First, cocoa prices and export earnings were not in a state of steady and long-term decline, such as coffee prices and earnings were at the time the coffee market came under regulation. Secondly, the Coffee Agreement had provided only for arresting severe price declines, and provided for no price targets. By contrast, the draft cocoa agreement provided for a target price range, and contained permissive guidelines for market intervention at any price level. The Coffee Agreement provided for emergency intervention at 1962 price levels, the draft cocoa agreement, theoretically, at any level.

Thirdly, the industry brief observed that proponents of the ICA had identified overproduction as the root problem in the coffee market. In the case of cocoa, it said, consuming countries had always purchased all production, and since World War II the global level of inventories had never exceeded a six months supply.

Finally, proponents of the ICA had contended that consumers would be protected from price inflation by the availability of gigantic coffee stocks (estimated to be a two year's supply for total global needs). By contrast, there was no surplus cocoa stocks to defend consumers against either price manipulation or price increases.

While the industry position paper asserted "that there is no economic need for an international cocoa agreement," it declared that it was "essential" for the United States to insist on certain provisions in any agreement it might sign "for other reasons." Generally, the industry-recommended provisions called for fixing regulatory objectives more explicitly in the agreement, for reducing the

---

[515] "Comparison of Cocoa and Coffee," Appendix A, in Ibid., 18-21.

discretionary powers assigned to the cocoa council by the draft agreement, and for strengthening U.S. voting power in the proposed council.[516]

As events actually developed, the industry recommendations on price targets and market intervention were most critical. Here it was recommended that the price at which market intervention occurred should not exceed 18 cents per pound, and that sales quotas should be automatically suspended when price returned to a level above 18 cents.

The industry's economic analysis, as expressed in the Clifford firm's background paper, but also in the intensive personal contacts between Finney and the industry advisers with the State Department, probably influenced, to a considerable degree, the official conceptions of what price and other terms might reasonably be accepted in an agreement in 1963, and subsequently. In this way, of course, the industry also influenced the general posture of the U.S. towards the cocoa negotiations, for example, its readiness to compromise or even to make unilateral concessions, and indirectly, the outcome of the negotiations themselves.

This analysis, as it was carefully conceived to do, made a great deal of sense to official policy-makers who otherwise were lacking in enthusiasm for an agreement, and who were, for their own reasons, oriented to a type of agreement that would protect producers against excessive price instability and price lows. Also, as one of the latter has indicated, officials, very few of whom knew anything about the complexities of the cocoa trade, welcomed expert advice from the industry.[517] While for foreign policy reasons, the policy-makers were not deterred

---

[516] Ibid., 13-14.

[517] Interview, Paul Callanan, January 26, 1972. Callanan observes that the Clifford firm helped facilitate communication between the State Department and the industry. He intimates that the State Department used Finney as a bridge to the industry, and "we didn't have to pay for his services."

from entering negotiations— the industry had expressly opposed even the idea of an agreement in 1963— accommodating industry preferences concerning the terms of the pact seemed imperative to an attempt to bring the industry around to tolerating an agreement, even if it would not actively support one.[518] The attempt to accommodate industry views on the minimum price issue at the 1963 Conference, and thereby assure, at least, its neutrality towards an agreement, probably lent inflexibility to the American position.

It is at the 1966 Conference, among the four cocoa conferences, that American industry opposition to an agreement was clearly decisive in the outcome of the negotiations. The Conference had resolved all the other critical issues, so that agreement or disagreement on a price minimum would determine the outcome. Importantly, the producers were in a mood of compromise, and prepared to accept a minimum price which many consumers, but not they, would have agreed to in 1963.

U.S. policy-makers were divided on the merits of pushing through to an agreement, although leaning heavily in that direction. If, in the scales of indecision, the industry advisers, or possibly even Hershey Corp. alone, had accepted a 19 minimum price compromise, the United States would probably have signed an agreement. While considerable political effort was made to secure industry support— Permanent U.N. Representative Arthur Goldberg personally pleaded with the industry advisers to consider the political benefits of U.S. support for an agreement— the government was not, in the final analysis, prepared to sign an agreement without that support. Under exceedingly propitious circumstances for interest group intervention, the cocoa industry was able to "veto" U.S. entry into an agreement.

---

[518] Interview, Henry Brodie, June 30, 1971.

By 1966 the industry was striking an ostensibly different posture towards the cocoa negotiations than it had several years earlier. Rather than voicing a strident, uncompromising opposition to any agreement, it was more apt to assert that it was, despite honest misgivings about market regulation, prepared to "co-operate with our Government," by not opposing a "GOOD agreement."[519] Extensive interviewing among cocoa businessmen, however, indicates that there was over time a shift of tactics, but little or no change of sentiment about cocoa agreements as such.

At the advent of the Kennedy Administration cocoa businessmen had been genuinely anxious that the government might cave into LDC pressures, or stumble into an agreement. Julian Hemphill, for example, was impressed with what he perceived as a propensity on the part of State Department officials for "image building," without regard for the "positive programs" to help the cocoa trade.[520] Businessmen, at first, were also less certain of the efficacy of their standing with the State Department than had been their coffee peers.

Under the tutelage of the Clifford firm, which was particularly helpful in developing sophisticated policy analysis for the industry, and with growing experience of the fragility of cocoa negotiations, the industry became increasingly confident of its capacity to thwart any inclinations that might develop among policy-makers for an agreement. While it has consistently maintained a healthy respect for the possibility that government might seek an agreement, even against industry wishes, it has grown more confident that businessmen and government officials "think alike" on the issues.

This confidence has been borne partly of its success in developing a close advisory relationship with the Bureau of Economic Affairs, but undoubtedly too,

---

[519] New York Cocoa Exchange, Inc., Report of the Board of Managers, 1966, 3.

[520] Interview, Julian Hemphill, February 9, 1972.

out of some fortuitous changes in the "objective" political environment of policy-making. From the late sixties political conditions in the United States have become increasingly unfavorable to new departures in U.S. cocoa policy. The election of a Republican Administration, Vietnam disengagement, inflation, and Executive-Congressional conflict related to Indochina and the Watergate affair, have probably enhanced the credibility of the argument that industry support would be essential to any successful bid for U.S. entry into an agreement. The industry, and its Washington lobbyist, have always been mindful that policy-makers are sensitive to a commodity agreement's vulnerability in Congress.[521] And the political events in the U.S. of the late sixties and early seventies could not have but assured the cocoa industry on this point.

Neither the Conference of 1967 nor of 1972 was particularly demanding on industry political resources. In 1967 negotiations failed, as much as anything, because several key producers were momentarily not interested in having regulations. In 1972 some key terms finally accepted by producers and the European consumers were considerably outside the ambit of anything U.S. officials were prepared to consider. In both instances, the industry advisers could safely lay back and profess their willingness to support a "reasonable" agreement.

Over the fifteen years of serious cocoa negotiations U.S. industry leaders have become "tired and bored" of the issue of market regulation, but have always been vigilant against it. Despite minor adjustments of stance, the major firms and associations of the industry have been persistent and consistent in their views of how market regulation would adversely affect preferred ways of doing business and their material interests. The Confectioners and Merchants Associations have been vociferously opposed to an agreement, although only the latter has consistently participated in joint industry efforts to prevent one. The few and already hard-pressed members of the Merchants Association fear, with substantial

---

521 Ibid.

justification, that a substantive agreement would snuff out the commodity exchanges through which they make and hedge their transactions. Market regulation, to them, spells their demise, or at least, the expansion of direct transactions between producer marketing boards and the processing corporations, at their expense.

Nestle (US), General Foods, and especially Hershey, hold the reins of policy-making for the chocolate manufacturing industry, and to a large degree, for the whole cocoa industry. Although each is, to varying degrees, reliant on the operations of the commodity exchanges, and has preferred free market mechanisms, they could theoretically adjust successfully to a regulated market, even to the demise of the exchanges. General Foods is the most reliant on the Cocoa Exchange for management purposes, and its cocoa operatives, who maintain a low profile in industry politics, are known to strongly oppose an agreement. The managers of Nestle (US) have tended to oppose a cocoa agreement, but periodically they have been reminded by the multinational's headquarters in Vevey that the company must maintain a "statesman-like posture" towards the cocoa negotiations.[522]

The Hershey Corporation has been the bellwether of the cocoa industry throughout the cocoa agreement negotiations. To some degree, "industry support" for one or another national policy can be translated as "Hershey support," although the company has hardly been in a position to dictate industry policy on commodity agreements. It is probable, nevertheless, that had the Hershey Corporation ever taken the view that the United States should enter a given agreement, that the dynamics of industry-government relations in policy-making would have been considerably different. It is substantially more likely, for example, that the United States would have signed an agreement at the 1966 Conference, if the Corporation's

[522]Interview, Johann Scheu, September 20, 1971.

management had supported the concessions that its Director of Purchasing, Julian Hemphill, was prepared to make.

Actually, of course, Hershey has been a leading architect of the industry consensus that has always viewed the cocoa negotiations with the deepest skepticism, if not outright aversion. At least until the mid-sixties its management was strongly imbued with the free enterprise orthodoxy of its Pennsylvania founder. Government intervention in the free market was seen as intrinsically objectionable.[523] More pragmatically, the corporation had developed a lucrative business based on skillful use of the Cocoa Exchange, on employing the services of numerous cocoa traders, and on maintaining large inventories of cocoa purchased in periods of low or relatively low prices. To Hershey, cocoa proposals, particularly those advanced by the producers, have portended higher prices for its raw material, and probably the demise of its traditional and preferred way of doing business, on the Exchange and through the cocoa traders.

Hershey has had objective material "interests" in fending off market regulation. Its conception of these, however, phases into a set of convictions that both producers and consumers are better off with a free market system. The system has performed very well, it contends, in expanding consumption, in increasing the revenues of both producers and consumers, and in absorbing potential surpluses. Market regulation, on the other hand, would likely upset a smoothly functioning system, and by fostering higher prices, risk product substitution for cocoa.

Neither Hershey nor the industry, at large, has been much swayed by political arguments for cocoa market regulation, such as the coffee processors had been, to a considerable degree, in 1962. Industry leaders acknowledge that government officials have sometimes rather feebly tried to persuade them of

---

[523] Interview, Julian Hemphill, February 9, 1972.

various political imperatives for supporting regulation, but they also say that they have never been at all impressed by political arguments.[524] In fact, officials themselves have been too little convinced of the political value of a cocoa agreement to convey any sense of political conviction to businessmen.

The industry, however, has worried that officials might succumb to LDC political pressures and enter an agreement out of political expedience. This explains why it has maintained continuous and expensive advisory and lobbying relationships with key sectors of government. These relationships have partly shaped government views of cocoa agreement proposals. To a greater extent, they have reinforced official views that have derived from other sources. Persuasion has been a primary medium of industry influence on policy. But the wild card for the cocoa industry has been that commodity agreements are vulnerable in Congress. The executive branch would have to have strong reasons— reasons that so far have not obtained—for sending an agreement to Congress, in the face of industry opposition.

---

[524] Interview, Julian Hemphill, February 10, 1972.

CONCLUSIONS

Two types of conclusions are suggested by this analysis of the role of business in U.S. policy-making for the Coffee Agreement, the cocoa negotiations and the soluble coffee dispute. First, conclusions can be drawn concerning the role of business in deciding U.S. policies for these particular issues. Second, other conclusions about business and policy-making, in general, can link this study and its findings to generalizations from other studies of business, or more broadly, of interest groups and policy-making.

Business and the Coffee and Cocoa Cases. U.S. support for the International Coffee Agreement (1962), not to mention outright leadership to secure it, represented a substantial departure from past American orientations—indifference or opposition—to LDC appeals for agreements for coffee and other products. Why the U.S. volte face? And how, and with what impact, did the American coffee industry relate to this change?

Raul Prebisch, the former Secretary-General of UNCTAD, seems to suggest that a combination of favorable factors in the early sixties induced the U.S. government to override business opposition to a coffee agreement. "It appears," he has written, "that for several years it was impossible to negotiate a commodity agreement for coffee because the point of view of the importing countries was largely influenced by commercial interests." The declining coffee prices of the 1950's, he continues, and their "serious impact upon a large number of Latin American countries," created a favorable political context for the change of government policies in the consuming countries. In his view, "the importing countries began to take a broader view of the problems relating to the regulation of world trade in coffee."[525]

This study has developed a somewhat different thesis concerning the relationship of business to policy-making in the development of the Coffee Agreement. Prebisch is correct that a variety of factors were peculiarly conducive to U.S. support of a coffee agreement at the turn into the sixties. There was a crisis in the global coffee market, that virtually no one could fail to perceive, or did. Coffee trade was susceptible to effective regulation; and there already had been considerable international experience of market regulation, among the producers, and some between the United States and Latin America. Producers had already exhibited the capacity and inclination to control the market. Scores of LDCs depended heavily on coffee exports for national earnings, if not for economic viability itself. And Brazil, Colombia and several Central American countries were among these.

Also the coffee market crisis and years of preparatory consultations on market regulation coincided with what U.S. policy-makers perceived as a phase of political and economic instability within the LDCs, particularly within Latin coffee-producing countries, that might be exploited by an aggressive Soviet Union or Castro Cuba. Fortuitously, from the standpoint of the proponents of a coffee agreement, a new President came to office in 1961, whose advocacy of an Alliance for Progress, was almost bound to encompass support for a coffee agreement. In the event, the Kennedy Administration's commitment to direct the "inevitable" Latin American economic and social revolution into acceptable

---

525 UNCTAD, Towards a New Trade Policy, 56.

channels gave fresh and timely impetus to bureaucratic and diplomatic initiatives for assistance to LDC commodity trade, and finally resulted in U.S. entry into the Coffee Agreement.

But as Prebisch's analysis does not suggest, the ICA case also calls into question the stereotype of consumer business invariably opposing commodity agreements for LDC products. That stereotype, ironically, tends to obscure the fact that the American coffee industry, or at least, its most influential segments, did have a significant voice in deciding that the United States should support the ICA, and specific terms thereof. Paradoxically, if business is credited with influence only when the U.S. government opposes or is cool towards an agreement advocated by the LDCs (e.g., the Cocoa Agreement), the nature of business influence for commodity agreement issues, in general, is apt to be misunderstood, and its extent underestimated.

Business firms and the National Coffee Association, strongly led by General Foods Corporation, several other large roasters, and some large trading firms, were prominently involved in the development of the ICA. Key business leaders, impressed by many of the same considerations that motivated the official policy-makers, were among the prime movers of the coffee agreement negotiations from the earliest stages of policy development. These same leaders worked closely with officials in building a supporting consensus in the representative, if roaster-dominated NCA, during the critical stages of actual negotiation and of consummation of U.S. participation in the ICA through Congressional legislation.

As events actually developed, substantial business support was only one of several factors favoring U.S. leadership for the Agreement; but it was a major factor. Analysis of actual policy development, including all phases such as securing Congressional approval, indicates the strong likelihood that the U.S. government would never have signed the Coffee Agreement, had the NCA opposed it. At least, it is likely that opposition within Congress to the Treaty and implementing legislation would have been more pronounced, and probably decisive, if the government had, under hypothetical circumstances, tried to override unified business opposition.

Certain business organizations, it must also be concluded, helped shape official conceptions of the type of agreement that should be negotiated. Several factors, including the incrementalist proclivities of the officials, predisposed the United States to an agreement that would prevent market collapse, with as little government intervention in the market as possible. This study has shown how business positions on particular terms of the proposed agreement, for example, its opposition to the setting of explicit price objectives, reinforced this orientation.

The case of the cocoa negotiations, by contrast, illustrates a business interest group taking a prominent role in reinforcing otherwise existing U.S. government skepticism towards LDC proposals for a cocoa agreement, and more recently, towards the International Cocoa Agreement (1972) itself. In comparing the coffee and cocoa issues systematically, it became clear that several factors that were conducive to U.S. support of the Coffee Agreement have not obtained so far in the case of cocoa, at least, not with comparable weight. Even in the absence of industry opposition to market regulation, it is doubtful that American officials would have expressed much enthusiasm for a cocoa agreement during the past decade.

Several factors, besides industry attitudes, have contributed to official circumspection about cocoa agreement proposals. No protracted crisis has developed in the cocoa market, such as occurred in coffee. Fluctuating cocoa prices, policy-makers observe, have continually destabilized the bargaining situations in which agreements have been negotiated, and obstructed the unity among essential parties to an agreement that must be sustained for effective regulation. Simply stated, American officials have perceived no compelling economic reason for market regulation, and indeed some dangers in it. The free market, they believe, has performed relatively well for both producers and consumers. They believe too that the cocoa market would be technically more difficult to regulate. While they have been prepared to contemplate seriously a standby, emergency-type agreement, they have constantly been at odds with what they see as the producer conception of an agreement, one that would encourage price-raising measures.

Nor have there been strongly compelling political reasons for U.S. officials to overcome their reservations about having cocoa market regulation. While LDC pressures have undoubtedly kept the United States at the negotiating table, these have not registered strongly enough to impell decisive responses. Fewer LDCs depend upon cocoa exports than upon coffee exports, and since most of these are African countries, the United States has tended to defer to European "responsibility" for nurturing them. At no time have Cold War sentiments given impetus for U.S. entry into a cocoa agreement, such as they did in the case of the Coffee Agreement. If anything, the Kennedy Administration's initial preoccupation with securing a Coffee Agreement to complement Alliance for Progress distracted policy-maker attention from the contemporaneous demands for a cocoa agreement. And as the cocoa negotiations proceeded through the decade of the sixties, the concurrent difficulties of securing and maintaining Congressional support for the ICA tended to dampen interest in a cocoa agreement. By 1972 the domestic political climate, including serious inflation price controls, and the rise of consumer-interest groups, had become steadily less favorable to U.S. entry into a cocoa agreement.

Significantly, another decisive contrast between the cocoa and coffee cases is that the cocoa industry has generally opposed market regulation, while the most influential segments of the coffee industry favored regulation of their market in 1962. General Foods has opposed a cocoa agreement, although it was the single most important business proponent of the Coffee Agreement. Through strenuous lobbying with State Department officials, but also capitalizing on the bureaucrats' fear of Congressional obstruction of an agreement opposed by business, the cocoa industry has exerted a generally restraining influence on American cocoa agreement policy.

In the soluble coffee controversy between the United States and Brazil the U.S. government undertook an intensive, multi-pronged campaign to induce Brazil to abandon its "subsidization" of soluble coffee exports to the United States. This case, in some respects more than the other two cases, has afforded a vivid cutaway view of business relationships to policy-making.

Under General Foods and Nestle (US) leadership, the National Coffee Association played a major role in pressing the State Department into action against Brazil's instant coffee export practices. Although the State Department might have come to the same position it did anyway, independent of business pressure, this seems unlikely. Certainly, it would have done so more slowly.

NCA action flagged the "problem" of Brazilian imports at its onset, kept the pressure on State for its resolution, and helped shape the nature of the settlement of the dispute in 1972. More pointedly, it was General Foods, in collaboration with the Amalgamated Meatcutters and Butcher Workmen, that sustained pressure on the government, even when in 1970 Nestle and the NCA gave up the cause of stronger measures against Brazilian imports.

Two conditions favored State Department receptivity to business points of view in the solubles case. On the one hand, the dispute was inextricably related to the operations of the International Coffee Agreement; and satisfactory resolution of the dispute came to be seen as a precondition for the survival of the ICA, or at least, for the continuation of American support of the Agreement.

On the other hand, the solubles case demonstrates how business may gain leverage on policy-making in a government bureaucracy by capitalizing on Congress's participation in commodity trade politics. In the coffee and cocoa agreement cases business intervention in policy-making through Congress remained largely potential. However, the mere threat of that intervention helped the business interests involved to gain access to and to have influence on policy-makers in the bureaucracies. In the soluble coffee case, General Foods effectively intervened in Congress to advance its policy preference in the dispute.

Who Decides: Business or Government? Several conclusions, or additional lines of inquiry, are suggested by taking a systemic view of business-government relations in policy-making for the coffee and cocoa agreement cases. Prof. Stephen Krasner has recently posited two models that might theoretically explain the nature and impact of business relations with the U.S. government in the decision to join the Coffee Agreement (1962).

The "state centric" model, he suggests, depicts the "position of official actors" as prevailing over those of private groups in determining foreign policy. The "interest group" model, by contrast, calls attention to evidence that private groups prevail over official actors.[526] Regarding the Coffee Agreement case,

---

526 Stephen Krasner, "Business Government Relations: The Case of the International Coffee Agreement," Unpublished Paper, Center for International Affairs, Harvard University, 1963, 2.

Krasner concludes, "The behavior of the United States approximated the state centric model."[527] "The State Department," he explains, "initiated action for a coffee agreement. Industry backing came only after the government's position was established."[528]

This study indicates a different conclusion, and by considering two additional cases, calls for some qualification of Krasner's larger inference from the Coffee Agreement case that the "power of official agencies remains substantial in one important economic arena: relations between public agencies and private corporations [in the making of foreign economic policy]."[529]

Krasner observes that for national security issues there is a "clear a priori rationale for assuming that official agencies rather than private ones determine policy."[530] He seems to suggest, however, that the Coffee Agreement case warrants the further conclusion that officials have a relatively free hand in determining foreign policy for economic issues, although he adds as a minor point, under greater restraints imposed by interest group activity.[531] This might be so, but the argument is not easily sustained by evidence from the Coffee Agreement case alone, much less by the coffee and cocoa cases taken together. The relative paucity of studies of foreign policy-making for economic issues also cautions against expansive generalizations based on one, or even three cases.

Neither the state centric model nor the interest group model, as Krasner has defined each, is adequate by itself to interpret the policy consequences of business-government interactions for either the ICA case, or the cocoa agreement and soluble coffee cases. This may be seen by considering what has been

---

527 Ibid.

528 Ibid., 2.

529 Ibid. 2 and 34.

530 Ibid., 17.

531 Ibid., 1.

said about the policy-making actors, their capabilities, their goals, and the nature and conditions of their interaction for the coffee and cocoa issues.

In all three cases the primary official actors were the State Department and the Congress, with the Kennedy White House taking a strong initiative for the Coffee Agreement. The State Department was the primary bureaucratic actor, largely because demands for coffee and cocoa agreements originated outside the country, and cast the issues as essentially "foreign policy" issues from the beginning. Business demands for restraints on Brazilian soluble coffee imports were directed primarily to the State Department because the Department was already administering U.S. participation in the ICA, and because business wished to use the threat of destroying the Agreement as a means of compelling Brazilian concessions. There was only negligible inter-bureaucracy bargaining over what U.S. coffee and cocoa policies should be, and only in the case of soluble coffee any evident bargaining among different offices within the State Department. Essentially, the Bureau of Economic Affairs prevailed in the latter instance, and has formulated Department positions in these three cases.

Congress was a major participant in deciding policy for the Coffee Agreement and for soluble coffee, and its potential participation in cocoa policy-making, through its treaty and legislative functions, has indirectly affected interactions between the cocoa industry and the State Department. The views of the chairmen of the Senate Committee on Foreign Relations, of the Senate Finance Committee, and of the House Ways and Means Committee, as well as those of the "internationalists" in the Senate, have tended to decide Congressional positions regarding the issues.

In all three cases, it has been shown, individual business firms and associations may appropriately be considered actors which potentially have impact on policy-making. While the coffee and cocoa industries, respectively, are not monoliths, they have acted with a high degree of cohesion in advancing their claims upon policy. This analysis, however, has emphasized that the large processing corporations, and specifically General Foods Corporation (all three cases) and Hershey Corporation (cocoa agreement case), have been most decisive in determining industry positions for the issues.

What actor goals and capabilities help explain the impact of business-government relations on policy outcomes? In the Coffee Agreement case the State Department and Congress were primarily driven by political motives to support the Coffee Agreement. White House leadership, in the framework of general initiatives to bolster Latin America against radicalism or Communism, for the first time assured that government resources would be centrally co-ordinated and fully deployed to secure an agreement benefitting LDC producers.

What should not escape notice, however, is that General Foods, and other large corporations and trading firms that are most influential in deciding "industry" positions, simply "follow the initiative" of the State Department, as Krasner suggests.[532] General Foods executives shared official political goals, as well as had economic goals (e.g., market stability) which made an agreement tolerable, if not positively desirable. Indeed during the period 1958-1961, when the groundwork for the Kennedy efforts were laid, GF and other business firms took initiatives of their own for government action on coffee problems. They positively welcomed the Kennedy efforts for market regulation in 1961, and expended their own political resources to support them. GF, on the strength of its tremendous buying power, led the National Coffee Association into support of the ICA, and even brought pressure on certain skeptical LDC governments to join the Agreement.

---

532 Ibid., 2.

To ignore the fact that GF and other important coffee firms positively favored a reasonable coffee agreement, irrespective of the official initiatives in 1961, encourages a disregard for what policy consequences would have likely followed, if they had opposed one. These major firms could likely have thwarted the negotiation of a coffee treaty, or at last resort, blocked its passage through Congress.

The state centric model, in other words, does not adequately interpret the implications of positive industry attachment to the idea of market regulation in 1962, much less of the hypothetical absence of that support.

The insufficiency of the state centric model for explaining policy is even more evident in the soluble coffee case. Here the NCA goal, or in the end, the General Foods goal, was to eliminate the competitive advantage enjoyed by Brazilian soluble exporters to the United States. While the State Department supported LDC industrialization, in principle, doing so in this case was seen as an unacceptable risk to the Coffee Agreement. The Department's major goal, therefore, became to preserve industry support of the Agreement, with as little damage to American relations with Brazil as possible. Industry policy thereby became U.S. foreign policy, even though the State Department was only secondarily concerned to "protect" the U.S. industry.

Congress' participation enhanced GF capabilities to assure that the State Department would only settle for a resolution of the solubles dispute acceptable to it. The collaboration of the Amalgamated Meatcutters Union (AFL-CIO) further strengthened the capacity of GF to influence policy.

In the cocoa agreement case two policy-relevant factors contrast significantly with those in the Coffee Agreement case. First, there has been an absence of strong political motive to energize the U.S. policy-making system to favor any given cocoa agreement. Second, the cocoa industry, including the three largest chocolate manufacturers, and the confectioners, have generally opposed U.S. participation in an agreement. The official actors have had no political motives that compel them to overcome their economic and practical reservations about LDC proposals. And cocoa industry opposition has only reinforced the inertia of the official policy-makers.

The state centric and interest group models explain much more about the coffee and cocoa cases when employed together, because neither officials nor interest group actors have prevailed over one another decisively. That is, coffee and cocoa policies have evolved out of close and continual bargaining between interest group leaders and officials, with the support of both groups largely essential to the consensus for each of the policies.

On a scale of contrasts, however, the state centric model is somewhat more explanatory of Coffee Agreement policy than the interest group model. The interest group model is slightly more useful for tracing the U.S. stand on Brazilian solubles imports to its primary source, the domestic soluble producers and the related labor union. The two models are equally useful in explaining the "mixed" sources of U.S. cocoa agreement policy: officials without much enthusiasm for LDC proposals and cocoa industry leaders with a general aversion for such proposals.

Numerous empirical studies of the processes of foreign policy-making for various economic issues and issue-areas, as well as the development of theoretical frameworks for comparisons of cases, are required before there can be much confidence in generalizations about the relative potencies of officials and interest groups in determining policies in the broad field of foreign economic policy.

With respect to the issue-area of "commodity agreements for LDC-produced commodities," however, U.S. commodity consuming industries may be expected to have a pronounced, though not necessarily a controlling role in U.S. policy-making. The reasons for this may now be summarized. First, the industries will normally feel that their material interests are strongly and directly affected by market regulation, and will be well organized and single-minded in representing their concerns to government. They will tend to act without challenge from competing interest groups.

Second, official policy-makers are generally skeptical of the economic merits of such agreements, and are likely to seek them only if strong political motives warrant. For the immediate future the easing of Cold War competition in Africa, Asia, and Latin America, especially through the instruments of foreign aid and assistance to LDC trade, reduces the likelihood that such motives will be present in most instances. Under such conditions, policy-makers are more susceptible to business influence, especially business opposition to a given agreement.

Finally, the American system of policy-making, as a system, is likely to be conservative and unresponsive towards commodity agreement proposals, and susceptible to business intervention. Power to determine policy for commodity agreements is widely dispersed, and a substantial amount of political impetus is needed to assure consensus among many bureaucratic and Congressional participants in policy-making, and to galvanize them into concerted action. Since commodity agreements, by their nature, do not command enthusiastic support among Americans, the policy-making system tends to inertia when confronted with specific proposals for agreements. The system, therefore, is particularly susceptible to blocking actions by purposeful, well-organized business groups that oppose agreements under consideration.

Most of the literature on commodity agreements considers the economic advantages of market regulation by such agreements. This research has attempted to illuminate some of the political purposes and processes that determine whether the United States will actually support particular agreements.

Business and Foreign Policy. This study suggests the value of differentiating both business actors and foreign policy issues. "Business" has not been a monolith for the issues studied, and is not likely to be for other issues. Some firms and associations were found to be more influential than others; and some firms were discovered to have taken different stances towards ostensibly comparable issues. Similarly it was found that business has exercised a discrete role in the coffee and cocoa issues that may be like or unlike those that other studies have shown business to take for other foreign policy issues. For example, these commodity case studies reveal business having a more significant impact on policy-making in the trade field than the monumental American Business and Public Policy concludes business had in the case of the trade expansion issue of the 1950's.[533]

How does business approach the foreign policy-making process, and what factors favor its having an impact? First, these cases yield evidence to support Prof. LaPalombara's simple assertion that "Interest groups will gravitate to the critical points of political power."[534] And business is not likely to be intimidated nor necessarily disregarded if such "critical points" happen to be in the State Department.[535] In fact, business has developed quasi-institutionalized advisory relationships with the State Department for the coffee

---

[533] Bauer, et al, op. cit.

Joseph La Palombara, Interest Groups in Italian Politics (Princeton: Princeton University Press, 1964), 10.

[534] Harmon Zeigler reaches the dubious conclusion that the State Department is likely to be impervious to interest group pressures on foreign policy issues. Zeigler, op. cit., 223.

and cocoa issues, and a wider network of informal and formal relationships in conjunction with these. If the State Department is to be the locus of some kinds of important decisions affecting business, as it is increasingly for the New Diplomacy, it can be expected that business will seek effective access to its policy-making process, or seek removal of such decisions from the Department's purview.

It is recognized that interest groups attempt to work through all the major points of access to the governmental process.[536] In these coffee and cocoa cases business has shown a distinct preference for working directly with appropriate offices of the State Department, in the first instance, with the White House or other Executive departments, as necessary, and for resorting to Congress only as a last resort.[537]

However, as other studies of the American political system indicate would probably be the case, the coffee and cocoa industries have not been unmindful of the leverage that can be exerted on policy-making through Congress. In the American system of government, powers of policy development tend to be highly dispersed within and among the several branches of government. This is particularly true of trade issues including international commodity market regulation. One implication of this, of course, is that there is a "multiplicity of of coordinate or nearly coordinate points of access to governmental decisions." Such a system of government, David Truman adds, affords "luxuriant opportunities for defensive groups to delay or prevent action."[538] These opportunities,

---

536 For a statement of this view see Bernard C. Cohen, The Influence of Non-Governmental Groups on Foreign Policy-Making (Boston: World Peace Foundation), 14.

537 Cohen has found in a case study of policy-making for the Japanese Peace Treaty that the Pacific Fisheries Conference used Congressional representation to gain access to decision-making in the State Department. Ibid., 14.

538 David Truman, The Governmental Process: Political Interests and Public Opinion, Borzoi Books (New York: Alfred A. Knopf, 1971), xlii.

the study suggests, may also be transformed into opportunities to influence the actual content of policies.

The actual or potential participation of Congress in policy development for the coffee and cocoa issues has accorded business exceptional opportunities to influence the general orientation of bureaucratic policy-makers, and some specific aspects of policies.[539] Since Congressional support of executive initiatives has been essential to one or another aspect of policy-development for all three issues— and this support has, by no means, been foreordained— these businesses have benefitted by their presumed or real capacities to sway the key leaders of Congress. Business interests have gained access to and influence on the bureaucratic policy-makers, to a large extent, because the latter feel that substantial business support is imperative to develop and sustain desired coffee and cocoa policies that will be acceptable to Congress.

Among all the issues for which Congressional participation in policy-making is potentially conducive to interest group access and influence, these commodity agreement issues must be ranked among the most favorable to business intervention. Commodity agreements for LDC products do not excite great enthusiasm on the part of any segment of Congress, and the Congressional consensus that was developed for the Coffee Agreement, even as precarious as that was, could not be easily reproduced for another product. Some of the adventitious factors that favored Congressional support of the ICA in the early sixties have now receded; and factors that are likely adverse to that support, such as consumer-interest organization and consciousness, are now more substantially evident. Either under the "ideal" conditions that prevailed in the early sixties,

---

[539] Business does not always successfully capitalize upon opportunities to use the leverage of coordinate points of access to governmental decisions. Bauer et al, op. cit. In the cases under study the business actors do.

or under the less favorable conditions of today, business interests are in a strategic position to move an ambivalent policy-making system, if for no other reasons than that Congress is a participant in policy-making and that it is not likely to be easily persuaded of the desirability of any commodity agreement.

Thirdly, the business approach to and impact on policy-making for the coffee and cocoa issues have been partly a function of how officials have perceived their relationships to the two concerned industries. Bernard Cohen has suggested that a business group can exercise little influence on policy "unless its interest in the policy problem is recognized as legitimate by policy-makers."[540] There can be no question but that policy-makers have perceived industry representations for these issues as "legitimate." The establishment of formal advisory relationships attests to this. Or as Thomas Mann has indicated cryptically with reference to the case of the Coffee Agreement, "We would never have thought of not consulting with business."[541] By implication, American businesses were considered to have too much at stake in market regulation not to be consulted forthrightly.

Other factors seem to have reinforced this predisposition. These cases, for example, lend further evidence to support another observation by Bernard Cohen. "It would appear," Cohen asserts, "that when the 'attentive public' is very small, it is much easier for specific interest groups to establish their position as the representatives of the only sectors of the public that are vitally concerned about the policy in hand."[542] In these cases not only have the attentive publics been small, but the industries have been virtually the only sectors to organize effectively to press their views on government. In the seventies the prospects of

---

[540] Cohen, op. cit., 17.

[541] Interview, Thomas Mann, August 8, 1971.

[542] Cohen, op. cit., 12.

effective consumer-interest organization for this type of issue are greater; but during the period under study, the business interest groups, with one labor group in the solubles coffee case, did not have to compete with other organized groups for accommodation to their interests. As John Pincus has observed with specific reference to these commodity issues, one consequence of this state of affairs is that "State Department people get in the habit of deferring to business because it is the only active constituency."[543]

Joseph LaPalombara perhaps best summarizes how official perspectives can facilitate effective interest group participation in policy-making. "Interest groups," he asserts with relevance to this study, "afford a most convenient means for bureaucracy to effect stable and profitable relationships with relevant publics."[544] The authoritative coffee and cocoa associations, as La Palombara observes generally of numerous other cases, have offered the State Department a potentially important basis of support, and in the case of coffee, actual support for its efforts to assist LDC commodity trade. Officials have welcomed industry advice and expertise in developing effective commodity agreement policies; and for the most part, they have felt that substantial industry support would be essential to U.S. entry into any agreement.

Finally, what may be said about the nature of business influence in these cases? What Samuel Finer has said of relations between British lobbies and government departments seems aptly to describe relations between the coffee and cocoa industries and the U.S. government for these issues. Most contact, he asserts, is at department level and consists of an "exchange of views."[545] No evidence has been found in these cases of what Thomas Mann

---

[543] Interview, John Pincus, August 30, 1971.

[544] LaPalombara, op. cit., 257.

[545] S.E. Finer, Anonymous Empire: A Study of the Lobby in Great Britain (London: The Pall Mall Press Limited 1958), 25.

has termed "great influence," that is, of moments when business has decisively and dramatically persuaded officials to take a course of action not otherwise contemplated or intended.

The concepts of "accommodation" and "consensus-building" are as indicative of the relations that have obtained between business and government in these cases as are the more discrete, one-dimensional concepts of "influence" and "pressure." Although business has neither dictated nor controlled U.S. commodity agreement policies for coffee and cocoa, it has undoubtedly been a major force in shaping them.

APPENDIX

International Coffee Agreement: Chronology of Legislative History

1962 - 1972

<u>1962</u>

September 28	U.S. signs ICA, 1962.
October 4	President Kennedy transmits ICA to Senate for advice and consent to ratification.

<u>1963</u>

March 12	Senate Foreign Relations Committee hearings on ICA, 1962, Executive H.
May 13	Senate FRC reports favorably on ratification. Senators Carlson, Mundt, Williams submit minority views.
May 21	Senate passes resolution of consent to ratification, 69-20-11 (not voting). At least 6 not voting favorable.
June 24	U.S. becomes "provisional" member, signifying to U.N. depository authority that until implementing legislation secured "the United States does not assume any of the obligations for which such legislation is necessary."
July 1	ICA enters provisionally into force.
October 22	International Coffee Agreement Act to regulate trade pursuant to ICA, H.R. 8864, introduced in House and referred to Committee on Ways and Means. Hearings in Executive Session.
October 25	Ways and Means reports H.R. 8864 favorably to House, Congressmen Curtis and Alger submit minority views.
November 14	House debates and passes H.R. 8864, 181-145-109.
November 15	H.R. 8864 introduced to Senate and referred to the Committee on Finance.
December 19	<u>Washington Post</u> editorial charges Finance Committee Chairman (Byrd) with using coffee legislation to delay important tax hearings. Committee members "defend" Chairman on Senate floor, noting contradictory administration requests on bill priorities. Until December 12, administration had wanted coffee hearings first. From 12th asked deferral until after tax hearings.

December 27	U.S. deposits at U.N. instrument of ratification for ICA, 1962. ICA enters into force.

<u>1964</u>

February 24, 25 and 26	Senate Committee on Finance Hearings on H.R. 8864.
March 12	Committee on Finance reports H.R. 8864 favorably.
July 31	Senate debates and passes H.R. 8864 as amended (Dirksen) 58-27-15.
August 13	Conference committee reports acceptance of Dirksen amendment to Senate and House. Senate accepts by voice vote.
August 18	House rejects Conference Report 1803, 183-194-58. No further action and H.R. 8864 dies with adjournment of 88th Congress, October 3, 1964.
October 1	International Coffee Organization calls for enforcement of ICA provisions. U.S. must default temporarily, until implementing legislation secured.

<u>1965</u>

January 26	Implementing legislation reintroduced in Senate as S. 701. Referred to Committee on Finance.
January 27	Committee on Finance hearings on S. 701.
February 1	Committee on Finance reports S. 701 favorably, by a vote of 8-6.
February 2	Senate debates and approves S. 701, 56-23-21.
April 13 and 14	House Committee on Ways and Means hearings on S. 701. Executive session.
April 19	Ways and Means reports favorably on S. 701, with amendments (limit contribution to $150,000).
May 12	House debates and passes S. 701 with amendments (dollar limit on contributions; Findley amendment), 300-97-36.
May 13	Senate approves S. 701 as amended, 61-19-20.
May 22	President Johnson signs P.L. 89-23. In force through September 30, 1968.

<u>1968</u>

March 21	U.S. signs ICA, 1968.
April 23	President Johnson transmits ICA to Senate for advice and consent to ratification.
June 4 and 12	Senate Foreign Relations hearings on ICA, 1968, Executive D.
June 21	Senate FCR reports favorably on ratification.
June 28	Senate passes resolution of consent to ratification, 51-8-41.
July 2	International Coffee Agreement Act, H.R. 18299, introduced in House and referred to the House Ways and Means Committee.
July 8	Ways and Means hearings on H.R. 18299.
July 10	U.S. becomes provisional member of ICA, 1968.
July 11	Ways and Means reports H.R. 18299 favorably, with amendments (duration to September 30, 1973; safeguard against "unwarranted price increases").
July 16	Senate Committee on Finance reviews H.R. 18299 in executive session, decides Senate version should take form of addition to the Renegotiation Act of 1951, in process of being amended through H.R. 17324. Amendments to limit legislation to 2-year period and provide measures to counteract certain shipping practices of Brazil.
July 26	Committee on Finance recommends enactment of H.R. 17324, as amended by "Title III" to include original H.R. 18299 with amendments.
September 30	International Coffee Agreement of 1965 expires. Hiatus in U.S. enforcement begins.
October 3	House-Senate Conference reports recommends enactment of H.R. 17324 as amended by Committee on Finance.
October 7	Senate passes H.R. 17324 by voice vote.
October 10	House passes H.R. 17324, 199-44-188.
October 24	President Johnson signs P.L. 90-634.

November 1	U.S. deposits at U.N. instrument of ratification for ICA, 1968.

<u>1970</u>

April 7	H.R. 19567 to extend the authority of the International Coffee Act 1968, introduced in the House and referred to the House Ways and Means Committee.
May 13	Secretary of State promotes Coffee Act extension in Ways and Means hearings on trade.
June 30	Ways and Means Chairman Mills threatens H.R. 19567 will not be reported out until Brazil conforms to obligations of ICA, 1968, governing trade in processed coffee.
July 8	Ways and Means executive hearings on H.R. 19567.
July 15	Ways and Means announces indefinite delay in reporting out H.R. 19567, pending progress on negotiations with Brazil over soluble coffee.
September 30	International Coffee Agreement Act of 1968 expires. Another hiatus in U.S. Enforcement begins.
December 1	Ways and Means reports favorably on H.R. 19567 with amendment revising next termination date to June 30, 1971. "Requests" President to report by April 1 action by him or Brazil to terminate Brazil's discriminatory trade practices in soluble coffee. In the absence of such action, the Committee indicates it will not consider extending the implementing legislation for the Coffee Agreement.
December 18	House passes H.R. 19567 by voice vote.
December 31	Senate passes H.R. 19567 by voice vote.

<u>1971</u>

April 1	President Nixon reports to Congress on favorable settlement of soluble coffee dispute with Brazil.
May 3	H.R. 8293 to extend the authority of the International Coffee Act 1968 introduced in the House and referred to the Committee on Ways and Means.
June 2	Ways and Means reports H.R. 8293 favorably, to extend Act to close of September 30, 1973.
June 8	H.R. 8293 granted open rule for House debate. News of Brazilian "harrassment" of U.S. shrimp boats within

	Brazil's claimed 200 mile territorial sea limit prompts Ways and Means Chairman Mills to withhold bill from floor.
June 30	International Coffee Agreement Act of 1968 expires. Another hiatus in U.S. enforcement begins.
October 25-29	U.S.-Brazilian negotiations over dispute concerning U.S. fishing within Brazil's territorial sea limit.
November 5	House debates and passes H.R. 8293, 201-100-134. Extends Act until September 30, 1973.

1972

March 9	Senate Committee on Finance reports H.R. 8293 favorably. Senate passes H.R. 8293 by voice vote. Extends Coffee Act until September 30, 1973.

Sources: Numerous volumes of Congressional Quarterly Almanac, Congressional Record, and various Committee reports of House and Senate.

SOURCES CONSULTED

Books

Arthur, Henry B. Commodity Futures as a Business Management Tool. Division of Research, Harvard Graduate School of Business Administration. Boston: Harvard University, 1971.

Baranyai, Leon, and Mills, J.C. International Commodity Agreements. Mexico: Centro De Estudios Monetarios Latinoamericanos, 1963.

Bauer, Raymond A.; de Sola Pool, Ithiel; and Dexter, Louis A. American Business and Public Policy. New York: Atherton, 1963.

Cohen, Bernard C. The Influence of Non-Governmental Groups on Foreign Policy-Making. Boston: World Peace Foundation, 1959.

Davis, Joseph S. International Commodity Agreements: Hope, Illusion or Menace? New York: The Committee on International Economic Policy, 1947.

Eisenhower, Milton. The Wine is Bitter. Garden City, New York: Doubleday and Co., 1963.

Finer, S.E. Anonymous Empire: A Study of the Lobby in Great Britain. London: The Pall Mall Press Limited, 1958.

Fisher, Bart S. The International Coffee Agreement: A Study in Coffee Diplomacy. Praeger Special Studies in International Economics and Development. New York: Praeger Publishers, 1972.

Haas, Ernst B. Tangle of Hopes: American Commitments and World Order. Englewood Cliffs, New Jersey: Prentice Hall, Inc., 1969.

Herrington, E. Pendleton. Public Administration and the Public Interest. New York: McGraw-Hill Book Company, Inc., 1936.

Johnson, Harry G. Economic Policies Toward Less Developed Countries. New York: Frederick A. Praeger, 1967.

Killick, Tony. "The Economics of Cocoa." The Study of Contemporary Ghana. Vol. I: The Economy of Ghana. Edited by Walter Birmingham, I. Neustadt, and E.N. Omaboe. Published for the Ghana Academy of Sciences. London: George Allen and Unwin Ltd., 1966.

Kolko, Gabriel. The Roots of American Foreign Policy. Boston: Beacon Press, 1969.

La Palombara, Joseph. Interest Groups in Italian Politics. Princeton: Princeton University Press, 1964.

Lindblom, Charles E. The Policy-Making Process. Foundations of Modern Political Science Series. Englewood Cliffs, New Jersey: Prentice-Hall, Inc., 1968.

Lowi, Theodore J. The End of Liberalism: Ideology, Policy and the Crisis of Public Authority. New York: W. W. Norton & Company, Inc., 1969.

Oechslin, Marcel. Formation des prix du cacao et possibilité de leur stabilisation. Zuerich: Glaettli, 1965.

Outtara, Liliane Nicolas. Fondements économiques d'une organization du marché mondial du cacao. Toulouse: Faculté de droit et des sciences, Université de Toulouse, 1968.

Powelson, John P. Latin America: Today's Economic and Social Revolution. New York: McGraw-Hill, 1964.

Robinson, James. Congress and Foreign Policy-Making. Homewood, Ill.: Dorsey Press, 1962.

Rowe, John Wilkinson Foster. Primary Commodities in International Trade. Cambridge: at the University Press, 1965.

Schlesinger, Arthur M., Jr. A Thousand Days: John F. Kennedy in the White House. Greenwich, Connecticut: Fawcett Publications, 1967.

Schutjer, Wayne A., and Ayo, Edward Jide. Negotiating a World Cocoa Agreement: Analysis and Prospects. Bulletin 744, October 1967. University Park, Pennsylvania: The Pennsylvania State University, College of Agriculture, Agricultural Experiment Station, 1967.

Truman, David. The Governmental Process: Political Interests and Public Opinion. Borzoi Books. New York: Alfred A. Knopf, 1971.

Wagner, R. Harrison. United States Policy Toward Latin America: A Study of Domestic and International Politics. Stanford: Stanford University Press, 1970.

Weymar, F. Helmut. The Dynamics of the World Cocoa Market. Cambridge: MIT Press, 1968.

Wickizer, V. D. Coffee, Tea and Cocoa: An Economic and Political Analysis. Stanford, California: Stanford University Press, 1951.

Wootton, Graham. Interest Groups. Foundations of Modern Political Science Series. Englewood Cliffs, New Jersey: Prentice Hall, Inc., 1970.

Zeigler, Harmon. Interest Groups in American Society. Englewood Cliffs, New Jersey: Prentice Hall, Inc., 1964.

Periodicals

Bilder, Richard. "The International Coffee Agreement: A Case History in Negotiation." Law and Contemporary Problems, XXVIII (spring 1963), 328-377.

Blumenthal, W. Michael. "Coffee's Role in Foreign Affairs." Tea and Coffee Trade Journal, CXXII (March, 1962), 24ff.

Caine, Sydney (Sir). "Commodity Agreements—A New Look." Lloyds Bank Review, XV (January, 1963), 14-29.

"Cocoa Talks Collapse Again." West Africa (December 30, 1967).

Congressional Quarterly Almanac, 1963.

Congressional Quarterly Almanac, 1965.

Cordell, A. J. "Brazilian Soluble Coffee Problem: A Review." Quarterly Review of Economics and Business, IX (spring, 1969), 29-38.

Dahl, Robert A. "Business and Politics: A Critical Appraisal of Political Science." American Political Science Review, LIII (March, 1959).

Daniels, Paul C. "The Inter-American Coffee Agreement." Law and Contemporary Problems, VIII (autumn, 1941), 708-20.

"The Editor Interviews: Jack McKiernan." Tea and Coffee Trade Journal, CXXII (January, 1962).

Fried, Edward R. "Agreement is Still Part of U.S. Policy." Tea and Coffee Trade Journal, CXXXII (June, 1967), 24ff.

"Gbedemah's Second Budget." West Africa, XL (September 1, 1956), 655-656.

Gill and Duffus, Ltd. Cocoa Report. London: Gill and Duffus. September, 1965.

Haley, Bernard F. "Relation Between Cartel Policy and Commodity Agreements." American Economic Review, XXXVI (May, 1946), 717-734.

Haley, Bernard F. "United States Policy Regarding Commodity Agreements." Proceedings of the Academy of Political Science, XXI, No. 3 (May, 1945), 429-436.

Hanson, Simon G. "International Commodity Agreements: The 'Success' of the International Coffee Agreement: How the State Department Deceived the Congress." Inter-American Economic Affairs, XXI (autumn, 1967), 55-79.

"International Coffee Organization Arbitration of Brazil-United States Dispute in Processed Coffee." [February 28, 1969], VIII International Legal Materials, 564-78.

Jacobson, Jerome. "Difficulties in Framing Effective Commodity Agreements." International Development Review, X (June, 1968), 10-15.

Law, Alton. "International Commodity Agreements: Policies and Problems." Journal of Economic Issues, IV (September, 1970), 87-102.

Law and Contemporary Problems, XXVIII (spring, 1963).

Lenhart, Harry, Jr. "Economic Report/Domestic Producers Dominate Lobbying for Division of Sugar Market." National Journal, III, 24 (June 12, 1971), 1251-1265.

McKiernan, John F. "Equal Opportunity for All in the Trade." Tea and Coffee Trade Journal, CXX (May, 1961), 17ff.

--------, "First Let's See How Agreement Shapes Up." Tea and Coffee Trade Journal, CXXXII (June, 1967), 23ff.

--------, "A Goodwill Mission to Latin America." Tea and Coffee Trade Journal, CXX (June, 1961), 12ff

--------, "The 'NCA' and Free Enterprise." Coffee Annual, 1962. New York: George Gordon Paton & Co., 1963.

--------, "The NCA's Half Century of Service." Coffee Annual, 1959. George Gordon Paton, 1960.

--------, "One of Coffee's Most Eventful Years." Tea and Coffee Trade Journal, CXXIV (January, 1963), 26ff.

--------, "The Role of the N.C.A." Coffee Annual, 1961. New York: George Gordon Paton, 1962.

--------, "State Department Cooperates with NCA." Tea and Coffee Trade Journal, CXXX (March, 1966), 19ff.

--------, "The U.S. Coffee Industry's 'Diplomatic Task Force.'" Coffee Annual, 1969. New York: George Gordon Paton, 1969.

Mann, Thomas C. "The Coffee Study Group." Coffee Annual, 1958. New York: George Gordon Paton, 1959.

Meono, Charles J. "Who Will Benefit from the Agreement." Tea and Coffee Trade Journal, CXXII (March, 1962), 16ff.

"NCA Committee Report on U.N. Coffee Conference," Tea and Coffee Trade Journal, CXXIV (January, 1963).

"NCA Faces Challenges of Declining Consumption and the Coffee Agreement," (Editorial). Tea and Coffee Trade Journal, CXXIV (March, 1968).

"New York Talks Break Down." West Africa (July 2, 1966).

New York Times (Editorial). February 6, 1968.

Pan American Coffee Bureau. Annual Coffee Statistics, 1969. No. 33. New York: PACB, 1970.

Pincus, John A. "What Policy for Commodities?" Foreign Affairs, XLII (January, 1964), 227-241.

--------, "Commodity Agreements: Bonanza or Illusion." Columbia Journal of World Business, II (January, 1967), 41-50.

Price, David E. "The Politics of Sugar." Review of Politics (April, 1971), 212-232.

Robbins, George V. "Floor/Ceiling Coffee Prices." Coffee Annual, 1958. New York: George Gordon Paton, 1959.

Salera, Virgil. "The New Coffee Agreement— Facts and Issues." Inter-American Economic Affairs, XV (spring, 1962), 46-69.

Sivetz, Michael. "Export of Solubles from Brazil to U.S." Tea and Coffee Trade Journal, CXXXI (September, 1966), 16ff.

Tea and Coffee Trade Journal, CXVI (June, 1959).

--------, CXXIII (July 1962).

--------, CXXXIV (March, 1968).

"United States Coffee Policy." Coffee Annual 1961. New York: George Gordon Paton, 1962.

Wall Street Journal, November 28, 1961.

-------- (Editorial), February 26, 1968.

World Coffee & Tea: Guide to Coffee/USA, XII (August, 1971).

--------, XIII (August, 1972).

International Organization Documents

Baranson, J. "The Soluble Dispute and the Case of Reverse Protection." The Coffee Problem: Essays and Official Papers, Vol. II of The Coffee Papers: An Inquiry into the Economics of Commodity Markets. Edited by Dragoslav Avramovic. Washington: IBRD, 1969.

Coffee Study Group. "Conclusions Reached at the Coffee Study Group Meeting Concerning the Long-Term Agreement," CSG-69/62 (E), Rev. 2, March 28, 1962.

International Bank for Reconstruction and Development. The Coffee Papers: An Inquiry Into the Economics of Commodity Markets. Vol. I: The Coffee Problem Revisited. Edited by Dragoslav Avramovic. Washington: IBRD, February, 1969.

--------. The Coffee Papers: An Inquiry into the Economics of Commodity Markets. Vol. II: The Coffee Problem: Essays and Official Papers. Edited by Dragoslav Avramovic. Washington: IBRD, February 1969.

--------. International Coffee Agreement, 1968: Background and Analysis, Report EC-165. Prepared by Shamsher Singh. Washington: IBRD, August, 1968.

International Coffee Organization. Arbitration Panel on the Dispute Between Brazil and the United States of America under Article 44 of the Agreement. Verbatim Records. Records 1-20. February 17-28, 1969.

--------. International Coffee Council. History of Recent International Coffee Agreements: Their Background, Provisions, Operations and Related Developments, 1954-1963. ICC-1-1. June 28, 1963.

International Trade Center. UNCTAD and GATT. The Market of Soluble Coffee in Canada and Japan. Geneva, 1971.

Organization of American States. Alliance for Progress: Official Documents Emanating from the Special Meeting of the Inter-American Economic and Social Council at the Ministerial Level, ES-RE-Doc. 145 (English), Rev. 3 Corr., Punta del Este, August 16, 1944.

U.N. Conference on Trade and Development. Commodity Problems and Policies. TD/129. February 16, 1972.

--------. The International Organization of Commodity Trade: Case Study on Cocoa. Prepared by FAO. TD/B/Ac. 2/3. January 3, 1966.

--------. Conference on Trade and Development. The Significance of the Second Session of the United Nations Conference on Trade and Development. Report by the Secretary-General. TD/96/Rev. 1. 1968.

--------: Summary Records of Executive Committee, Tenth Meeting, December 15, 1967, TD/Cocoa .2/EX/SR.1-13.

--------. Conference on Trade and Development. Towards a New Trade Policy for Development. Report by the Secretary-General. New York: United Nations, 1964.

U.N. Department of Economic and Social Affairs. Towards Accelerated Development: Proposals for the Second United Nations Development Decade. Report of the Committee for Development Planning. ST/ECA/128. 1970.

U.N. United Nations Coffee Conference, 1962. Summary of Proceedings. E/Conf. 42/8. New York: United Nations, 1962.

U.S. Public Documents

Department of State Bulletin, XLIV (1961).

---------, XLVII (1962).

Dungan, Ralph A. Special Assistant to the President. "Memo to the Files: Re: Coffee Agreement." Unpublished White House Memorandum, January 15, 1964.

Gordon, Lincoln. Oral History Interview. John F. Kennedy Library, Waltham, Massachusetts.

Report to the President-Elect of the Task Force on Foreign Economic Policy. Submitted by George Ball (Chairman), January, 1961. Unpublished Document, John F. Kennedy Library, Waltham, Massachusetts.

Report to the President-Elect of the Task Force on Immediate Latin American Problems. Submitted by Adolph Berle (Chairman), January, 1961. Unpublished Document, John F. Kennedy Library, Waltham, Massachusetts.

Rupley, A.S. "Soluble Coffee." Unpublished Memorandum, 1962. Attached to Memorandum of Transmittal from Lewis Harris and Associates, Inc., to Ralph Dungan, Special Assistant to the President, White House, July 12, 1962. John F. Kennedy Library, Boston, Files (Tariffs) TA 1654, Box 1959.

U.S. Department of Agriculture. Economic Research Service. A History of Sugar Marketing. Agricultural Report No. 197. Prepared by Ray A. Ballinger. Washington: GPO, 1961.

U.S. Department of Commerce. 1967 Census of Manufacturers. Preliminary Report. Washington: Bureau of the Census, November, 1969.

U.S. Congress. House. Committee on Agriculture. The United States Sugar Program. Committee Print. 91st Cong.; 2d sess., 1971.

---------. House. Committee on Ways and Means. Continuation of the International Coffee Agreement Act of 1968. Report to accompany H.R. 8293. Report No. 92-242, June 2, 1971, 92d Cong.; 1st sess., 1971.

U.S. Congress. House. Committee on Ways and Means. International Coffee Agreement. Hearing, July 8, 1968. 90th Cong.; 2d sess., 1968.

--------. House. Committee on Ways and Means, International Coffee Agreement Act of 1968, Rpt. No. 1704, July 11, 1968. 90th Cong.; 2d sess., 1968.

--------. House. Committee on Ways and Means. International Coffee Agreement Act, Report No. 91-1641, December 1, 1970, 91st Cong.; 2d sess., 1970.

--------. House. Committee on Ways and Means. Tariff and Trade Proposals. Hearings, June 12 and 15, 1970, Part 14, 91st Cong.; 2d sess., 1970.

--------. House. 88th Cong.; 1st sess. Congressional Record. November 14, 1963.

--------. House. 89th Cong.; 1st sess. Congressional Record, May 12, 1965.

--------. House. 88th Cong.; 2d sess. Congressional Record, May 27, 1967.

--------. House. 91st Cong.; 2d sess. Congressional Record, December 18, 1970.

--------. House. 92nd Cong.; 1st sess. Congressional Record, November 5, 1971.

--------. Senate. Committee on Finance. Coffee. Hearings, February 25-27, 1964, 88th Cong., 2d sess., 1964.

--------. Senate. Committee on Finance. Coffee. Sen. Report 53, February 1, 1965, 89th Cong.; 1st sess., 1965.

--------. Senate. Committee on Finance. History of the Committee on Finance, Sen. Doc. 91-57, March 5, 1970, 91st Cong.; 2d sess., 1970.

--------. Senate. Committee on Foreign Relations. American Republics Corporation Act, Hearings, 86th Cong.; 2d sess., 1960.

--------. Senate. Committee on Foreign Relations. Brazil and United States Policies. Report of a Study Mission to Several of the American Republics. Washington: U.S. Government Printing Office, 1962.

--------. Senate. Committee on Foreign Relations. International Coffee Agreement, 1962. Hearing, March 12, 1963, 87th Cong.; 2d sess., 1963.

U.S. Congress. Senate. Committee on Foreign Relations. International Coffee Agreement, 1968. Hearings, June 4 and 12, 1968, 90th Cong.; 2d sess., 1968.

--------. Senate. Committee on Foreign Relations. United States-Latin American Relations: Commodity Problems in Latin America. Study, prepared at the request of the Subcommittee on American Republic Affairs of the Committee on Foreign Relations by International Economic Consultants, Inc., December 12, 1959, 86th Cong.; 1st sess., 1959.

--------. Senate. 75th Cong.; 2d sess. Congressional Record, February 3, 1941.

--------. Senate. 88th Cong.; 1st sess. Congressional Record, May 20, 1963.

--------. Senate. 88th Cong.; 1st sess. Congressional Record, May 21, 1963.

--------. Senate. 88th Cong., 2d sess. Congressional Record, July 13, 1964.

--------. Senate, 88th Cong.; 2d sess. Congressional Record, July 31, 1964.

--------. Senate. 89th Cong.; 1st sess. Congressional Record, February 2, 1965.

--------. Senate. 91st Cong.; 2nd sess. Congressional Record. December 31, 1970.

U.S. Department of State. Bureau for Economic Affairs. "International Commodity Policy and Commodity Agreements." Unpublished Memorandum, June, 1968.

--------. Bureau for Economic Affairs. "Meeting of the Advisory Committee on International Business Problems," June 13, 1968." Unpublished Memorandum from Anthony M. Solomon, Assistant Secretary of State, June 14, 1968.

--------. Bureau for Economic Affairs. "Office of the Deputy Assistant Secretary for International Resources and Food Policy (ORF)." Internal Memorandum. July, 1968.

--------. Bureau for Economic Affairs. Office of International Resources and Food Policy. Division of Tropical Products. "Briefing Book: ICA Act of 1968 (as amended in 1970)." Unpublished briefing booklet for State Department officials testifying before Congress, 1970.

U.S. Department of State. Commodity Agreements: A Partial Answer to the Trade Problems of Developing Countries. Henry Brodie. Commercial Policy Series Pubn. 200. Washington: GPO, 1965.

--------. "Report of the United States Delegation to the United Nations Cocoa Conference September 26-October 24, 1963." Unpublished report submitted to Secretary of State by the U.S. Delegate, Jerome Jacobson. Prepared by Paul E. Callanan, Chief, Tropical Products Division. 1963.

U.S. President's Commission on Foreign Economic Policy (Randall Commission). Report to the President and to Congress. Washington: GPO, 1954.

Business Documents

Chamber of Commerce of the United States. Commodity Agreements—Their Role in the World Economy. Report of the Committee on Economic Policy. Washington, D.C.: Chamber of Commerce, 1963.

Harvard Business School. General Foods Corporation. Case No. ICH/10G104/AM-P/188R2, 1964.

Letter from Johann Scheu, Nestle, to Jack Button, Assistant Chief, Sugar and Tropical Products, Bureau of Economic Affairs, U.S. Department of State. Unpublished letter, March 30, 1967.

Letter from Samuel E. Stavisky, President, to Jose Luis de Freitas Valle, President, Associacao Profissional de Industria de Cafe Soluvel, July 18, 1967. Attachment 1, Exhibit B, Registration Statement under Foreign Agents Registration Act of 1938, Registration No. 1531, August, 1967, U.S. Department of Justice, Washington, D.C.

National Coffee Association. News Letter, No. 468, February 3, 1956.

--------, News Letter, No. 539, June 7, 1957.

--------, News Letter, No. 612, October 31, 1958.

--------, News Letter, No. 617, December 4, 1958.

--------. News Letter, No. 629, February 27, 1959.

--------, News Letter, Supplement to No. 632, March 20, 1959.

--------, News Letter, No. 640, May 15, 1959.

--------. News Letter, No. 749, June 5, 1961.

--------, News Letter, No. 752, June 20, 1961.

National Coffee Association. News Letter, No. 754, July 10, 1961.

--------. News Letter, No. 757, July 31, 1961.

--------. News Letter, Special Bulletin, No. 31. September 8, 1961.

--------. News Letter, Special Bulletin, No. 4, September 27, 1961.

--------. News Letter, Special Bulletin, No. 12, March 15, 1962.

--------. News Letter, Special Bulletin, No. 18, July 17, 1962.

--------. News Letter, No. 1011, June 13, 1966.

--------. News Letter, No. 1035, November 28, 1966.

--------. News Letter, No. 1060, May 22, 1967.

--------. NCA Special Bulletin, No. 173, May 4, 1970.

New York Cocoa Exchange, Inc. Report of the Board of Managers, 1957.

--------. Report of the Board of Managers, 1958.

--------. Report of the Board of Managers, 1962.

--------. Report of the Board of Managers, 1963.

--------. "Firms, Corporations and Individuals Represented in Membership." Charter By-Laws and Rules, 1970, XIII-XXII.

Rashish, Myer. "The Proposed International Cocoa Agreement." Unpublished Background Paper Issued in Behalf of The New York Cocoa Exchange. The Cocoa Merchants' Association of America, Inc., The Chocolate Manufacturers Association of the United States of America, and the National Confectioners' Association of the United States, Inc. August, 1963.

Robbins, George V. Address to Convention of the Tea and Coffee Association of Canada, October 26, 1948. Mimeograph.

Samuel E. Stavisky & Associates, Inc. "Background Memorandum." Press release for Brazilian Soluble Coffee Industry, Sao Paulo, November, 1967.

--------. "U.S. Switches Tactics in Battle to Ban Brazil's Instant Coffee." Press release for Brazilian Soluble Coffee Industry. December 29, 1967.

Standard and Poor's. Corporation Records, October-November, 1971.

Tansley, Sir Eric. "Is a Cocoa Scheme Necessary?" Unpublished Paper. January, 1972.

World Coffee Information Center. "Coffee—Economic Impact. Washington, D. C. : World Coffee Information Center, Pan-American Coffee Bureau, 1970.

Other Unpublished Materials

Krasner, Stephen D. "Business-Government Relations: The Case of the International Coffee Agreement." Unpublished Paper, Center for International Affairs, Harvard University, spring, 1973.

---------. "The Politics of Primary Commodities: A Study of Coffee, 1900-1970." Unpublished Ph. D. Dissertation. Harvard University, 1972.

Vanderslice, Lane. "The International Coffee Agreement and Control of Coffee Overproduction." Unpublished Ph. D. Dissertation, University of Michigan, 1971.

Letters to Author

Blumenthal, W. Michael. Former Deputy Assistant Secretary of State for Economic Affairs. October 20, 1971.

Mann, Thomas C. Former Under Secretary of State for Economic Affairs. June 28, 1971.

Martin, Edwin. Former Assistant Secretary of State for Economic Affairs. February 11, 1972.

Solomon, Anthony M. Former Assistant Secretary of State for Economic Affairs. April 6, 1972.

Interviews

Edward Aborn. President, Coca-Cola/Tenco. Linden, N. J. October 4, 1971.

Peter Ady. Professor, Oxford University. New York City. January 5, 1972.

Gardner Ainsworth. Maritime Affairs, Department of State. Washington, D. C. July 27, 1971.

K. Aman-Koffi. Ivory Coast Stabilization Fund. New York City. February 25, 1971.

Frederick Arkhurst. Formerly Permanent Secretary, Foreign Affairs, Ghana. New York City. March 26, 1971.

Marshall Barrett. Merril Lynch, Fenner, Pierce and Smith. New York City. September 15, 1971.

Henry Bashkin. Bureau of International Commerce, Department of Commerce. Washington, D.C. April 29, 1971.

Edward C. Bittner. Bureau of Inter-American Affairs, Department of State. Washington, D.C. July 28, 1971.

Robert Best. Staff Member, Senate Committee on Finance. Washington, D.C. July 6, 1971.

W. Michael Blumenthal. President, Bendix International; formerly Deputy Assistant Secretary of State. New York City. October 13, 1971.

Henry Brodie. Former Director of the Office of International Resources, Department of State. Washington, D.C. June 30, 1971.

James Buckley. Vice President for Purchasing, Nestle (U.S.). New York City. September 30, 1971.

Paul Callanan. Former Chief, Tropical Products Division, Department of State. Washington, D.C. July 12, 1971 and January 26, 1972.

J.M. Clark. Clark, Anderson, Clayton & Co. New York City. September 28, 1971.

Edward Cohen. Tropical Products Division, Department of State. June 25, 1971.

Martin Coyne. J. Aron & Co. New York City. September 27, 1971.

William Diebold. Council on Foreign Relations. New York City. March 2, 1971.

Mario DiPasquale. Executive Secretary, Green Coffee Association of New York. New York City. September 28, 1971.

Paul Douglas. Former U.S. Senator. Washington, D.C. July 19, 1971.

Sam Ekuza. Deputy Manager, Uganda Marketing Board. New York City. October 19, 1971.

Thomas D. Finney, Jr. Clifford, Warnke, Glass, McIlwain & Finney. Washington, D.C. January 27, 1972.

Alwyn N. Fischel. A.C. and Leon Israel International. New York City. March 29 and 30, 1972.

Carmel Flynn. Editor, National Coffee Association Newsletter. New York City. June 17, 1971.

John W. Foley. Director, Office for Nigerian Affairs, Department of State; former DCM, Ghana. Washington, D.C. June 30, 1971.

Edward Fried. Brookings Institution; former Deputy Assistant Secretary of State. Washington, D.C. June 24, 1971 and July 12, 1971.

Jose Gemeil. Samuel E. Stavisky & Associates, Inc. Washington, D.C. July 11, 1971.

Ruth Gold. Special Assistant, Bureau of Economic Affairs, Department of State. Washington, D.C. January 25, 1972.

Julian Hemphill. Director of Purchasing and Board Member, Hershey Food Corporation. New York City. February 8, 9 and 10, 1972.

Leslie Hurt. Foreign Agricultural Service, Department of Agriculture. Washington, D.C. April 29, 1971.

Sam Israel. A.C. and Leon Israel International. New York City. October 12, 1971.

Jerome Jacobson. Robert Nathan and Associates; formerly Deputy Assistant Secretary of State. Washington, D.C. July 12, 1971.

Perce Judd. United Nations Conference on Trade and Development. New York City. November 24, 1971.

Julius Katz. Deputy Assistant Secretary of State. Washington, D.C. July 15, 1971.

George R. Kenney. Director, Economic Policy Staff, Bureau of African Affairs, Department of State. Washington, D.C. January 25, 1972.

Harold Lamarr. Staff Member, House Committee on Ways and Means. Washington, D.C. July 6, 1971 and January 25, 1972.

Richard E. Lippincott. Deputy Director, Office of Brazilian Affairs, Department of State. Washington, D.C. July 28, 1971.

Virginia McClung. Special Assistant, Office of International Resources and Food Policy, Department of State. Washington, D.C. July 27, 1971.

George McEvoy. J. Aron & Co. New York City. September 23, 1971.

George Maciel. Ambassador of Brazil to Organization of American States. Washington, D.C. July 16, 1971.

John McKiernan. Former President, National Coffee Association. New York City. November 23, 1971.

Arnold Mayer. Amalgamated Meatcutters and Butcher Workmen (AFL-CIO). Washington, D.C. November 23, 1971.

Thomas Mann. Under Secretary of State for Economic Affairs (ret.), Department of State, Austin, Texas. August 20, 1971.

William J. Mennert. Merrill Lynch, Fenner, Pierce and Smith. New York City. September 15, 1971.

Ari Nugterren. A.C. and Leon Israel International. New York City. January 30, 1971.

Frederick Otterbein. Vice President, General Foods Corporation. New York City. September 22, 1971.

Len Parry. Produce Unitrade. New York City. October 5, 1971.

Kenneth H. Paton. George Gordon Paton. New York City. February 25, 1971.

John A. Pincus. Rand Institute; former consultant to Department of State. New York City. August 30, 1971.

Raul Prebisch. Former Secretary General, United Nations Conference on Trade and Development. New York City. February 2, 1971 and April 20, 1971.

Albert M. Prosterman. Albert M. Prosterman & Associates, Inc. Washington, D.C. January 24 and 27, 1972.

Arthur R. Ransohoff. Arthur R. Ransohoff & Co. New York City. September 14, 1971.

Michael Riess. AGRIMET, Metal Traders, Inc. New York City. June 7, 1971.

Nicolas Rivero. Economist, Organization of American States. Washington, D.C. July 13, 1971.

George Robbins. Former Director of Green Coffee Operations, General Foods Corporation. New York City. February 25, 1971 and August 11, 1971.

J. Phillip Rourk. Foreign Agricultural Service, Department of Agriculture. Washington, D.C. April 29, 1971.

Joao Oliveira Santos. Operations Manager, Inter-American Development Bank; former Secretary General, International Coffee Organization. Washington, D.C. April 30, July 28 and 29, 1971.

Johann J. Scheu. Director of Purchasing, Nestle (U.S.). New York City. September 20 and 24, 1971.

Mark Schneider. Legislative Assistant to Senator Edward Kennedy. Washington, D. C. July 8, 1971.

Richard C. Scissors. Department of State. Washington, D. C. April 29 and June 25, 1971.

Shamsher Singh. International Economist, International Bank for Reconstruction and Development. Washington, D. C. July 26, 1971.

Andrew A. Scholtz. Scholtz and Co. New York City. June 17, 1971.

Helena Stalson. Council on Foreign Relations. New York City. March 2, 1971.

William Stern. General Cocoa Co. New York City. September 21, 1971.

William J. Struning. Director of Research, Pan-American Coffee Bureau. New York City. February 25, 1971.

Franklin Williams. President, Phelps-Stokes Foundation. New York City. March 26, 1971.

Charles York. Chief, Tropical Products Division, Department of State. Washington, D. C. July 2, 1971.